Sacred Scripture, Sacred War

Sacred Scripture, Sacred War

The Bible and the American Revolution

JAMES P. BYRD

OXFORD
UNIVERSITY PRESS

OXFORD
UNIVERSITY PRESS

Oxford University Press is a department of the University of Oxford.
It furthers the University's objective of excellence in research, scholarship,
and education by publishing worldwide.

Oxford   New York
Auckland   Cape Town   Dar es Salaam   Hong Kong   Karachi
Kuala Lumpur   Madrid   Melbourne   Mexico City   Nairobi
New Delhi   Shanghai   Taipei   Toronto

With offices in
Argentina   Austria   Brazil   Chile   Czech Republic   France   Greece
Guatemala   Hungary   Italy   Japan   Poland   Portugal   Singapore
South Korea   Switzerland   Thailand   Turkey   Ukraine   Vietnam

Oxford is a registered trademark of Oxford University Press
in the UK and certain other countries.

Published in the United States of America by
Oxford University Press
198 Madison Avenue, New York, NY 10016

© Oxford University Press 2013

Library of Congress Cataloging-in-Publication Data
Byrd, James P., 1965–
Sacred scripture, sacred war : the Bible and the American Revolution / James P. Byrd.
pages cm.
Includes bibliographical references (pages) and index.
ISBN 978–0–19–984349–7
1. War—Biblical teaching.   2. United States—History—Revolution, 1775–1783—
Religious aspects—Christianity.   3. Bible—Theology.   4. War—Religious aspects—
Christianity.   5. United States—Church history—18th century.   I. Title.
BS680.W2B97 2013
261.8′73—dc23
2012038604

1 3 5 7 9 8 6 4 2
Printed in the United States of America
on acid-free paper

To Karen, Olivia, and Caroline

Contents

Acknowledgments

I AM THANKFUL for the advice of friends and colleagues who helped to make this a better book than it would have been otherwise. Edward J. Blum, Dale A. Johnson, Thomas S. Kidd, Kenneth P. Minkema, Harry S. Stout, and Douglas A. Sweeney have been incredibly supportive of this book. While researching, I had the opportunity to attend a month-long seminar on "Religion, War, and the Meaning of America," led by Harry S. Stout at Calvin College. My conversations with colleagues at that seminar greatly helped me to think though this project. I am thankful to all the participants, and to the Seminars on Christian Scholarship at Calvin for that opportunity. Since this project involved work with both printed and unprinted sermon manuscripts, I am grateful for the expert assistance of archivists at the American Antiquarian Society, especially Diann Benti, and Moira Fitzgerald at the Beinecke Rare Book & Manuscript Library at Yale University. I have been privileged to work with excellent research assistants at Vanderbilt. Matthew McCullough, a PhD student who has since graduated, was very helpful in assisting me with this project from its beginning. Jimmy Squibb also contributed much to this work, offering many valuable suggestions as I was bringing the book to its conclusion. My thanks go to the professionals at Oxford University Press who did a wonderful job. I am especially grateful to Theo Calderara, senior editor at Oxford, who has believed in this project for several years. He is an exceptional editor who made excellent suggestions at every point in the process. I want to thank all of my colleagues at Vanderbilt for their friendship, support, and advice. I have learned much from conversations about this book with several colleagues, especially those in American religious history, Dennis Dickerson, Kathleen Flake, and my dean and faculty colleague, James Hudnut-Beumler. I am also thankful that Vanderbilt has given me the opportunity to work with outstanding graduate students in religious

history, and I thank all of them for all they have taught me. I would probably not have finished this book without the excellent work of my adminis-
trative colleagues, especially Marie McEntire and Karen Eardley. Since my
research involved designing a database, I am grateful for the technical help
provided by Eric Hood, Erik Johnson, Clayton Bollmann, and Nick Cavin.
Most of all, I am grateful to my wife, Karen M. Byrd, and our daughters,
Olivia and Caroline. They inspire me in everything I do.

James P. Byrd
Nashville, TN
November 2012

Sacred Scripture, Sacred War

Introduction

ON JANUARY 17, 1776, exactly one week after Thomas Paine's enormously influential *Common Sense* was printed in Philadelphia, Connecticut minister Samuel Sherwood preached a sermon that likewise addressed the American Revolution. While the minister Sherwood equaled Paine's devotion to patriotism, the deist Paine rivaled Sherwood's biblical repertoire. In 1776, Paine was certainly no minister, but his brief stint behind a Methodist pulpit in England may have taught him something about how to use scripture to make a convincing argument. *Common Sense*, which most historians agree was "the most brilliant pamphlet written during the American Revolution," had the feel of a sermon as Paine employed the King James Bible against King George's tyranny.[1] The ancient Hebrews, Paine argued, were models for the American patriots.[2] Sherwood, by contrast, looked to the New Testament to defend the patriotic cause, specifically, to the book of Revelation. As the only apocalyptic book in the New Testament, Revelation was, in the view of many colonists, a symbolic description of the end of the world, climaxing in the final victory of Christ over the powers of Antichrist. The American Revolution, Sherwood believed, was a climactic event in this apocalyptic scenario, and the American cause was the cause of Christ against the tyrannical influences of Antichrist. "God Almighty, with all the powers of heaven, are on our side," Sherwood preached. "Great numbers of angels, no doubt, are encamping round our coast, for our defense and protection. Michael [a mighty angel of God] stands ready; with all the artillery of heaven, to encounter the dragon, and to vanquish this black host."[3]

Despite their differences, Sherwood and Paine, the preacher and the political pamphleteer, proclaimed American patriotism through scripture and contributed to an American tradition. From the Revolution through the War on Terror, the Bible has been a constant presence in American wars. Americans have cited scripture to justify violence, praise heroes, vilify enemies, celebrate victories, and rationalize defeats. Americans often think of the United States as "God's New Israel," a blessed nation on a divine mission, its wars blessed by God.[4]

By focusing on how the Bible inspired patriotism in Revolutionary America, this book addresses an important but neglected topic. As Harry S. Stout has observed, historians have largely overlooked the "symbiotic" relationship between religion and war throughout American history. As Stout argues, "American wars are *sacred* wars and American religion, with some notable exceptions, is martial at the very core of its being." American wars became sacred largely with the help of scripture, for the Bible has long been America's Book—the collection of texts Americans have most read and referenced—and as such the Bible has maintained a consistent and respected status in most of America's wars.[5]

Scripture was everywhere in Revolutionary America. As historian Gordon S. Wood aptly summarized, "it was the clergy who made the Revolution meaningful for most common people," because "for every gentleman who read a scholarly pamphlet and delved into Whig and ancient history for an explanation of events, there were dozens of ordinary people who read the Bible and looked to their ministers for an interpretation of what the Revolution meant."[6]

Even colonists who normally had no use for the Bible often found much use for it during the Revolution. Consider again the case of Thomas Paine. After *Common Sense* was published, John Adams confronted Paine, told him "that his Reasoning from the Old Testament was ridiculous," and questioned Paine's sincerity. According to Adams, Paine "laughed...and then expressed a Contempt of the Old Testament and indeed of the Bible at large, which surprized me." Paine quickly recognized that Adams did not appreciate his disdain for scripture. Indeed, Adams once told Thomas Jefferson that "the Bible is the best book in the World." But Adams had not seen anything yet of Paine's religious radicalism.[7] In his *Age of Reason* (1794, 1795), Paine asserted that the Old Testament was "a history of wickedness," more appropriately judged "the word of a demon than the Word of God." Even so, Paine had quoted generously from the Old Testament to arouse patriotic opposition to British tyranny in *Common Sense*. Paine may not have believed in biblical truth, but he clearly recognized biblical persuasiveness. Paine knew that a convincing argument for American patriotism required a dose of scripture that would sustain patriots during what he later described as "the times that try men's souls," when "the summer-soldier and the sun-shine patriot" would abandon the cause. In effect, *Common Sense* had to make biblical sense.[8]

But what kind of "sense" did the Bible make of the American Revolution? Like almost everyone at the time, Paine knew that most colonists took the Bible seriously in pondering questions about war, politics, and patriotism. Despite the variety of studies on religion in the Revolution, however, we have no comprehensive analysis of how revolutionary Americans defended their patriotic convictions through scripture, which texts they cited and how they used them. As a result, any conclusions historians have drawn about the Bible in Revolutionary America have been necessarily tentative. In this book, I draw on an analysis of over 17,000 biblical citations in over 500 sources from New England, the middle colonies, and the South (see appendix). Through a reading of the sources and an analysis of their biblical citations, I have identified the biblical texts that colonists cited most often to inspire troops to fight for God and country. Although historians have known for years that the Bible was present in the American Revolution, this book reveals *how* it was present, specifically how it was used to make the patriotic case for war. It, for the first time, provides an analysis of the biblical texts and themes that rose to the forefront as American patriots rose to the task of challenging the British Empire. This book is not only about the Bible and the American Revolution; it is also a book about the patriotic Bible *of* the American Revolution.

Most of the sources are sermons, because colonists shaped patriotic interpretations of scripture mainly through preaching. Certainly, ministers were not the only colonists who looked to the Bible to make patriotic arguments for the Revolution. Nearly everyone, including the founders, employed patriotic views of the Bible, and this book therefore engages some of the biblical ideas of Abigail and John Adams, Benjamin Franklin, and, of course, Thomas Paine, among others. George Washington is an important presence here, not only for his biblical ideas, but because of his nearly biblical status in Revolutionary America. But this book does not focus primarily on the founders. The founders certainly quoted scripture to illustrate political ideas and to persuade the population, but to nowhere near the extent that the clergy did. Again Gordon Wood was correct: the clergy translated the Revolution's meaning to most people, and they were successful in doing so largely because they spoke in the all-persuasive stories and images from scripture. In the biblically saturated American colonies, ministers were the agreed-upon experts on the Bible; their sermons were the most serious engagements between scripture and war in America, both before and during the Revolution.

Certainly, not everyone paid attention to sermons. But the evidence indicates that wartime was prime time for preaching. The more war raged on, the more authoritative sermons became, to the point that the most productive year for preaching in colonial America was 1776. Sermons led the way in applying the Bible to the American Revolution. Even Thomas Paine's *Common Sense* seemed to be an exception that proved the rule, because historians often attributed its extraordinary success to the fact that it was much like a sermon. As historian Robert Middlekauff put it, Paine's *Common Sense* was "a sermon disguised as a political tract."[9]

The Bible and Pre-Revolutionary Patriotism

Biblical patriotism did not begin with the American Revolution. The colonists' views on war, government, and the Bible drew largely from European and British conflicts. Describing the centrality of scripture in the English Revolution of the seventeenth century, Christopher Hill pointed out that scripture was "accepted as the ultimate authority on economics and politics no less than on religion and morals." It made sense, therefore, that John Locke, the great philosopher of the Enlightenment, supported his influential *Two Treatises on Government* with ample biblical references to Moses, Abraham, Adam, Eve, Esau, and Cain.[10]

Even if biblical patriotism was not an American invention, wars in the colonies were unique, and they shaped unique perspectives on scripture. The Revolutionary War erupted in an America that was well accustomed to conflict. Nearly every colonist before the Revolution had been affected by war in some major way. The American colonists were uniquely militant, and we cannot understand the place of scripture in the Revolution without coming to terms with the colonists' wartime experiences. In these wars, American Indians were sometimes allies, but they were most often the colonists' enemies.[11]

A century before the Revolutionary War began, New England colonists fought the destructive King Philip's War against the Wampanoags and their allies. Later colonists engaged in a succession of wars against combined forces of France, sometimes Spain, and a variety of Native American peoples, culminating in the Seven Years' War (1756–1763), which had an American component, often called the French and Indian War (1754–1763). These wars were not particularly American but European. The real decision makers were across the Atlantic, calling on British colonists to sacrifice themselves on the battlefield without much support from England. In these engagements, many colonists believed they were fighting evil on a massive scale, an alliance of the French Catholic influences of "Antichrist" and devilish "savagery" that threatened God's Protestant, British forces.

Anti-Catholicism was a central biblical conviction for colonial Protestants, an inheritance from Europe that had its origins in the Reformation. For most colonial Protestants, Catholicism was "excellently calculated to make men slaves," as Massachusetts minister Peter Thacher preached in an unprinted sermon. Indian-hating was a newer conviction, forged in war on the American frontier. But like anti-Catholicism, Indian-hating became a biblical idea for Protestants, and it reached new heights during the Seven Years' War. As colonial Protestants went to war against the French and Native Americans, they believed they were fighting against the forces of hell; ministers preached that these wars were reminiscent of the most dramatic wars of scripture. As future president of Yale Ezra Stiles stated in an unprinted sermon, the American Indians were like the Canaanites of the Old Testament—they had to be wiped out so that God's people could take the Promised Land. Here Stiles celebrated the quick and "constant vanishing of the natives" from the land, along with the British victory over the French at Montreal in September 1760. With "the French removed," Stiles preached, "the Indians will be convinced" that the colonists "are [their] Masters in America."[12]

But even these conflicts against the forces of "papacy" and "savagery" did little to prepare colonists for the reversal of the Revolutionary War, when their own homeland became the tyrannical enemy, and Catholic France became an American ally. Through all these wars, many colonists revered the Bible not only as a moral and religious guide but also as an authority on warfare, and they ignited patriotic zeal with a patriotic Bible.

Biblical Obstacles to Wartime Patriotism

What historian Drew Gilpin Faust said of the American Civil War applied also to the Revolution: convincing soldiers to kill for their country was more difficult than inspiring them to die for it. Motivating soldiers to kill "required the more significant departure from soldiers' understandings of themselves as human beings and . . . as Christians."[13] Much of the Bible, and of Christianity in general, seemed to be antiwar—and anti-revolutionary. In the American Revolution, wartime motivation required biblical inspiration, as colonists mustered the biblical passages through which they justified war, waged it, coped with defeats, and celebrated victories.

Ministers knew well the obstacles patriots faced in the Revolutionary War, just as they knew better than anyone the value of scripture in overcoming such challenges. Most seriously, ministers recognized that both pacifists and loyalists could quote scripture to defend their positions. Pacifists often quoted the Sermon on the Mount, when Jesus commanded his followers to turn the other cheek rather than resist evil (Matthew 5:38). This text was a major challenge to patriots. They spent so much time refuting it that it became one of the most cited biblical texts in Revolutionary America (see appendix). Some loyalists even claimed that the Bible condemned the American Revolution as a satanic scheme, equating American patriotism with witchcraft.[14] Among British Methodists, for instance, John Wesley adamantly opposed the Revolution, and John Fletcher, in his sermon *The Bible and the Sword,* called on British Redcoats to execute biblically inspired warfare to suppress "the epidemical fever of wild patriotism," asserting that the American "patriots" were in reality "the mobbing sons of Belial" (a demon from the Old Testament).[15] For many American patriots, therefore, successful warfare required biblical warfare, and they had to make the most persuasive case they could for a patriotic Bible.

Another challenge that faced wartime preachers was the troubled condition of the soldiers they addressed. Most colonial soldiers were not professional military men and they were almost proud of their unprofessionalism. After all, most colonists were wary of anything that smacked of a "professional" military. Standing armies and hired mercenaries bred more corruption than protection, many believed, and they much preferred a virtuous and patriotic citizen army. So colonial soldiers were mostly younger than average (typically in their early twenties) and mostly poorer than average, and together they comprised what historian John Ferling called "armies of amateurs," ordinary citizens, many of whom had never set foot on a battlefield. Colonial soldiers were not only ill prepared, they were often outnumbered. At one point in the Revolution, the British had some 50,000 regular troops in the colonies, not counting 30,000 mercenaries, compared with fewer than 4000 American soldiers in the Continental Army, supplemented by an irregular number of militia men.[16]

Such inexperienced and overmatched soldiers needed instruction and inspiration, both of which ministers used the Bible to provide. Precisely because they were amateur soldiers, their ministers warned them not to be amateur Christians, since their success on the battlefield depended on spiritual and military training, and both relied on biblical wisdom. As army chaplain and Dutch Reformed pastor William Linn preached in

1776, the "American troops" were "raw and undisciplined," mostly "unaccustomed to horror and bloodshed." And yet "the Lord has made them strong in battle." Inspired by godly courage, Linn implored the army to "let your hearts betray no unmanly fears in our glorious cause. When you come to be drawn in battle array, let your breasts rise high and your joints stand firm; let a generous indignation sparkle in your eyes and flush on your cheeks...behave like men, and fight for your people, and for the cities of your God."[17]

Much was at stake in military preaching, which is why George Washington was skilled chaplains' strongest defender and inept chaplains' harshest critic. Whether he was commanding troops from Virginia in the French and Indian War or leading the Continental Army in the Revolutionary War, Washington wanted chaplains to accompany him. Patriotism, Washington knew, required commitment to virtuous discipline and sacrificial loyalty, and he needed preachers who could command patriotic fervor from the Bible to the battlefield.[18]

Assessing Biblical Patriotism: The Bible as War Story, the Revolutionary War as Biblical

Even before the Revolution, many colonists could not assess their wars without citing scripture, and they could not comprehend scripture without referencing war. For them the Bible was not a distant, ancient text; it was an engaging, universal drama, relevant and realistic, and interaction with scripture—whether through preaching, hearing, writing, or reading—was an engrossing exercise. Certainly, not all colonists agreed on how to interpret the Bible. The American Revolution was deeply rooted in ideas derived from the Enlightenment, and these ideas included new, critical questions about the Bible and its historical accuracy. Several of the founders, for instance, doubted the historical validity of much of scripture, including its stories of miracles. Even so, biblical skepticism did not interfere with biblical patriotism. Regardless of any doubts the founders and some ministers may have had, many of them still turned to scripture to inspire support for the Revolution.

The vast majority of Revolutionary-era Americans, however, were hardly biblical skeptics. They shared what theologian Hans Frei called a "pre-critical" view of scripture. That is, they believed the Bible to be "strongly realistic" and that scripture was both historically reliable and primarily "literal" in its meaning.[19] Moreover, for most Americans, not only was scripture mainly historical, but history's development since biblical times had, like scripture, been ordered by divine providence. Many revolutionary Americans, including George Washington, saw providence at work everywhere during the war. Providence helped make sense of the war, just as it helped make sense of scripture.[20]

One way in which providence worked through scripture was in the use of biblical typology, an ancient and popular means of interpreting the Bible. Interpreters viewed events and persons in the Old Testament as "types" that symbolized events and persons in the New Testament. In his defense of the Great Awakening revivals against both radical enthusiasts and rationalist doubters, Jonathan Edwards interpreted the story of David and Goliath as a "type" symbolizing Christian salvation. Just as God saved David from Goliath in a miraculous way, so, too, Christ saved his people "from their spiritual enemies." So David's military victory over Goliath prefigured Christ's spiritual victory over sin on the cross. Because God ordered history though providence, the various events of scripture held a larger meaning that even the participants in those events were unaware of. The same biblical text could also have multiple meanings. On another occasion Edwards used the story of David and Goliath to warn military officers and soldiers to trust in God, not in their own efforts, when going to war. David, Edwards preached, won the duel with Goliath because of God's deliverance, not because of David's own skill with the sling and the stone. In both contexts, the story of David and Goliath emphasized the power of God over human effort. Edwards's concern was that people would disregard the powerful work of the sovereign God and attempt to save themselves through their own prideful delusion. The results would be disastrous, both spiritually and militarily.[21]

One of the most important biblical models for war and for politics in general was Old Testament Israel. Colonists, from Puritan New England through the Revolution, drew numerous comparisons between their societies and ancient Israel. Most often, revolutionary ministers did not claim that Israel was a "type" that was finally fulfilled in the United States. Instead, most ministers agreed, the church was the ultimate fulfillment of Israel.[22] That did not stop Americans, however, from viewing Israel as an important example for the colonies, especially in wartime. In 1777, for example, Cyprian Strong of Chatham, Connecticut assumed that "there is no one (I trust) whose mind is not at once struck with the description of Israel, as being a most perfect resemblance of these American Colonies: almost as much so, as if spoken with a primary reference to them."[23]

Understandably, then, revolutionary patriots justified their actions by citing examples from biblical Israel, including the actions of war heroes such as Deborah and David. Through various types and examples, therefore, scripture gave people a dramatic, realistic, and historically reliable view of the world—one to which war was central.[24]

The Bible was seen, primarily, as a vast assemblage of war stories. Americans in a biblically literate society knew that the Bible was full of war—armies, battles, heroic warriors, and cowardly villains. But not all aspects of biblical warfare impressed Americans equally. Colonists reflected on the many narratives of war in the Bible through a variety of traditions and convictions—frameworks through which they selected biblical texts and applied them to experiences in wartime. Three interconnected themes were particularly important.[25]

Republicanism

In Revolutionary America, the Bible was one ancient authority to which patriots could appeal to reject British authority. Another was the classical world. Historians have demonstrated how founders and patriots of all varieties looked to ancient Rome and other classical republics to find political models of true republican governments. The Revolution's debt to the Bible has not received as much attention, prompting historian Joyce Appleby to vouch for the Bible's importance alongside classical influences. As Appleby noted, "Classical republicanism did not reign alone. The most important source of meaning for eighteenth-century Americans was the Bible." As well-known as classical history was in Revolutionary America, it certainly was not as widely known as scripture.[26]

Revolutionary patriotism was therefore both classical and biblical, and a variety of patriots, from founders to preachers, drew liberally from ancient Rome and ancient scripture to defend the American Revolution. Whether they were citing classical or biblical sources, patriots often read these sources through a political ideology known as "republicanism."

Republicanism was both central to the Revolution and notoriously hard to define—even the learned founders disagreed over what it meant. John Adams, who knew as much about republican ideas as anyone, once claimed neither he nor anyone else "ever did or ever will" know the full meaning of republicanism.[27] Despite its complexity, republicanism at least included a firm belief in virtue and liberty, and a fear that liberty was always threatened by vice and tyranny.

This sense that all governments, like individuals, were prone to corruption was critical. Both the classical world and scripture overflowed with
examples of how even the best nations, and the best individuals, could
fall. Greece and Rome were prime examples. Most revolutionary patriots agreed with the statement of Connecticut minister Levi Hart in 1775:
"Those ancient, renowned States of Greece and Rome" achieved "their
greatest luster from a set of public spirited, patriotic men, whose hearts
glowed with the love of liberty," and who influenced history "long after
those once mighty empires are gone to decay" by "neglecting to follow
the maxims of those wise men, those patriots of liberty."[28] Influenced by
republican ideas, citizens needed always to be on the lookout for what New
Hampshire Congregationalist and Harvard president Samuel Langdon
called out in the title of his Revolutionary-era sermon *Government corrupted by Vice*. These republican ideas influenced founders and ministers
alike, convincing them that they always needed to be aware that oppressive governments would overstep their bounds and infringe upon individual rights.[29]

Republicanism, colonists agreed, was definitely biblical—the Bible
"is the most Republican Book in the World," John Adams wrote.[30] Many
seventeenth-century figures who influenced republican thought, thinkers
like the English poet John Milton, used scripture to support their political
concepts.[31] Moreover, in America, New England Puritans developed a system of covenant theology from scripture that shaped their political struc-
tures, and this concept may well have influenced republicanism. Puritans
believed that God aligned with nations through covenants, with the classic case being ancient Israel, though New England Puritans saw themselves in covenant with God in a similar way. Nations that obeyed God
and honored the covenant, avoiding vice and promoting virtue, enjoyed
providential blessings while nations that disobeyed the covenant suffered
devastation and defeat. Covenant theology's teaching that moral nations
prospered while immoral nations suffered fit with the republican idea that
virtue was the key to success in government.[32]

The republican idea of a conflict between liberty and tyranny is essential to understanding the way many colonists read the Bible. In wartime,
liberty and tyranny were constantly at odds, they believed, not only within
governments, but also within the soul. This conflict was multifaceted,
both personal and social, and it was ancient and biblical. In the Seven
Years' War, as colonists fought against the French and their Indian allies,
clergy were especially adept at merging their view of the biblical warfare

of God's people with the republican cause of liberty. Soon, they would turn their Heaven-assisted weapons against the British forces of tyranny.[33]

Republican concepts of liberty, therefore, shaped colonists' views of themselves and their wars in relation to the ancient wars of scripture. Liberty was a multifaceted idea, however, both in scripture and in colonial America. So while most colonists were able to find republican liberty in scripture, they discovered that different biblical texts offered different definitions of liberty—the liberty of the Exodus differed from the liberty of Paul's teaching to the Galatians, for example.

Moreover, colonists disagreed on how to apply the Bible's teachings on liberty to their world—did they apply only to revolt against a monarch, or did they also imply revolt against African slavery in Revolutionary America? Some colonists used the Bible to oppose slavery, but most did not. Despite the flurry of revolutionary arguments for freedom, slavery prospered. White preachers dominated the pulpits, just as they led the way in defining (and limiting) what the Bible said about liberty. Moreover, most denominations did not allow women to preach. Historian Catherine Brekus well expressed the harsh reality: "In Revolutionary America, only white men were created equal."[34] Another limitation on liberty was denominational. Protestantism was dominant in the Revolutionary era. Of some 3200 communities of worship in the colonies in 1775 only about sixty were Catholic churches, and five were Jewish synagogues.[35] For many non-Protestants, as well as for some Protestants (including Baptists), both scripture and republican ideas fueled arguments for religious liberty against the official (and tax-supported) churches in the states. By the end of the Revolution, colonists had not shaped one republican Bible but many republican Bibles. Over time, the flexibility of freedom—and its engagement with diverse views of scripture—only expanded exponentially in the early republic.[36]

Martyrdom

The ideal of sacrifice was central to the republican concept of virtue. Liberty came only when people of integrity sacrificed themselves for their nation. This was the essence of patriotism.[37] The virtue of sacrifice was not new for colonial Protestants. Likely influenced by martyr stories such as those featured in John Foxe's *Actes and Monuments,* many had what historian Susan Juster called an "oversized colonial martyr complex"; they believed that suffering was central to their faith. And though Juster argued that actual martyrdom was "a textual experience in colonial America"—more read about than experienced—experiences in war were an exception.³⁸ Colonial wars not only generated heroic acts of sacrifice and martyrdom but also produced sermons that heralded the virtues of suffering for the faith.

During the American Revolution, references to martyrdom were every-where. Fallen soldiers under Washington's command were martyrs, sev-eral ministers proclaimed, and their heroism would rank them alongside the heroic martyrs of church history. In his dramatic sermon after the war *America Saved, or Divine Glory displayed, in the late War with Great Britain,* Connecticut minister Thomas Brockway preached that American soldiers had "nobly died martyrs to liberty." As such, all Americans should celebrate the memory of these revolutionary martyrs, Brockway preached. Shame on any "unfeeling wretch that refuses to drop a tear upon the urn of" these "officers and brave soldiers, that have spilt their blood in the cause of liberty." Let the memories of these martyrs "be held dear to pos-terity, and the liberties of our country" and let "the price of their blood, be ever treated as sacred," Brockway asserted.³⁹

Likewise, in a sermon delivered after the battle at Yorktown, Israel Evans, one of George Washington's favorite chaplains, praised the "mar-tyrs for the cause of freedom," and proclaimed that, if heaven would allow it, he would call them to rise from the grave "and animate your country-men to finish the glorious work of liberty! Arise, and lead on your brother soldiers to dreadful deeds of death and slaughter, until the ruthless hand of Britain shall no more disturb the peace of men." These patriotic mar-tyrs were blessed by God, and contrasted sharply with villainous traitors such as Benedict Arnold, who, as chaplain George Duffield of Philadelphia preached, was "cursed and detested of God and of men."⁴⁰

Military and Spiritual Warfare

Even when preaching on war or summoning troops to battle, ministers connected their martial zeal to a higher priority: salvation. Understandably, therefore, the ideas of sacrificial martyrdom and Christian republican-ism gained coherence alongside a third conviction, the belief that biblical warfare integrated spirituality and violence, the spiritual struggles of the soul with military struggles on the battlefield. That is, biblical warfare was waged on two fronts. The Bible's most fundamental war was spiritual war-fare, a struggle for salvation that pitted Christ versus Satan, virtue versus vice—a conflict that entangled every human soul. But biblical warfare was not merely a metaphor for spirituality. Many clergy connected spiritual and military warfare, violent conflicts between God's chosen people and their enemies. Biblical wars were both military and spiritual, and the two were mutually reinforcing.[41]

As ministers asserted, skillful soldiers in spiritual warfare could be the most vicious fighters in military wars. Though God granted victory, he did not win military battles alone. As in spiritual warfare, in military warfare God worked through human efforts or "means," so military expertise was critical. As Israel Evans preached just before Washington's army began its famous winter encampment at Valley Forge, "the only means to procure" military success "are the sharpness of your swords,...your skill in war, and your invincible courage in battle."[42] Here again, the pious could reap benefits in battle. Vibrant spirituality could reinforce martial discipline—Christianity made better soldiers. Authentic faith could bring success on the battlefield, and military prowess was a spiritual gift.[43] As Massachusetts Congregationalist Eli Forbes preached in 1771, "I would not intimate that every good Christian is of consequence a good soldier,—an accomplished man of war; but this I will venture to say, there cannot be a good soldier, an accomplished man of war, destitute of the principle and practice of Christianity."[44] When ministers connected spiritual and military warfare, therefore, they made patriotic service in war a sacred virtue. Ministers hoped that soldiers, inspired by the spiritual nature of patriotic duty, would overcome their natural aversions to dying—and especially killing—in battle.

Americans envisioned a patriotic Bible through the potent synthesis of these convictions: political liberty was a divine cause against tyrannical evil, sacrifice and martyrdom for God's chosen nation were virtues, and there was an intimate relationship between spiritual and military warfare. Inspired by these ideas, colonists selected the biblical passages through which they made sense of war. While all wars require explanation—narratives that distinguish just warriors from unjust aggressors—colonial American wars also required biblical interpretation. In battles against the Indians and the French, and in the later Revolution against the British, wars influenced which biblical texts colonists saw as being most important and how they applied those texts in their political and spiritual lives.

This book examines the biblical texts that colonists found most productive in waging American wars and in proclaiming American patriotism. Obviously, one book cannot possibly cover all the biblical texts that

American patriots took with them to war. What it does offer, however, is an unprecedented analysis of the most cited and the most discussed biblical texts that shaped wartime patriotism. These scriptures were popular for a reason. They were, in the view of many patriots, the most useful in making the case for war. Following chapter 1, which narrates the important context of biblical patriotism in the military sermon, the remaining chapters focus on these prominent scriptures and themes. In assessing the popularity of these texts and themes in Revolutionary America, we gain for the first time a reliable account of how patriots used the Bible. Despite the variety of texts applied to numerous battle situations, consistent themes emerge that allow one to grasp a militant view of scripture, a patriotic Bible *of* the American Revolution.[45]

I

"The Curse of Cowardice"

THE MARTIAL POWER OF THE SERMON

Is the Work of Peace...our only Business? No; in such a
Time even the God of Peace proclaims by his Providence,
'To Arms!' Then the Sword is...consecrated to God; and
the Art of War becomes a Part of our Religion.
SAMUEL DAVIES, *The Curse of Cowardice* (1759)

"AS THE SKILL of a pilot in a storm, and the worth of a Christian in a time of trial, so the valor of a soldier is best seen in a day of battle," preached Nathan Perkins, a Congregationalist pastor from Hartford, Connecticut. The problem was, as Perkins knew well, most of the soldiers he addressed had never seen "a day of battle." It was June 2, 1775. The Revolutionary War had started less than two months earlier. Thirteen days later George Washington would be appointed commander in chief of the Continental Army. In the meantime, a war that many never thought they would see was raging. The duty of the preacher was to summon martial courage in the place of military experience. "The most of you are strangers to the dreadful horrors of battle," including "the roaring of cannon, the smoke and confusion, the cries of the wounded," and the "groans of the dying." Even so, "be courageous," Perkins charged. "You fight not for your daily bread," but you fight for "your just rights, all you hold dear as men and sacred as Christians, your all." What greater motives could any soldier have? "If these motives do not fire your souls in your country's cause, what can! Indeed you have every thing before you to rouse up the soldier, warm the man and animate the Christian." Even with motives galore, however, Perkins knew that inspiring soldiers for battle required replacing the fear of war with the fear of being branded a coward. "Cowardice is as unseemly in a soldier, as ignorance is in a statesman," he implored.[1]

In the colonies, sermons were the most important tool for disseminating biblical interpretation. Both before and after the Revolution, sermons were preached on appointed days of fasting or thanksgiving in times of crisis, days on which even presidents such as Thomas Jefferson saw the political value of biblical rhetoric.[2]

The influence of the sermon was never more powerful than in wartime, when communal values, social identity, and unifying purpose were critical. Many viewed the sermon as an important tool for combating the chronic problems of soldier recruitment and morale. In sermons, colonists heard that courage was indispensible—faith itself implied struggle, which required courage. In times of war, faithful courage meant the readiness to fight. Sermons were social acts, able to unite people into a courageous force. More importantly, though, sermons were messages of salvation. Although practical matters entered sermons, the gospel remained. Most preachers were adept at reinforcing the connection between military sacrifice and authentic faith. Through hundreds of martial sermons, ministers, who were among the more educated and more respected colonists, led the way in interpreting the Bible and proclaiming its relevance—both politically and spiritually—for American wars.

It is therefore not surprising that preaching intensity increased as the Revolutionary crisis escalated. As Harry S. Stout determined, "more sermons were preached in 1776 than in any previous year in New England's history."[3] The statistics are impressive. In Revolutionary America, Congregationalist ministers alone preached over 2000 sermons each week. Sermons were published at four times the rate of political pamphlets and were more influential as well. Whereas pamphlets were aimed at an elite readership, sermons began as an oral communication for everyone and, as such, proved even more persuasive in printed form.[4] The sermon buttressed the Revolution in ways that the pamphlet could not match. The most radical exception was, of course, Thomas Paine's bestseller *Common Sense,* published in 1776. But it was the exception that proved the rule. Paine's pamphlet was effective in part because it was a not much like a pamphlet at all. It was more like a sermon, filled with biblical references in a common style and noticeably lacking Latin quotations and classical forms. Its sermonic style had much to do with its success.[5]

Ideas mattered, whether printed in pamphlets or delivered in sermons, but just as important were their modes of expression. Delivery was critical, which may be why revivals were a driving force for the Revolution. Certainly, not all patriots were revivalist Protestants, and not all revivalist

Protestants were patriots, although many were. Moreover, many revivalist patriots saw a connection between their zeal for the gospel and their zeal for the American cause. For many revivalist Protestants, it was natural to assume that great preachers would be great patriots. We find an instance of this confidence in Presbyterian minister Nathaniel Whitaker's eulogy of George Whitefield, who died in 1770. Whitaker, a pastor in Salem, Massachusetts, was a devotee of Whitefield, and had traveled to Britain with him on one of his preaching tours. In the eulogy, while celebrating Whitefield's unrivaled spiritual influence, Whitaker also asserted Whitefield's patriotism. Whitefield, Whitaker preached, "was a patriot, not in shew, but reality, and an enemy to tyranny." Whitaker even credited Whitefield with contributing to the repeal of the Stamp Act.[6] Whitaker was not alone in believing that Whitefield had serious patriotic credentials.

Whitefield's patriotic reputation did not rest completely on political preaching. His sermons certainly had political ramifications, but he rarely addressed politics directly. Typically, he preached on the spiritual "New Birth" of salvation. Still, Whitefield became a source of patriotic authority. In September of 1775, five months into the Revolutionary War and five years after Whitefield's death, a group of Continental Army officers visited Whitefield's tomb in Newburyport, Massachusetts. They were looking for inspiration for battle, but in an unusual way. They asked that Whitefield's coffin be opened. When the sexton complied, the officers removed the famous evangelist's collar and his wristbands and took the relics with them. The army officers may not have known much about Whitefield's political preaching, or the relative lack thereof, but they knew Whitefield as an evangelist who appealed to the people and resisted traditional authority.[7]

Some historians have claimed that the revivals influenced the Revolution not so much intellectually as rhetorically. That is, revivals did not directly "cause" the Revolution. But revivalists, especially Whitefield, developed new methods for drawing large crowds and persuading them through zealous, biblical rhetoric.[8] As historian Thomas Kidd has persuasively argued, "Evangelicalism bred an egalitarian spirit that fed a deep social transformation, that revolution in 'hearts and minds' accompanying the military and political rebellion." Much of this "egalitarian spirit" came from revivalist preachers' skillful use of the Bible.[9]

Sermons could also inspire patriotism, many believed, because biblical preaching shaped virtue, and patriotism could not exist without virtue. A good patriot was often assumed to be a good Christian. Perhaps that explains why Abigail Adams saw more of Christianity in Benjamin

Franklin than he ever saw in himself. In November 1775, after she had enjoyed a nice dinner with Franklin, Adams wrote to her husband that Franklin was "social, but not talkative, and when he spoke, something useful dropped from his tongue." She also said that Franklin was "grave, yet pleasant and affable." What most impressed Abigail Adams, however, was Franklin's character. She saw it all over his face—literally. "I thought I could read in his countenance the virtues of his heart, among which patriotism shone in its full lustre, and with that is blended every virtue of a Christian: for a true patriot must be a religious man." First impressions can be deceiving of course, and years later she would recant this positive impression of Franklin. Possibly her first impression of Franklin deceived her because she shared the widespread assumption that patriotism could not thrive in a soul lacking Christian convictions. As she expressed it, "He who neglects his duty to his Maker may well be expected to be deficient and insincere in his duty towards the public." Without Christianity to support virtue, "revenge or ambition, pride, lust, or profit" would corrupt would-be patriots. Once such corruption set in, "you may as well hope to bind up a hungry tiger with a cobweb, as to hold such debauched patriots in the visionary chains of decency, or to charm them with the intellectual beauty of truth and reason."[10]

Preaching supported patriotism, therefore, in part because virtue was a critical wartime asset. No authentic republic could be conceived without virtue, which was the safeguard of liberty. Virtue, however, was always contested, and the only assured test of it was struggle.

This message of republican virtue and the struggles needed to sustain it was much on the minds of people in Revolutionary America. It was the primary concern in a sermon preached one month after the Boston Massacre. The preacher, Judah Champion, a Congregationalist pastor from Litchfield, Connecticut, took the pulpit to proclaim that liberty often required war and that virtue always required sacrifice. There was no easy way for the people to maintain their freedoms. What the people needed above all, Champion preached, was a lesson in liberty that dwelt, not on rights and privileges, but on hardship and history—on, as he put it in the title of his sermon, *The Distresses, Hardships and Dangers our Ancestors Encounter'd, in Settling New-England.* This story of hardship was often told, but it could not be told often enough, Champion asserted, especially in troubled times. The people of 1770 were "very much unacquainted with the distresses their ancestors encounter'd, whose zeal and virtue should not be forgotten." In fact, these "trials, hardships and perils" could not be forgotten if the people were to protect their liberties, both "civil and religious" from violation. What inspired Champion, therefore, and what he hoped would inspire the people in the days after the Boston Massacre was a war story, actually a story of several wars and hardships, all of which had shaped the character of the people as they earned their freedoms in covenant with God.[11]

This narration of wars and struggle began as mainly a New England story, but it eventually involved all the colonies. Early in the Revolution, New England was the site of the most intense conflict between Britain and the colonies. The "massacre" happened, after all, in Boston, and that was no accident. Massachusetts was the home of the most radical agitators against Britain, to the point that the British saw the budding conflict as a regional one. It made sense, then, that Champion looked to New England's history to inspire patriotism.

As the conflict escalated, colonists from other regions would claim the New England story as their own. It made perfect sense that the Second Continental Congress would summon this story when it presented the Declaration of Taking up Arms on July 6, 1775. "Our forefathers," they wrote, "left their native land to seek on these shores a residence for civil and religious freedom." As always, the search for freedom demanded struggle: "At the expense of their blood . . . they effected settlements in the distant and inhospitable wilds of America, then filled with numerous and warlike nations of barbarians."[12] The story needed to be told, the Congress realized, because it proved that the colonists had earned their freedoms. Patriotic preachers like Champion drew the same lesson.

In fact, Champion's sermon was no less than a litany on war, a proclamation of the colonists' struggles, one after another, from the first settlements to the present distresses. Champion described wars with Native Americans filled with "shocking instances of savage cruelty," which were "enough to chill the blood in every vein. How many of our ancestors, who came into America, as an asylum for liberty, have fallen sacrifices to Pagan cruelty! How many little ones have had their brains dashed out against the stones! Nevertheless our progenitors, through the good hand of GOD upon them, nobly surmounted all those pressing difficulties they had to encounter." Champion's descriptions of such wars were hardly a fair representation of events. With all its biases and limitations, however, Champion put history to use in shaping an effective argument for revolutionary patriotism.[13]

Wartime occasions were almost always preaching occasions in colonial America. Champion's sermon shows how the history of the Bible in Revolutionary American patriotism is unintelligible without recognizing the place of the sermon in colonial American wars.

Frontier Warfare and the Rise of Martial Preaching

War, as historian Jill Lepore has written, always involves "wounds and words."[14] War requires both violence and discourse—words to justify killing, to cope with destruction, and to give meaning to victory and defeat. In colonial America, the words that gave meaning to war were often religious ones, especially words from the Bible and wartime sermons. Sermons powerfully shaped how colonial societies came to terms with their martial identities. It is no accident that New England was both the most sermon-saturated and the most militant region in colonial North America.

Nothing strengthened the sermon in New England more pervasively than war. In the catastrophic destruction of King Philip's War in 1675, the most destructive war between colonists and Native Americans in the seventeenth century, preaching helped colonists to shape their identity as "a people of war." Times of crisis naturally increased the power of the pulpit. But during King Philip's War, ministers were not only comforting; they also seemed prophetic. Preachers had been delivering warnings about God's impending punishment of a wayward people. That punishment now arrived in the devastation wrought by war. King Philip and his allies were merely the agents of God's wrath. As the war raged, the sermon was the ultimate providential guide and justifier of New England's punishment and eventual deliverance. Deliverance would come, ministers preached, when the people recognized that they were fighting not only the Native Americans but their own sins. If the people renounced their wicked ways, the covenant between God and New England would survive, as had the covenant between God and ancient Israel. God required of his people obedience—and that obedience included the willingness to wage war.[15]

Preachers had many opportunities to address war and issues of national concern in annual election sermons, which were attended by governors and legislators. In artillery election sermons, delivered to commemorate the election of militia officers, the people learned that "the art of war" was a divinely approved virtue, and that Christ required them to fight. As King Philip's War ended, chaplain Samuel Nowell's artillery election sermon *Abraham in Arms* set the tone for martial preaching for years to come, using as a text one of the most popular martial scriptures, Exodus 15:3 "The Lord is a Man of War."[16]

Through the power of sermons like *Abraham in Arms*, preachers found ample biblical resources to reinforce the colonists' identity as a martial people. A few colonists even believed that the Bible itself was a sacred object with strange wartime powers. A soldier named Goodman Wright believed that holding the Bible protected him from Indian attacks. Apparently the Indians knew this, because those who killed him in battle "rippe[d] him open and put his Bible in his Belly."[17]

We know of this graphic story through one of many Puritan narratives about King Philip's War. It seemed that New England colonists could not write or preach enough about war. And they not only wrote about violence, they committed their share of it too, even in its most extreme forms. New England colonists were not above torture, and they offered rewards for scalps of their Indian enemies. When Metacom (King Philip) was finally captured, New Englanders decapitated him and quartered his body, actions that the renowned minister Increase Mather justified by saying that Philip was "hewed in pieces before the Lord."[18]

Through various wars with the American Indians, therefore, colonists developed their own unique ways of fighting, often called the "American way of war." They sometimes employed "terror tactics," including violence against noncombatants. Not only did colonists kill American Indian women and children, but they also destroyed their villages, executed those captured in war, and even sold some as slaves.[19] Colonists who employed these military tactics often did so because they believed they were fighting savages who did not play by normal military rules. Why, then, should the colonists fight fair? To do so would be to handicap themselves in battle. In the King Philip's War, some Puritans observed that wars against Indians did not deserve the dignity of being called legitimate wars, because the term "war" assumed a conflict between civilized nations, fought according to normal rules of combat.[20] Whether or not the "troubles" with the Indians in 1675 deserved to be called a war, they certainly called for martial preaching, finding defenses in scripture to support New England's covenant with God in violent times. In New England, therefore, the prestige of the sermon and the militancy of society were mutually reinforcing.[21]

This reciprocal interplay between the sermon and war developed over the next century both in and beyond New England, culminating in the Revolution. Preachers had plenty of opportunities to hone their wartime skills, for war was never far from the colonies in the eighteenth century. Most of these colonial wars were extensions of larger European conflicts, particularly between England and France. In America, they were known as King William's War (1689–1697), Queen Anne's War (1702–1713), King George's War (1744–1748), and the French and Indian War (1754–1763), which was the American stage of a war known in Europe as the Seven Years' War (1756–1763). Through these wars, preachers preached as soldiers fought, and, influenced by war sermons, colonists understood their patriotic service as a spiritual duty. Sermons punctuated all the diverse activities of war—electing militia officers, summoning troops to battle, and making biblical sense out of victory and defeat.

Sermons played a prominent role in one of the great moments of colonial American patriotism before the Revolution. In June 1745, New England militia under the command of William Pepperrell attacked the French fort at Louisbourg, on the island of Cape Breton in Canada. In preparing for the attack, military leaders called upon the clergy for support. Pepperell even enlisted the help of George Whitefield, who supported the campaign and even provided a motto for it: *Nil Desperandum, Christo Duce* (Christ leads, never despair!). This attack, in the midst of King George's War, proved dramatically successful, and the victory aroused the colonies—especially in New England, but in the middle colonies as well. It was a miraculous victory, many colonists believed, and most importantly, it displayed God's military might on behalf of his Protestant British forces. God even seemed to side with the colonists in battle, as a storm destroyed a fleet of French ships that had been sent to retake the fort.

Many of the clergy were ecstatic, and they preached sermons that celebrated New England's triumph over the French Catholic power. Preaching in July 1745, in celebration of the dramatic Cape Breton victory, renowned Boston pastor Charles Chauncy lauded the Song of Deborah because it "gives the principal Glory" of military success to God, but did not neglect "to give all just Applause to the Officers and Troops that acquired it under the divine Conduct and Blessing." In wartime, therefore, Whitefield (the most famous revival preacher) and Chauncy (one of revival's harshest critics) spoke in patriotic unison.[22]

We see in these sermons a rising intensity in the developing alignment between Protestantism and republicanism. Historically, many colonists considered republicanism a radical political ideology that clashed with traditional Protestant theology. In the midst of war with France, however, preachers increasingly linked religious and political liberty, and envisioned the Protestant struggle against Catholicism as parallel to Britain's struggle for freedom against French tyranny.[23]

Republican convictions, then, which so influenced eighteenth-century wars, developed from war and turmoil in the seventeenth century. Particularly important was the crisis of 1649, when the English people beheaded King Charles I and waged a civil war. The next crisis occurred in 1688, when King James II was dethroned and replaced by William III and his wife, Mary II. Queen Mary was James's daughter and King William was his nephew. More importantly, William and Mary were Protestant and King James had been Catholic. British citizens, most of whom were Protestant, called his dethroning the "Glorious Revolution," and it was glorious primarily because it had removed a Catholic from the throne. Catholicism, most British Protestants believed, was inherently tyrannical, so they instinctively feared Catholic monarchs. During the reign of William and Mary, Parliament gained expanded powers. A Bill of Rights was passed that ensured many English liberties, included safeguards against a Catholic retaking the throne, and forbade any monarch from instituting a standing army in peacetime. The Glorious Revolution inspired a political perspective known as "Real Whig," which guarded British rights against tyrannical threats, especially from any unchecked political authority, whether a monarch or Parliament. In this way their government, the English people believed, stood in stark contrast with the tyrannical Catholic monarchies of France and Spain.[24]

The alliance of colonial American Protestantism and republicanism expanded in the Seven Years' War, the fourth and most critical war in which England and France battled for dominance in northeastern America. It far surpassed in scope any war that had affected the colonies, though the war in the colonies was only one segment of a massive conflict that was, as Winston Churchill said, "the first world war." The Seven Years' War expanded beyond the colonies and even beyond France and England to encompass West Africa, the Caribbean, the Philippines, and India. On the American stage, it involved three empires—England; France; and the Iroquois Confederacy, an alliance of the Mohawk, Oneida, Onondaga, Cayuga, and Seneca nations. Today, we may have difficulty thinking of the Iroquois Confederacy as an empire comparable to those of France and England. But, as historian Fred Anderson has argued, "the Iroquois

League had been practicing its own brand of imperialism for more than a century before the Seven Years' War began."[25]

The war started when a little-known twenty-two-year-old Virginian named George Washington launched his military career with a victory that spun out of control into a bloody massacre. In 1754, Washington was a lieutenant colonel of a Virginia militia, charged with countering the French threat in the Ohio Country—a large area between the Blue Ridge Mountains and the Great Lakes that was fiercely contested between the French and British. Along the way, Washington joined an important British ally, Tanacharison (also spelled Tanaghrisson), a Seneca leader and diplomatic representative of the Iroquois Confederation. On May 27, Washington and his forces, joined by Tanacharison and his warriors, surrounded some thirty-two French troops led by Joseph Coulon de Villiers de Jumonville, attacking and quickly defeating them. After the battle was over, Tanacharison attacked Jumonville with a hatchet, bashing in his skull and then pulling out his brains. His warriors responded by scalping nearby French soldiers. Tanacharison's act was a clear declaration of war.[26]

A little over a month after the massacre, Washington, newly promoted to colonel, suffered two devastating defeats: the first at the Battle of Fort Necessity on July 3, 1754, and the second at the Battle of the Monongahela six days later. The defeat at Monongahela was an unabashed disaster. General Edward Braddock, the commander in chief of the British troops, had little respect for the American Indians as soldiers. He once told Benjamin Franklin that "savages...may indeed be a formidable enemy to your raw American militia; but upon the king's regular and disciplined troops, Sir, it is impossible they should make any impression." Braddock could not have been more wrong. Ironically, he was killed by a mostly American Indian force at the Monongahela River. Reflecting on the battle almost a half century later, Baptist pastor Richard Furman of South Carolina blamed the defeat on Braddock, the "haughty, confident commander," and said that Braddock could have avoided "the fatal and shameful defeat" if he had listened to the advice of Washington. After Braddock fell, Washington took charge of the troops—fortunately for them, Furman surmised. Had it not been for Washington's "courage and conduct," the remaining British troops would "have been cut to pieces." At least Washington survived the debacle, along with Daniel Boone, who would later achieve fame as a hero of the American frontier.[27]

Twenty-two years later, just after the new nation had issued its Declaration of Independence, Washington recalled how happy he had been just to have survived these crushing defeats. In that celebrated July of 1776, Washington wrote that he "did not let the Anniversary of the 3d or 9th of this [month] pass off without a grateful remembrance of the escape we had at the Meadows and on the Banks of Monongahela. [T]he same Providence that protected us upon those occasions will, I hope, continue his Mercies, and make us happy Instruments in restoring Peace & liberty to this once favour'd, but now distressed Country."[28]

Here, then, Washington, not known for his piety, expressed his faith in, perhaps even anxieties about, divine providence. For Washington, as for nearly everyone else in Revolutionary America, war and divine providence were inextricably connected. Facing the challenges of the Revolution, Washington turned to God, and to his memories of the Seven Years' War. Just as he had earned his heroic reputation in that war, so did it profoundly shape the tradition of colonial American religious patriotism that Washington exemplified.

The religious patriotism formed in the Seven Years' War was fiercely anti-Catholic and often anti–American Indian.[29] One of the masters of patriotic preaching in this war was Samuel Davies, a revivalist Presbyterian from Hanover County, Virginia. Davies was impressive. No less great an orator than the revolutionary patriot Patrick Henry called Davies the best speaker he had ever heard. In August 1755, one month after the disastrous defeat at the Monongahela River, Davies used his famous oratorical skills to inspire a company of Virginia volunteers to go to battle. He titled his sermon *Religion and Patriotism the Constituents of a Good Soldier*, and his biblical text was "Be of good Courage, and let us play the men, for our People, and for the Cities of our God" (2 Samuel 10:12). Zealous religious patriotism was the only appropriate reaction to Braddock's defeat, Davies preached. Playing "the men" on God's behalf required a righteous loathing of the French and their "savage" accomplices in crime. "Our Frontiers" are "ravaged by merciless Savages, and our Fellow-Subjects" were "murdered with all the horrid Arts of Indian and Popish Torture." These "Indian and Popish" adversaries were the "eternal Enemies of Liberty."

Davies's goal was not only to mourn the loss of Braddock and his troops, but to use that embarrassing defeat to ignite a righteous patriotism among Virginians. The problem was that the people had been neither patriotically zealous nor spiritually faithful. "Alas! Our Country has been sunk in a deep sleep: A stupid Security has unmanned the Inhabitants." They had been inflicted "with an effeminate, cowardly Spirit." They had left their fellow subjects "to fall a helpless Prey to Blood-thirsty Savages, without affording them proper Assistance." What was Virginia to do, he implored, about "the hairy Scalps, clotted with Gore! The mangled Limbs! The ript-up Women! The Heart and Bowels, still palpitating with Life, smoking on the Ground!" What was Virginia to do about the "savages swilling their Blood, and imbibing a more outrageous Fury with the inhuman Draught! Sure these are not Men; they are not Beasts of Prey; they are something worse; they must be infernal Furies in human shape." Given such atrocities, "with what Horror must we look upon ourselves, as being little better than Accessories to their Blood?" What will the future of Virginia be? "Shall Virginia incur the Guilt and the everlasting Shame, of tamely exchanging her Liberty, her Religion, and her All, for arbitrary Gallic Power, and for Popish Slavery, Tyranny and Massacre?" These rhetorical questions called for righteous courage—not a rash, "savage ferocious Violence," but true "fortitude"—"the courage of a Man, and not of a Tyger."[30]

The next year Davies published *Virginia's Danger and Remedy*, which included reflections on Braddock's defeat and the need for patriotism. Two years later he preached the sermon *The Curse of Cowardice* to the militia in Hanover county. Here, he selected as his text Jeremiah's command "cursed be he that keepth back his Sword from Blood" (Jeremiah 48:10). Courage in warfare was the only Christian option, he preached. No substitute would do. To be sure, God was the Lord of peace. But how could peace be shared with "cruel invaders?" In the Seven Years' War, "the Sword is...consecrated to God; and the Art of War becomes a Part of our Religion." In such times, "even the God of Peace proclaims:...'To Arms!'" In these and other patriotic sermons, Davies's blending religion and republicanism was typical of the time. The Protestant and British cause of liberty faced attack on two sides—from Catholic tyranny and from American Indian "savagery."[31]

Throughout the conflict, sermons punctuated the decisive battles. In the latter years of the war, when the fortunes of the British improved, preachers responded with patriotic praise. General James Wolfe's dramatic victory at Quebec in 1759 prompted several celebratory sermons, many of them printed. When Montreal fell in September 1760, pulpits and presses erupted in jubilation.[32] Even segments of the American Jewish population were caught up in the religious patriotism. A published prayer service from a New York synagogue offered thanks "to Almighty God, for the Reducing of Canada to His Majesty's Dominions."[33] Just as all previous wars the colonists had fought paled in comparison to this war, so did the religious arguments in support of this war surpass all previous attempts to bring religion to bear on colonial wars. The Seven Years' War took republican Protestantism to new heights.

Martial Preaching in Revolutionary America

It is one of the great ironies of American history that the colossal British victory in the Seven Years' War set the stage for American Revolution. Few could at the time have imagined the sea change that was to come. As the Seven Years' War drew to a close, the colonies pulsed with British patriotism; colonists had never been prouder of their British identity. Finally, it seemed, they would be free to enjoy all the rights of loyal British subjects. At the same time, victory in war impressed many colonists with what they could accomplish when they united around a glorious cause.

But victory had its costs. The Treaty of Paris officially ended the war in 1763, and British war debts reached catastrophic heights, adding up to over 137 million pounds, far surpassing the normal British budget of 8 million pounds. Adding to the cost was the expense of maintaining security in America. The French and American Indians were still a threat—treaties could be signed, but only military presence ensured compliance. The British government decided that maintaining American security required a standing army, and a substantial one. Lord Jeffery Amherst, hero of the war and North American commander in chief, believed that 10,000 soldiers should be stationed in America.[34] War debts and postwar security demanded revenue. Taxes would be required, and the British government believed that colonists should pay many of them. After all, the war had been fought in large part to liberate the colonies from the French. The colonists agreed, but also felt that they had spent more than their share of blood helping to win the British victory, and that blood ought to count for more than money. To impose a standing army on America was unprecedented and, to many colonists, unwanted and even hostile. To impose heavy taxes on them was also unprecedented and equally hostile. These moves, which the British saw as necessary and right, seemed arbitrary and oppressive to the colonists.

Sermonizing the Stamp Act

The trouble accelerated with the Stamp Act of 1765, with which Parliament taxed the colonies directly on paper products, including pamphlets, newspapers, and almanacs. This was a radical change from the Crown's usual means of raising revenue by imposing customs duties on goods imported to the colonies. Most colonists did not like the duties, but they saw the need for them. Besides, many had become expert smugglers to avoid paying the duties. But the Stamp Act imposed a direct tax, not a duty, and the colonists believed that it violated their rights as British subjects. After all, the people elected their representatives and assemblies, and only those representatives had the right to tax them. The colonists did not consider themselves to be truly represented in Parliament; so, Parliament had no right to tax them. Moreover, they were in no mood to pay draconian taxes. The colonies were suffering an economic downturn—their markets were filled with products they could not sell, diminishing the value of their goods. Bankruptcy was rampant. To make matters worse, in 1764 the British had issued the Currency Act, which forbade the colonists from printing their own money, and the Sugar Act, which hampered their smuggling trade by vigorously enforcing the collection of duties on sugar, molasses, and other imports. With the Stamp Act, however, the colonists believed that Parliament had crossed the line between just rule and tyrannical imposition.[35]

The typical response, heard throughout the colonies, was emphatic: "no taxation without representation." The British had not anticipated the fiery reception the Stamp Act received in America. In one of the most famous responses, Patrick Henry of Virginia wrote several resolutions, one of which asserted that to support Parliament's authority to tax the colonies was to brand oneself a traitor to the colony. Other reactions were just as extreme. Some colonists rioted, and some organized into patriotic societies, the most famous of which was the Sons of Liberty. Such reactions made it dangerous to support the act. In Boston, a band of protesters took out their hostility on Andrew Oliver, the agent whose job it was to enforce the act, by burning him in effigy.[36]

In responding so strongly to the Stamp Act, colonists revealed themselves to be fierce advocates for the Real Whig political perspective. Yet Americans did not consider themselves to be radical thinkers. In their view, they were holding England accountable to the unwritten English "constitution," or vision of government, which they believed the nation had drifted away from. Not only the Real Whigs but nearly everyone in Britain had deep respect for the country's heralded constitution. It was the English constitution that had made the British Empire the world's foremost bastion of liberty. Its brilliance was in its balance of the three main orders of society: monarchy, nobility, and common people. Under the English constitution, each of these orders had its own place in the government. The power of the monarch was balanced by the two houses of Parliament—the House of Lords, which represented the nobility, and the House of Commons, which represented the people. The best form of government was mixed, part monarchy and part republic, an idea the British found well expressed in French political philosopher Montesquieu's *Spirit of the Laws* (1748) and other works.[37]

The people knew this was a delicate balance, however, and that tyranny was always a threat. Many revolutionaries believed that England had gradually upended that balance and impinged upon the rights of its citizens. In claiming to restore the true meaning of the English constitution, American revolutionaries were actually positing a new, somewhat radical interpretation of the constitution that separated them from the mainstream views of other English citizens.

This Real Whig perspective had many influences, including the seventeenth-century thinkers Algernon Sidney, who was executed in 1683 for conspiring against King Charles II, and John Milton, England's most renowned author since Shakespeare. More recent influences included John Trenchard and Thomas Gordon, who collaborated on many Whig writings in the early eighteenth century, including *The Independent Whig* (1720–1721), and a series that was especially popular in America, *Cato's Letters* (1720–1723).[38]

Politics, according to these Real Whig authors, was rarely a civil affair. Politics meant conflict, a constant struggle between the rulers and the ruled, centralized power versus the rights of the people. This fear of centralized authority made sense to many colonists, mainly because they were far removed from their king and their Parliament, and that distance had forced them to devise means of governing themselves. So when Thomas Gordon wrote that "whatever is good for the people, is bad for their governors; and what is good for the governors, is pernicious to the people," many revolutionaries agreed.[39]

Many ministers adopted the Real Whig political views, and did their share to fuel the violent reaction to the Stamp Act. In August, Boston minister Jonathan Mayhew preached a rabble-rousing sermon using Paul's declaration to the Galatians, "I would that they were even cut off which trouble you." This sermon, which has not survived, aroused the ire of loyalist Peter Oliver, who wrote that Mayhew's sermon was "so seditious" that it inspired a mob to attack the homes of several Massachusetts officials, including the house of Thomas Hutchinson, the deputy governor. The mob had left Hutchinson with little more than "bare walls and floors," and it left Mayhew regretting the wrath his sermon had provoked. The sermon, it seemed, could be more politically subversive than even preachers realized.[40]

Opposition to the Stamp Act brought the colonies together. In October 1765, representatives from nine colonies met in New York City and issued resolutions against the act, while insisting that they remained loyal to Britain. All the while, the Sons of Liberty continued their work, often aided by ministers, many of whom, like Charles Chauncy in Boston and Stephen Johnson in eastern Connecticut, preferred to do so covertly.

In Johnson, the Sons of Liberty found one of their strongest supporters. He was a graduate of Yale (1743), a pastor in Lyme, Connecticut, and counted himself among the New Divinity followers of Jonathan Edwards. No minister was more opposed to the Stamp Act, and few wrote half as much as Johnson did to inflame the population against this travesty of British injustice. Not only did Johnson preach against the act, but he published a series of articles in the *New London Gazette*—though he did so under a pseudonym. Other newspapers picked up his articles, helping spread throughout New England his assertions that Parliament had violated the essence of the British constitution. Johnson strongly condemned the British Empire's claim that the colonists were "virtually" represented in Parliament, even though they had no voice in electing any of the representatives.[41]

In his sermon of December 18, 1765, also published anonymously, Johnson blended the political arguments from his newspaper articles with a strong biblical condemnation of British policies. These two authorities, scripture and the British constitution, claimed the loyalty of all good British subjects. The authority of scripture went unquestioned, and Britons prized their "excellent constitution...very highly, next to our bibles."[42] Indeed, the Stamp Act was equally offensive to scripture and to the British constitution, Johnson believed. He and many other preachers typically blended constitutional arguments and the philosophy of John Locke and others with biblical exhortations to liberty. Certainly, one could make the political arguments that Johnson made without referencing scripture, but biblical support, especially delivered in the persuasive rhetoric of the sermon, made these arguments stronger.[43]

Johnson drew on a prominent biblical argument, asserting that the colonists were held in unjust slavery, much like the Israelites had been held by the Egyptians. Even so, George III was no pharaoh—at least not yet. At this point, most colonists still thought highly of their sovereign. He was still, as Johnson wrote, "our gracious King" and a great defender of the British constitution. Later interpreters of Exodus in the Revolution would change their minds on this point—by 1776, King George III would be a pharaoh personified.[44] In 1765, however, the true pharaohs, in Johnson's view, were the corrupt British lawmakers, especially the prime minister, George Grenville. The colonists were loyal British citizens, Johnson asserted, and desired reform, not revolution. To be sure, Johnson was offended by the accusation that the colonists were using the Stamp Act as an excuse to rebel and declare their independence. It was a vile lie, fabricated by British conspirators to divert attention away from their unjust policies. Surely, the service of the colonists, all their sacrifices in war and peace, should "fully vindicate them from this idle scheme of 'independency.'"[45]

And yet, Johnson's protests included a threat: though neither wanted nor declared, independence might be the last resort for the oppressed colonies. The colonies had "no temptation to independency," but that temptation could develop "if the British empire" were to "become ripe for ruin." Johnson fired off a repertoire of wreckage toward which Britain seemed to be heading: "a proud, arbitrary, selfish, and venal spirit of corruption"; a "policy of government" based on "bribery and corruption"; and a conviction "to support these shocking enormities and corruptions" by oppressing the Empire's loyal subjects. If these trends continued, Johnson preached, then the colonists would have one "dreadful alternative—slavery or independency." The colonists would not need long to decide.[46]

But it would not come to that, at least not yet. Colonial fury convinced Parliament to repeal the Stamp Act. The colonists rejoiced at their victory, while Parliament compensated by issuing the Declaratory Act, which reasserted Parliament's absolute authority over the colonies. The repeal of the Stamp Act was a seminal moment in the colonists' growing sense of patriotic identity. To be sure, they still thought of themselves as British subjects, but they were ever more aware of their own separate identity as Americans. In the Stamp Act, they had been challenged, and they responded by calling their nation back to its own constitution.

Jubilant sermons resounded throughout the colonies, praising the repeal of the Stamp Act and the return of the prodigal nation to its constitutional roots.[47] It was a great moment for American patriotism, and sermons helped to make its greatness clear to all. Even supporters of the Stamp Act who were horrified by the colonists' opposition to it recognized the power of preachers in stirring up colonial protests. Peter Oliver lamented that "it was in vain to struggle against...the Gospel of...[the] black Regiment." Clergy fed "the Frenzy of Anarchy" into such a "political Enthusiasm, that the Minds of the most pious Men seemed to be wholly absorbed in the Temper of Riot." Oliver even pointed to one minister who called on the people to "Fight up to your Knees in Blood."[48] Many feared that the repeal of the Stamp Act would do little to "repeal" the enthusiasm of colonial American patriotism, an enthusiasm that preachers did much to ignite.

Those who held these suspicions found much evidence for them in the late 1760s. The repeal of the Stamp Act proved that the colonists, when united in protest, could change British policies. Meanwhile, the British government seemed ever more determined to assert its authority and to raise revenue. If direct taxes, like the Stamp Act, would not work, then they would stay the course with duties, such as those imposed in the Sugar Act. In June 1767, Parliament implemented the Townshend Revenue Acts, which would raise money by collecting duties on various goods, including tea and paint. Some of this money would go toward paying the salaries of the Crown's officials in the colonies, whose presence would prevent the colonies from becoming dependent on colonial legislatures. Overall, the British Empire was looking for ways to better keep order in and secure revenue from the colonies. To the British, the moves were sound policy.[49]

The Stamp Act, though, had changed colonial attitudes. Many colonists were suspicious of any of Parliament's means of raising money, even in the innocuous form of duties. Printing presses hummed, churning out pamphlets of protest. Most famous was John Dickinson's *Letters from a Farmer in Pennsylvania*. Dickinson was no rural farmer; he was a rich Philadelphia lawyer, but his argument against British taxation seemed authentic to many colonists. He contended that the Townshend duties were no better than the Stamp Act, because both were geared specifically toward raising revenue from the colonies. Taxation solely for the purpose of raising funds rather than to regulate trade was "a most dangerous innovation." Parliament was taking money from the colonists without their permission, treating them as slaves, not citizens.[50] Such "enslavement" would hurt Britain as well as America, some colonists warned. Presbyterian minister John Zubly of Savannah, Georgia, illustrated the point: a large tree, he said, could fall on its surrounding shrubs and crush them, but not "without tearing up its own roots."[51]

"Innocent Blood Crying to God from the Streets of Boston"

The greatest eruption in patriotic pulpits after the Stamp Act came in response to the famous Boston Massacre. The "massacre" (it was colonial patriots who labeled it such), occurred on March 5, 1770, when, after several days of tense verbal exchanges between British soldiers and Boston citizens, the soldiers fired their muskets into a crowd, killing five colonists. British officials were hardly surprised that violence had finally erupted in Boston. Many in the British Empire considered New England to be the center of their troubles with the colonies. Samuel Adams and the Sons of Liberty had been outspoken in their objections to British tyranny, and they were not alone. Boston was the center of protests, pamphlets, circular letters, and various other means of spreading a message of defiance of what colonists considered to be the unconstitutional tyrannies of British polices.

The British government's response escalated the situation dramatically: it increased the presence of British soldiers in Massachusetts. In Boston alone, a city of some 15,000 residents in 1769, the British had deployed almost 4000 redcoats. The presence of so many armed soldiers was bad enough in any population. But in a city filled with citizens who had a long-standing suspicion of standing armies, it was particularly offensive. This volatile combination of protest against tyranny and harsh responses from the British government made the Boston Massacre almost inevitable.[52]

The very name colonists gave to this incident, Boston Massacre, communicated well their immediate response. They were already on the lookout for signs of British violence, and when the shots fired into a crowd verified these suspicions, their outrage reverberated through the presses and pulpits. They would not allow the crisis to diminish, and they vowed to remember it. Preachers and citizen orators would commemorate the massacre for years with annual sermons and speeches. In fact, "March 5, 1770 would stand as the most important commemorative date on the New England calendar until it was replaced by July 4, 1776."[53]

Sermons on the Boston Massacre set a new precedent for violent rhetoric and righteous rage, and they began the first Sunday following the shootings.[54] Perhaps the most well-known was delivered by John Lathrop of the Old North church, *Innocent blood crying to God from the streets of Boston*. This was a sermon about murder—"the horrid murder...by a party of troops under the command of Captain Preston." Appropriately enough, Lathrop based his sermon on the first murder recorded in scripture, in which Cain killed his brother Abel. Most of all, it was a sermon about blood—the blood of Abel that cried out to God from the ground (Genesis 3:10). Blood certainly did cry out in this sermon. Lathrop mentioned "blood" over thirty times in twenty-one pages. The blood spilled in Boston, he preached, was not the blood shed by a brother but the blood shed by a diabolical standing army commissioned by a tyrannical government. "The unparalleled barbarity of those who were lately guilty of murdering a number of our innocent fellow-citizens will never be forgot," he preached. One could hardly forget such a sight, he lamented, "when our brethren were murdered before our eyes, and our most public streets were deeply dyed with innocent blood. How affecting, unutterably affecting, to see our fellow citizens shot to death—their garments rolled in blood, and corpses wallowing in gore, upon our Exchange, the place of general concourse, where our most respectable inhabitants meet every day!" This vile attack, Lathrop warned, could be part of an orchestrated plan for "nothing less than a general slaughter."[55]

As Lathrop saw it, the only response to the blood that cried out from the streets of Boston was vengeance. "To refuse, or unreasonably delay doing justice upon the murderer, is to let the blood of the innocent, like that of Abel, cry unto God for vengeance." That could not happen in America, Lathrop insisted. Boston blood must be accounted for. This was bloody preaching for desperate, violent times. Lathrop knew this, and he knew how offended some were that a preacher would proclaim such a gory cry for violent justice. But how could he not respond to a government-sponsored massacre? It was his duty in this case to preach the vengeance of God to an unjust power. "Can it be thought that the heralds of the Almighty, whose commission obliges them to cry aloud, and not to spare! . . . Can it be supposed, that [ministers] will be silent when the blood of the people of their charge is spilled as water, and their carcasses strewed in the streets? Verily no! For to do this were a great evil, and such as could not escape the righteous judgment of Almighty God!" The preacher who did not address the Boston Massacre was shirking his duty. The clergy had clear political responsibilities, including the duty to address all forms of injustice and oppression. Not only were ministers responsible for this kind of political speech, but they were leaders in it. Nonministers certainly gave political speeches, and they did so more than ever in the many commemorations of the Boston Massacre. But even lay speakers often used the sermon as their model.[56]

A little over two years after the Boston Massacre, another incident provoked revolutionary rage. On June 10, 1772, the British customs ship *Gaspee* was attacked and burned in Narragansett Bay. Some colonists tried to blame the attack on American Indians, but most everyone knew that the real culprits were colonial merchants. What enraged the colonists most was not the attack but the British response to it. The British government vowed to force the accused to stand trial in Britain. Americans, believing that they had a right to be tried before their peers, were enraged.

This rage was best expressed by a Baptist who delivered "the most widely read and reprinted sermon" early in the Revolutionary era.[57] John Allen was an eccentric preacher with a checkered past. In 1772, he had recently arrived from London where he had been accused of forgery three years before. In response to the burning of the *Gaspee*, he preached *An Oration, Upon the Beauties of Liberty, or the Essential Rights of the Americans*. This sermon had a huge impact. Published in seven printings and in five editions by 1774, Allen's sermon made a radical statement for opposing British tyranny. Scholars have even called Allen "New England's Tom Paine" because he actually called for America to reject King George III, a view that was radical even when Paine made the famous case for it nearly four years later in 1776.[58]

Allen voiced the colonists' outrage better than anyone. The British had denied Americans their natural rights, and this was a sacred violation. "A fly, or a worm," Allen wrote, "has as great a right to liberty, and freedom...as the most potent monarch upon the earth."[59] This sacred liberty was natural, but it was also biblical. Allen juxtaposed the prophet Micah, God's "son of liberty," against the evil tyrant King Ahaz. An evil king like Ahaz proved that God sometimes had endorsed kings but that he hated tyranny. God created kings to serve the people; he did not create people to serve kings. "Was not David made a king for the people?" A king "is not worthy to reign, that does not make the *rights* of his people the rule of his actions." A king who abuses power loses authority, Allen preached. "Whatever power destroys [the peoples'] rights, destroys at the same time, his right to reign."[60]

Even at this early date, therefore, Allen endorsed resistance against the king if the British continued their tyrannical course. "Stand alarm'd!" Allen preached. "Ye sons of America...guard your freedom, prevent your chains; stand up as one man for your liberty."[61] Allen even uttered the dreaded word "rebellion." "It is no rebellion to oppose any king...that destroys by...his violence the rights of the people." After all, Allen asserted, "the blessing of freedom we do not receive from kings, but from heaven."[62]

Tea Party Preaching

If anyone needed more proof that New England was the center of patriotic resistance to Britain, they would find it in the famous "Boston Tea Party" of December 16, 1773. They did not have that clever name for it at the time—no one called it a "tea party" until later. But contemporaries knew that something important had happened when a band of colonists, disguised as Mohawks, climbed aboard a ship and threw loads of tea into Boston Harbor. The tea was worth more than its estimated value of 10,000 pounds.[63]

For British officials and colonial protesters alike, the tea represented the authority of the empire. Would it be respected or rejected? Colonists had protested the Stamp Act and had gained a victory, albeit a qualified one. Could they repeat their success with much higher stakes after the Boston Massacre?

Many colonists felt that Britain had thrown down the gauntlet with the Tea Act, which imposed a tax on tea and made the East India Company the exclusive provider of tea to the colonies. From the British perspective, this was a wise investment in rescuing the East India Company from financial ruin. Besides, the net effect would be to lower the price of tea for Americans. Given the great amounts of tea the colonists drank, surely they would let the technicality of an imposed duty, and an imposed monopoly, pass in return for the lower cost of tea. From the colonial perspective, this was yet another example of British coerciveness. The British had no right to impose such taxes, the colonists repeated; moreover, Britain had no right to grant a monopoly to the East India Company.[64]

It was in a spirit of absolute defiance that some 200 colonists raided the three ships to destroy the tea. "We wore ragged clothes and...smeared our faces with grease and soot," one tea partier later reported—"surely we resembled devils...rather than men." This group of patriotic "devils" included such famous patriots as Paul Revere and Samuel Adams; and equally famous patriots had mixed responses to the audacious act. Reacting negatively was Benjamin Franklin, who called it "an act of violent injustice." John Adams, however, who always seemed to disagree with Franklin, said that the destruction of tea by men in Indian disguises was actually dignified. "There is a Dignity, a Majesty, a Sublimity" in it, he wrote. It was "notable and striking." Indeed "this Destruction of the Tea is so bold, so daring, so firm...that I cant but consider it as an Epoch in History."[65]

Adams may have been overly dramatic, but not by much. Almost everyone recognized that the "tea party" was a daring act that signaled a new era. By destroying the shipment of tea, New Englanders also seemed to be destroying any chance of easy reconciliation with Britain. This was the opinion of Israel Holly, an evangelical minister from Suffield, Connecticut. Preaching eleven days later, Holly admired the principle that led the Sons of Liberty to cast the tea into Boston Harbor, but he warned that the British government would have to respond with all its fury to protect its honor. This time "the colonies, Boston in particular," had "gone too far" in acting against British rule for Britain to allow them to get away without punishment. The situation was serious. The colonies and the British government were headed for a face-off, and neither side would be willing to back away. The colonists would have to insist on their liberties out of their convictions about constitutional freedom and basic rights. The British government would have to insist on its authority and right to punish subversive acts. Seeing the situation in a cosmic perspective, Holly wondered if this was God's chance to punish both Britain and the colonies for their sins. Perhaps this "increasing resolution, and recollecting strength on both sides" would be God's chosen "means of mutual ruin," God's way to "scourge a wicked nation and a sinful land." Holly hoped that would not be the case. But if it were, one of the chief sins New England would suffer for was hypocrisy: for crying out for their liberties while denying religious liberty to dissenters.[66]

Holly was one of these dissenters. During the revivals of the Great Awakening, he had been a Separate, one of those whose revivalist zeal drove them to break from the established Congregationalist churches. For Holly and many other revivalist Protestants, including many Baptists, the developing crisis was as much about religious liberty as it was about civil liberty. Both were natural rights, granted by God. To deny one was as bad as to deny the other. Many revolutionaries would have agreed that religious liberty was a sacred right, but they disagreed on exactly what religious liberty meant. For many dissenters, including Separates and Baptists, religious liberty meant that the colonies were wrong to tax all citizens to support the official churches. The practice was no more than religious taxation without representation. To Separates like Holly, therefore, New England, though leading the charge of civil patriotism, had proved to be a religious tyrant. The government of New England colonies had been "guilty of exercising the same arbitrary power, to abridge" people of "their natural and constitutional liberties and privileges," one of which was "a liberty to choose, in matters of religion, that way, mode, form and worship which a man in his conscience thinks most is agreeable" to God.[67]

Holly hoped that the destruction of the tea would signal the beginning of a consistent patriotism in the colonies, an embrace of both civil and religious liberty. His fear, and the fear of many colonists, was that Britain had struck a deal with tyranny, both civil and religious, and had even allied itself with the diabolical evil represented by the Catholic Church. England, then, was in danger of a complete reversal, turning from combating Catholic tyranny in the Seven Years' War to aligning with Catholic powers in the 1770s. If the colonists submit to Parliament's draconian acts that "bind the colonies," then "where will they stop?" If colonists do not resist, then "perhaps our religious privileges and liberties will be call'd for next, and in lieu thereof Popery enjoin'd." This was purely a logical assumption for Holly and other colonists: the alternative to Protestantism was Catholicism. And as surely as Protestantism meant liberty, Catholicism meant tyranny. "Popery" and "arbitrary government" shared "such a kindred and likeness...that they who are friendly to the one, cannot be enemies to the other." The possibilities terrified Holly. Not only would the colonists lose their property and their power, they would have their consciences "bound by Popish chains." Consequently, "away must go our bibles"; in their place would be "the superstitions and damnable heresies and idolatries of the church of Rome," including the demand to "pray to the Virgin Mary, worship images, believe the doctrine of Purgatory, and the Pope's infallibility," not to mention "the deepest plot of hell and Rome, the holy inquisition" and "all its terrors and cruelty."[68]

Preaching for "Intolerable" and "Coercive" Acts

The British response to the destruction of the tea seemed to confirm Holly's fears. Not surprisingly, King George III demanded a strong response to "the violent and outrageous" behavior of the Sons of Liberty. "We must master them or totally leave them alone," he said, but obviously the latter was not truly an option.[69] What was needed was a decisive and firm response. If they could stamp out the rebellion in Massachusetts, British officials thought, the other colonies would learn from that example and forego further rebellious schemes.

So Parliament moved quickly, passing four acts that would both retaliate for the destruction of the tea and make it clear that rebellion would not be tolerated. The Massachusetts Government Act wrested the colonial government from the control of elected officials and handed it over to a royal governor. The Administration of Justice Act, which some colonists called "the Murder Act," declared British officials immune from prosecution in local courts when enforcing British law, including quelling rioting patriots. If any officials faced charges, they could be tried in another colony or in England. The Quartering Act, which had expired, was reinstated. It forced colonists to house British soldiers on demand. Finally, the Boston Port Act closed down the shipping business in Boston until colonists reimbursed the government and the East India Company for the tea they had dumped into Boston Harbor.

Parliament passed these acts in March 1774. The response was outrage, not only in Massachusetts, but in other colonies as well. Collectedly, colonists called these acts the "Coercive Acts" or the "Intolerable Acts." To make matters worse, in May, Parliament passed the Quebec Act, which expanded the British-controlled Canadian boundary southward into lands that several colonies had claimed. Not only that, but the Quebec Act allowed the French inhabitants of the territory to practice Catholicism freely, with the support of the British Empire.[70]

Colonists everywhere erupted in anger. For a largely Protestant population, many of whom were convinced that the Pope wielded the power of Antichrist, the Quebec Act confirmed their suspicions that the British government had betrayed Protestant civil and religious liberties for Catholic tyranny.

Strong opposition came from colonists as diverse as Richard Furman, the Baptist minister from South Carolina, and Alexander Hamilton, then a student in New York. Hamilton charged that it was an act of religious and political aggression, for it established "arbitrary power, and its great engine the Popish religion" in America. "I imagine it will clearly appear," Hamilton wrote, "that the Roman Catholic religion" is not only "tolerated" but "established" in the Quebec Act, while Protestantism "has been left entirely destitute and unbefriended in Canada." A Catholic nation, with British support, had imposed itself on the colonies. "This act," Hamilton asserted, "develops the dark designs of the [British] ministry more fully than any thing they have done, and shows that they have formed a systematic project of absolute power." "We should consider" it, he concluded, "as being replete with danger to ourselves, and as threatening ruin to our posterity."[71]

Such reactions to the Coercive Acts and the Quebec Act proved Britain wrong—resistance to Parliament was not limited to Massachusetts or even to New England. Nor was opposition limited to political grievances. Religion was at the core of the dispute with British policies, and Hamilton's assertions were only one of many signals that ministers were not alone in seeing religious issues at the center of the resistance. But ministers led the way, and they did so by engaging the crisis in the light of scripture.

It is all the more appropriate, then, that one of the Revolutionary era's most famous sermons bore the title *Scriptural Instructions to Civil Rulers, and all Free-born Subjects*. Published in response to the Coercive Acts, it was one of hundreds of sermons that inspired patriots by exalting the biblical terms of freedom. Its preacher, Samuel Sherwood of Fairfield, Connecticut, included an appendix (written by Sherwood's ministerial colleague, Ebenezer Baldwin of Danbury) that described in detail "the heavy Grievances the Colonies labor under from several late Acts of the British Parliament." The problem was that good citizenship, the very character they had celebrated as good British subjects, could lead the colonists astray. They had been so loyal in fearing God and honoring the king that they could be overly trustful of Parliament and the Crown. What was needed, Sherwood intimated, was a healthy suspicion of the wiles of tyrannical governments. The colonists should not be "innocent and unwary," lest they be led "into snares"; they had to be informed, and reminded, of these grievances and their severity. Here, then, Sherwood symbolized the logic of revolutionary preaching: the crisis, closely narrated to include every offence of a British government growing more tyrannical by the day, demanded a biblically inspired patriotism. "This manly, this heroic, and truly patriotic spirit, which is gradually kindling up in every free-man's breast, through the continent, is undoubtedly a token for good; and will, if duly regulated by Christian principles and rules, ensure success to American liberty and freedom."[72]

Conclusions: The Sermon's Patriotic Authority in the Revolutionary War

It was the "regulation" of patriotism by "Christian principles," so essential to the Revolution in the minds of many, that made preaching all the more critical in the Revolutionary War. Once the war had begun at Lexington and Concord in April 1775, theoretical arguments about rights and privileges became more urgent. When battles had to be fought, preachers took up arms—sometimes literally, but more often by turning their pulpits into weapons. Pulpits fumed with rage as preachers lambasted British atrocities and proclaimed God's martial deliverance. "Let Lexington proclaim afar, the honors of the God of war," wrote David Tappan, pastor at Newbury and future professor at Harvard. Likewise, "in the late battle at Concord and Lexington," preached Connecticut minister Joseph Perry in May of 1775, the Redcoats "have imbrued their hands in the innocent blood of their fellow subjects with a relentless cruelty and inhuman barbarity, too much like that which we have experienced from the merciless savages of the wilderness." America had long been a land of war, mostly fought by colonists to defend British rights against what they called "savagery." Now, however, the tide had turned and savagery took a British form, patriots believed, and preachers were the staunchest defenders of the cause of America, which was "the cause of religion, of liberty" and "the cause of God!"[73]

Many patriotic ministers felt obligated to defend the martial function of the ministry. Pointedly, they often defended themselves against charges that spiritual ministers had no business advocating bloody warfare. "We own it is rare for soldiers to ask counsel of gospel Ministers," said Presbyterian John Carmichael in his sermon to a Pennsylvania militia company on June 4, 1775. But Carmichael quickly justified his martial authority as a gospel minister. "I am not called to address Red-Coats, but Christian Provincials," and, after all, he was doing no more than John the Baptist, who had given sound advice to soldiers when they asked for it (Luke 22:36).[74] Ministers typically argued that, when facing war against an unjust aggressor, spirituality demanded courageous battle, even from the clergy.

Some ministers took this advice literally, leaving the pulpit for the battlefield. But even as they did they often noted the apparent conflict, and revealed how they overcame it. Consider the story of Phillips Payson, pastor of the church at Chelsea, Massachusetts. He initially refused to support war, holding out hope for reconciliation with the British. He stood firm for patience over revolutionary patriotism until the battle of Lexington and the brutalities of the British convinced him to put aside his aversion to bloodshed and take up the musket himself. He proved to be a model soldier. As the Redcoats headed toward Boston after attacking Lexington and Concord, Payson led an attack on twelve British troops, killing one and capturing the rest. Years later, in a sermon commemorating the battle at Lexington, Payson heralded God's providence in the Revolution, and the crucial role of a spiritually inspired military.[75]

Chaplains played a vital role in the Revolutionary War effort. Chaplaincy was nothing new, of course, but a national chaplaincy to coincide with the new nation found its way on the agenda of the Continental Congress from the first few months of the war. On July 29, 1775, the Continental Congress established the chaplaincy. Chaplains would carry a rank equivalent to captain, and would serve the Continental Army.

Though the Congress set the standard pay for chaplains, George Washington protested that it was too low. The pay was "too small to encourage men of abilities," Washington wrote to Congress in December 31, 1775. Consider, Washington wrote, that many chaplains had left their churches to take on the chaplaincy, and that patriotic service left them responsible for paying for another clergyman to take over their congregations. Often, Washington noted, chaplains had to pay their replacement ministers more than their congressional pay for taking on the dangers of chaplaincy service. "I need not point out," Washington continued, "the great utility of Gentlemen whose Lives & Conversation are unexceptionable, being employed for that Service, in this Army." But Washington knew that he did need to point it out, because not all Americans, or even all congressmen, shared his opinion of how important chaplains were to the war effort.

Washington respected the chaplaincy because he wanted a disciplined, moral army, but also because he respected providence. Here, Washington touched on a crucial point that chaplains preached incessantly: the revolutionary cause needed both human and divine weapons. If the patriots lacked either God's blessing or heroic soldiers, the cause was doomed. As Massachusetts Congregationalist Peter Thacher put it in his unprinted sermon from 1777, "We are to be workers together with God to accomplish these great and good events." Washington ordered his soldiers and officers to attend "divine service, to implore the blessings of heaven upon the means used for our safety and defense."[76]

Washington had high expectations for chaplains and was often disappointed by those who were not up to the task. Other chaplains impressed him greatly, however. One such chaplain was Abiel Leonard of Woodstock, Connecticut. In a letter to Jonathan Trumbull, governor of Connecticut, Washington praised one of Leonard's sermons, in which he asserted "the necessity of courage and bravery, and at the same time of obedience and subordination to those in command." Washington needed such chaplains, and was worried that Leonard was about to leave the field. He wrote to Trumbull, expressing "concern, as I think his departure will be a loss," for

Leonard had proven to be "a warm and steady friend to his country and [had] taken great pains to animate the soldiers, and impress them with a knowledge of the important rights we are contending for."[77] In another letter, written in March of 1776 to Leonard's church, Washington wrote that the chaplain's "usefulness in this Army is great—he is employed in the glorious work of attending to the Morals, of a brave people who are fighting for their Liberties,...the Liberties of all America."[78]

Washington trusted Leonard, held him in high regard, and seemed to like him personally. Leonard's story did not end well, however. On July 27, 1777, he slit his own throat and died two weeks later. Chaplains as well as soldiers could be casualties of war, and Leonard was one especially tragic case among many. As historian Charles Royster observed, notwithstanding Leonard's status as "the preeminent chaplain in the Continental Army," still, "the failure of the chaplaincy troubled him."[79] The challenge of proclaiming patriotism under a higher authority, namely, a biblical authority, and often doing so with meager resources could prove too much to bear.

Though they usually were not soldiers, chaplains and other wartime preachers had their own unique struggles in the war. War was hell, everyone agreed, and chaplains were charged with providing moral and spiritual stability amid the stresses of the army camp and the battlefield. In their journals, chaplains recorded how stressful and important this work was. Not only regular troops but officers as well were vulnerable to pressures of the military life, and many of them lost control. In one instance, recorded by Baptist minister and chaplain Hezekiah Smith from August 1777, General Philip John Schuyler "acted more like a mad Man than the Commander in Chief." According to Smith, General Schuyler "beat some of the soldiers" then "cursed, damned swore, profaned the Name of God in a most horrible manner, and Swore by his Maker that if he could" he would attack "the Major of our Brigade," splitting "his Head Open and scatter his Brains about the Ground." Then Schuyler "attempted to thrust an Officer thro', and afterwards made his brags of it."[80]

Chaplains were particularly sensitive to this kind of bad behavior and wartime atrocities, and their journals abound with vivid details. One such account from William Rogers, Baptist minister and chaplain in the Continental Army, described a revolutionary Cain and Abel story in July 1779. Two brothers, John and Henry Pensell, were on opposite sides in the war, with John on the British side and Henry a patriot. They met in battle near the Susquehannah. Henry, having lost his gun, begged his brother for mercy. Instead, John loaded his gun and told his brother he would kill him because "you are a damned rebel." John then shot Henry, then "struck him four or five times with a tomahawk and scalped him."[81]

But if Rogers was appalled by such incidents of inhumanity, he seemed undisturbed by the Continental Army's attacks on Iroquois villages, attacks in which American troops burned everything in sight.[82] Chaplains were not morally neutral in the conflict. They were advocates of the cause above all, and sometimes their patriotism overcame their commitment to the standards of morally just warfare.

As the century between King Philip's War in 1675 and the beginning of the Revolutionary War in 1775 revealed, we cannot understand how pervasive the Bible was in Revolutionary society without recognizing the power of preaching in colonial America. Wartime events were preaching events. As we have seen, years before the Revolution, ministers had become primary authorities on war in colonial America. By the time of the Revolution, few public voices rivaled those of ministers. Even enemies of the Revolution often gave ample evidence of how powerful ministers were in supporting patriotism. After the battle of Bunker Hill, for instance, one British major harshly scolded colonial prisoners for listening to patriotic preaching. "It is your...damned Religion of this Country that ruins the Country; Damn your Religion." Echoing this sentiment, one loyalist reported to the earl of Dartmouth that "Your Lordship can scarcely conceive, what Fury the Discourses of some mad Preachers have created in this Country."[83]

What some loyalists called "mad preachers" many patriots considered prophetic messengers in a time of crisis. Ministers played a critical role in providing religious motivation for soldiers, officers, and even civilians as they embraced the war with Britain. By preaching sermons on the spiritual importance of martial service, ministers became authorities on war. There was little question, however, where their authority came from. It depended on the Bible—an ancient source of strength and persuasive revelation that people never depended on more than in times of war.

2

"The Lord is a Man of War"

MOSES, THE EXODUS, AND THE SPIRIT OF '76

IN REVOLUTIONARY AMERICA, when the rhetoric of liberty reverberated through the colonies, one of the most well-known narratives of liberation was the Exodus story. Patriots often compared themselves to the Israelites, God's chosen people, who were enslaved by the Egyptians much as the colonists were oppressed by the British, personified by King George III, whom Thomas Paine called the "hardened, sullen-tempered Pharaoh of England." No biblical narrative was more influential or more diverse in its applications than the story of Exodus and its intrepid if inarticulate hero, Moses.[1]

The Exodus of the Founders

The Exodus story seemed to capture the spirit of '76. As revolutionary patriots in a biblically literate society recognized, it all began when "there arose up a new king over Egypt, which knew not Joseph" (Exodus 1:8)—that is, a new Pharaoh who did not recognize the Israelites as loyal and productive citizens. Instead of respecting the Israelites for all they had contributed to the empire, the new Pharaoh saw them as enemies and conspired against them. Worried that the Israelites might become too powerful and either escape from the empire or ally themselves with another nation to overtake Egypt, Pharaoh put taskmasters over the Israelites "to afflict them with their burdens," and the Israelites diligently obeyed. They built Egypt's "treasure cities, Pithom and Ramses." Instead of gratitude for their loyal service, however, the Israelites received more severe afflictions from the Egyptians. "But the more they afflicted them, the more they multiplied and grew," and the more the Israelites prospered, the more the ruthless and conspiring Egyptians resented them. So the Egyptians treated the Israelites more severely than ever, and "made their lives bitter with hard bondage, in mortar, and in brick, and in all manner of service in the field." Still, the Israelite population increased. Desperate to quell the Israelite growth, Pharaoh conspired with midwives to kill Israelite males upon birth, and then commanded that all Israelite baby boys be thrown into the Nile. Moses was born into this situation. Instead of throwing him into the Nile, his mother put him in a basket and placed him in the river, where he was rescued and raised by Pharaoh's daughter. When God called Moses to deliver the people from slavery, Moses resisted, trying to back away from the dramatic call of the moment. But God persisted, and Moses complied. Moses first tried to negotiate with Pharaoh for the Israelites' freedom, but Pharaoh only treated them more harshly than ever, forcing them to meet their brick-production quota without straw. Only when God intervened by sending a series of ten plagues on the Egyptians did Pharaoh relent. But when Pharaoh reneged on his promise to free the people, God proved himself to be the ultimate "man of war" by drowning Pharaoh and his army in the Red Sea (Exodus 14–15).

Along with clergy, the founders saw revolutionary meaning in the inspiring Exodus narrative.[2] The letters between Abigail and John Adams have been recognized for their political insights and their candid personal reflections, but not for their biblical commentary. Perhaps they should be. In the space of a few months in 1776, the Adamses' correspondence reflected the influence of the story at the same time that the founders were considering the ramifications of rebellion.

In a letter to Abigail on May 17, 1776, John commented on a sermon that featured "a Parallel between the Case of Israel and that of America, and between the Conduct of Pharaoh and that of George. Jealousy that the Israelites would throw off the Government of Egypt made him issue his Edict that the Midwives should cast the Children into the River, and the other Edict that the Men should make a large Revenue of Brick without Straw. He concluded that the Course of Events, indicated strongly the Design of Providence that We should be separated from G. Britain." Such was the case, in Adams's view, for "G[reat] B[ritain] has at last driven America, to that last Step, a complete Separation from her, a total absolute Independence, not only of her Parliament but of her Crown."[3]

Adams was not the only revolutionary who thought of the Exodus when pondering the war and the prospects of independence. Almost four months later, John wrote another letter to Abigail, again with the Exodus on his mind. In this letter, he reported that both Benjamin Franklin and Thomas Jefferson wanted to feature the Exodus in the design for a

"Great Seal for the confederated States." Franklin had proposed a seal with "Moses lifting up his Wand, and dividing the Red Sea, and Pharaoh, in his Chariot overwhelmed with the Waters." Franklin wanted this seal to include the motto, "Rebellion to Tyrants is Obedience to God." Jefferson countered with a proposal for a Great Seal that would feature another image from the Exodus, a scene depicting the Israelites "in the Wilderness, led by a Cloud by day, and a Pillar of Fire by night," accompanied by images of "Hengist and Horsa, the Saxon Chiefs, from whom We claim the Honor of being descended and those Political Principles and Form of Government We have assumed."[4] Adams preferred an image of Hercules. But despite his preference for the classical over the biblical, Adams was no less affected by the revolutionary meaning of the Exodus. Eventually all three designs were discarded. But the fact that Adams, Jefferson, and Franklin all pondered the Exodus narrative in those decisive months in 1776 indicates that no biblical narrative surpassed the Exodus in identifying the major themes, plots, characters, and subplots of the Revolution. Revolutionaries could not get enough of the Exodus story. They saw in the Exodus the providential hand of God, which would orchestrate the Revolution.

Pharaoh, Providence, and Patriotic Paranoia

Even as muskets were firing in 1775, American patriots struggled to understand how King George III could become a modern Pharaoh. How could the government of Britain, the very birthplace of liberty in the Atlantic world, transform itself into a tyrannical menace? And if this issue puzzled colonists, the way in which it puzzled them has generated discussion among historians. Some argue that colonial patriots were paranoid, obsessed with deep, dark conspiracies hatched by the British Empire to reduce their colonies to slavery. "Were the American Revolutionaries mentally disturbed? Was the Revolution itself a consequence of anxieties buried deep in the psyches of its leaders?"[5] Although today we may be tempted to answer yes to these questions, assuming as we do that events do not always have direct, conscious causes, people in the Revolutionary era believed strongly that events did have direct and discoverable causes. As Gordon Wood has observed, conspiratorial, what we might even call paranoid, thinking, was actually a direct result of Enlightenment rationality and belief in the power of human decisions to influence great events. As Wood explains, "belief in plots was not a symptom of disturbed minds but a rational attempt to explain human phenomena in terms of human intentions and to maintain moral coherence in the affairs of men." The typical patriot in the Revolutionary era, therefore, had come to believe "that the British actions were indeed linked in what Jefferson called 'a deliberate, systematical plan of reducing us to slavery' and that this plan could be explained in terms not of the intentions of providence but of the intentions of British officials."[6]

For many patriots, however, providential designs and British intentions meshed seamlessly. When ministers looked to explain the dramatic British shift from liberty to tyranny, they often did so by pondering the mysteries of divine providence and evil intent in the Exodus story. If, as Jefferson said, the British had hatched "a deliberate, systematical plan of reducing us to slavery," they could have found no better model than the treacheries of Pharaoh. The Exodus began, as American revolutionaries knew, with a diabolical conspiracy in which Pharaoh devised a plan to oppress the Israelites. "Come on, let us deal wisely with" the Israelites, Pharaoh schemed, "lest they multiply" (Exodus 1:10).

American patriots often applied this verse to the conspiracies George III and his ministers hatched against the colonies.[7] As Nicholas Street, Congregationalist minister from East Haven, Connecticut, preached in 1777, "The British tyrant is only acting over the same wicked and cruel part, that Pharaoh king of Egypt acted towards the children of Israel above 3000 years ago." Like the Egyptians who conspired against the Israelites' prosperous growth, Great Britain was trying "to prevent our building ourselves up into Free, Independent States."[8] In Revolutionary America, as in ancient Israel, this conspiracy was nothing more than a "wicked, mischievous plot."[9] Seeing the British conspiracies through the lens of the Exodus, patriots found the narrative to be an important biblical motivator for revolution. They called on their fellow colonists to take up arms, fueling their zeal by stating that they were God's afflicted people, suffering unjustly under Britain's Egypt-like slavery.

Battles often brought to mind these ideas of British conspiracy and patriotic resolve, and sermons devoted to them drew comparisons to the Exodus. Consider the sermon by Massachusetts minister Elijah Fitch, *A Discourse . . . following the Precipitate Flight of the British Troops from Boston.* Fitch delivered this sermon on March 24, 1776, which was a week after the British abandoned Boston, ending an eleven-month siege. The siege had begun just a few days after the battles of Lexington and Concord, in April 1775. The British had also suffered heavy losses nearby at the battle of Bunker Hill on June 17, 1775, which further boosted the Americans' confidence. Then, when Washington's commanding position atop Dorchester Heights forced the British out of Boston, American patriots were thrilled.

Fitch celebrated this remarkable event, convinced that the Redcoats' abandonment of Boston was a providential episode—the mighty British had met opposition from God's armies, and more opposition was needed. He asserted that his hearers should make no mistake: the British were no longer fellow countrymen; they were enemies who had betrayed their colonial brothers and sisters. Despite the clear fact that the colonies had been fully loyal to the homeland, the British had turned on them, conspiring against them. The British had been "gnashing upon us with their teeth," and "preparing every instrument of cruelty and death" they could devise "to strike dread and terror into our hearts, to frighten, and thereby bring us" to surrender "to their unjust requisitions." The acts of Parliament alone, from the Stamp Act to the Coercive Acts, were enough to prove that the British had wicked designs for enslaving the colonies. "What could be more cruel, unmerciful and unjust, than their several acts against us?" They had worked "by deep laid plots," conspiring "in the dark, out of sight; and tried every method, that their cunning and subtlety could invent, to make us implicitly acknowledge, that they had a right to put their hands into our pockets...without our consent."[10]

Such unjust acts of Parliament led to even more atrocities and malicious warfare. In fighting the war, "what cruel and barbarous schemes and hellish plots have they laid?" Specifically, Fitch complained that the British had aroused "the Negroes...to cut our throats...and [had] set the Savages and Roman Catholics, like blood-hounds on our backs, while they like lions...came to meet us with open mouths, gaping for their prey; most furiously and maliciously gnashing upon us with their teeth; filled with rage and indignation, threatening...to devour us at a mouthful." Such wartime atrocities, such unjust acts as burning towns with little children and women in them, were "acts of cruelty...without a parallel among civilized nations." And yet, such uncivilized methods of war had not gained them victory, even over an overmatched opponent. Fitch was telling only one side of the story. Actually, both sides in the war tried to recruit Native Americans to their cause and both sides committed great atrocities. At times, it was the patriots who burned Indian villages, not the other way around. But in Fitch's providential view, God had delivered the patriots at Boston.[11]

Though Fitch saw the influence of providence in the outcome of battles, he insisted that the British were not mere pawns. On the contrary,
they were active agents of deceit and tyranny. Fitch warned Americans
of "the deep laid plots, the dark and cunning devices of those who once
ruled over us, to bring ruin and destruction upon this whole land" and
to "fasten our feet in the fetters of slavery."[12] Fitch foregrounded the
revolutionary import of the Exodus story. It was a story of liberation, to
be sure. But it was also a rumination on the mysteries of divine providence. God hardened Pharaoh's heart, meaning that he had allowed
Pharaoh to do what he wanted to do: enslave the Israelites. The plots,
the conspiracies, the inhumane treatment of God's people were, therefore, Pharaoh's design—just as the designs of the modern pharaoh,
George III, were the deliberate plots and conspiracies of his ministers
and Parliament.[13]

And yet Pharaohs—both in ancient Egypt and modern Britain—were
tyrants caught in the web of God's greater purposes. God turned Pharaoh's
evil intent to good ends in a grand, providential irony. Here, in the midst of
war against the mighty British, wartime ministers turned to theodicy—the
study of the problem of evil. Explanations for why and how God hardened
Pharaoh's heart paralleled explanations for why such a freedom-loving
and Protestant nation as Great Britain could transform itself into an agent
of civil and religious tyranny.[14]

In Fitch's view, God's providential plan for American liberty had been
at work in the conspiracies and oppressions of Britain from the beginning.
"Look upon wicked Pharaoh," Fitch preached, focusing especially on how
the Israelites misread Pharaoh's treatment of them as God's punishment.
Not so, Fitch surmised. Certainly, Pharaoh was God's tool, but Pharaoh's
harsh treatment of the Israelites was the only way to awaken them to seize
their freedom. If their burdens had not been "beyond what they were able
to bear," Moses may not have been able to persuade the Israelites to flee
from "the tyrant's service." So Pharaoh wanted to oppress the Israelites,
but in God's providential maneuverings, Pharaoh succeeded only in liberating them. In enslaving and oppressing the scattered Israelites, he united
them under Moses's command.

Fitch saw exactly the same process at play in the Revolution. In the
"grievous" treatment of Britain, the colonists should see God pushing
them toward their own deliverance. By reading British tyranny through
the Exodus story, American patriots found divine sanction of American
resistance.[15]

The Holy *"Man of War"*

Just as important as the goal of liberation, however, was God's *means* of liberation—a dramatic scene of divine violence. As clearly as any text in scripture, Israel's deliverance at the Red Sea revealed God to be a warrior: "The Lord is a man of war" (Exodus 15:3). No verse in scripture held more crucial implications for religious violence. God was a fighter—not just a sovereign deity who approved of violence but an active participant in combat. Just as many colonial wartime writings identified the Bible as primarily a book of war, they also stressed God's character as a warrior above most if not all his other attributes.[16]

From King Philip's War through the American Revolution, colonial ministers could not quote this verse often enough. In over a century of colonial American war sermons, Exodus 15 was the third most-cited biblical chapter, largely because of its stirring proclamation that God was a warrior.[17] Ministers often quoted Moses's proclamation that "the Lord is a man of war" to reinforce God's endorsement of warfare, and God's blessing on soldiers who fight for just causes. "The Lord is a man of war" became a prominent text to cite against pacifists, especially those who proclaimed God's preference for peace in all cases.

In the providentially charged culture of Revolutionary America, the militant God of the Exodus seemed to fight in impressively creative ways. God not only endorsed the Revolution, he also fought it, waging war alongside the Continental Army and state militias. God, therefore, was a patriot. Sometimes he fought for American patriots literally, just as he had done for the Israelites at the Red Sea. In that climactic scene, the Lord directed the wind to blow, opening up a path through the sea that allowed the Israelites safe passage. When the Egyptians pursued, however, God stopped the wind, causing the waters to engulf the path and drown the Egyptians. So the Lord killed Pharaoh and his army, literally fighting for the Israelites.

Above all, this biblical scene opened up possibilities for understanding divine intervention in the American Revolution. When the weather hampered British troop advances or naval assaults, patriotic ministers saw God's direct intervention on behalf of the patriots. As Presbyterian minister William Foster preached to soldiers in Pennsylvania in February 1776, "see how Pharaoh's chariots and his hosts were cast into the sea...they sank as lead in the mighty waters." Just as he had done for the Israelites, God moved "great waters" to defend American patriots—"what a signal display of his power in our behalf at the Newfoundland fishery." Here Foster referenced the famous "Independence Hurricane" that struck Nova Scotia and Newfoundland in September 1775. In that great storm, some 4000 mariners, many of them members of the British Royal Navy, were killed. From the perspective of patriots such as Foster, this was a providential drowning of the British that paralleled the drowning of the Egyptians in the Red Sea. God could still wage war with weather.[18]

God's timing at the Red Sea was impeccable, miraculous, and powerfully dramatic. It is no wonder, then, that seemingly miraculous deliverances brought the episode to mind. One of the most miraculous deliverances was when the British abandoned Boston on March 17, 1776. After that pivotal moment, when the revolutionary cause seemed destined for success, celebrations ensued. Amid the celebrations, however, General Washington, whose own reputation was being secured by providential victories like this one, took his seat at Cambridge to hear a sermon. The text chosen by chaplain Abiel Leonard, appropriately enough, described the moment when the Egyptians were mired in the middle of the Red Sea, unable to move forward and moments from being drowned in the flood when God, at Moses's prompting, closed the waters. There, in that moment of horrified realization, the Egyptians saw that the mighty God of Israel opposed them. They panicked, and "said, Let us flee from the face of Israel, for the Lord fighteth for them against the Egyptians" (Exodus 14:25). No text was more appropriate for America's "Israelites," who believed—or at least hoped—that God was on their side, and that their might, with God's help, had pushed the British to flee from Boston.[19]

By constantly proclaiming this image of God as a man of war, revolutionaries raised the religious stakes of their political conflict with Britain. Given these biblical sentiments of divine devastation and militant action, was the Revolution a just war, or was it a holy war, executed with divine vengeance upon the minions of Satan? Certainly, one could quote the Bible to support either view. But even though the Bible had often supported holy wars, eighteenth-century ministers hoped to avoid them. They hoped to fight only wars that met just war criteria, which included having a just reason for waging the war and civilized methods of fighting it. But just wars were not completely secular wars. Patriots fought for their political rights, but these rights were both civil and religious. Moreover, God was on the side of justice and supported righteous causes. Colonists did not see a contradiction in calling for God's support in waging war for a cause that was both just and holy.

The pressing issue regarding just war criteria was not the rationale for the war but the methods of engagement. Any violation of just war rules was obviously uncivilized barbarity, something well beneath the dignity of any nation that claimed virtue and honor. For many patriots, the British had clearly violated these criteria. The British, according to some ministers, had lost any pretense of civilized status and had degenerated into flagrant barbarism on the battlefield. But such accusations required proof. Ministers produced it by turning their sermons into commentaries on battlefield atrocities.[20]

Jonas Clark's *The Fate of Blood-thirsty Oppressors, and God's tender care of his distressed People* commemorating the first anniversary of the start of the war at Lexington and Concord was one such sermon. As pastor of the church in Lexington, Clark had a superior vantage point from which to interpret the religious importance of the battle and the war that it ignited. As British troops approached Lexington on the night of April 18, 1775, Clark was waiting with John Hancock and Samuel Adams, who were both hiding in Clark's house for protection. When the battle began, Clark was there.

Reflecting on the battle a year later, he referred often to Egypt as the first, great oppressor of God's people. God avenged the "innocent blood" of his people by freeing them of their "cruel bondage" and had done the same ever since, throughout scripture and throughout history. The American Revolution, especially the battles of Lexington and Concord, fit this pattern.[21] Within this providential framework, God brought good out of evil, converting tyrannical oppression into divine liberation. He cared for his people by turning "the violence and oppression of their enemies, to operate for their advantage, and promote their more speedy deliverance." Pharaoh and the Egyptians were the pivotal example. Their lust for power, their infatuation "to pursue their measures of oppression and violence," even when it was clear that God opposed them, led to their dramatic drowning in the Red Sea.[22]

Clark recognized that same Pharaoh-like lust in the avaricious policies of the British King and Parliament. "New acts" were "passed to distress and enslave us. The lust of domination appears no longer in disguise, but with an open face," as in the Coercive Acts and the Quebec Act, which was no more than a "bill for establishing the popish religion in Canada, contrary to the faith of the crown and the statutes of the kingdom."[23] At Lexington and Concord, however, the British nation proved itself to be not only tyrannical in its policies but also savage and barbaric in waging war. On April 19, the British "approached with the morning's light; and more like murderers and cut-throats, than the troops of a Christian king, without provocation, without warning, when no war was proclaimed, they draw the sword of violence, upon the inhabitants of this town, and with a cruelty and barbarity, which would have made the most hardened savage blush, they shed INNOCENT BLOOD!" From that moment on, the blood of patriots who died at Lexington cried out "unto God for vengeance from the ground!"[24]

Clearly, the battle of Lexington and Concord became a moment of sacred importance for patriots, and Clark's sermon is just one example of this. Two years later, another sermon commemorated the third anniversary of the beginning of the war, again preached, appropriately, in Lexington, and again Moses played a central role. Here was a religious condemnation of the British in the strongest terms. The British were no more than savages, preached Jacob Cushing, who chose his main text from one of the harshest holy war texts in scripture, which was also one of the most popular during the Revolution: the Song of Moses from Deuteronomy 32.

Cushing, who hailed from Waltham, Massachusetts, centered his sermon on Moses's proclamation of divine vengeance: "Rejoice, O ye nations, with his people, for he wilt avenge the blood of his servants, and will render vengeance to his adversaries" (Dt. 32:43). Cushing argued that the Revolutionary War began as uncivilized murder, hardly a war justly fought by the supposedly civilized British Empire. The battle at Lexington, as Cushing's title made clear, was a *Murderous War and Rapine, inhumanly perpetrated, by two brigades of British troops.* On that fateful day, the British "enemy came upon us like a flood, streaking a march from Boston, through by-ways, and under the darkness and silence of the night; and, like cowards and robbers, attacked us altogether defenseless; and cruelly murdered the innocent, the aged and helpless." From the beginning of the war, he preached, the British had defiled their hands with the blood of unjust atrocities. God would not let such murderous actions rest unpunished, however; he would execute vengeance on behalf of America's virtuous patriots. God would, Cushing predicted, "appear still for us, under all our distresses and oppression," and God would "*avenge the innocent blood* of our brethren, inhumanly shed in the beginning of the present unjust war."[25]

In executing divine vengeance, God did not always choose to fight alone—divine assistance from the weather in crucial battles notwithstanding. More often, God fought through the devotion of his patriotic people, and he required of them two things. First, they had to remember the atrocities that had spurred them to military action. They had to recall, even meditate on, Lexington and Concord in "remembrance of the origin of the present murderous war...the innocent blood wantonly shed around this sacred temple; and the subsequent slaughter and desolation by British troops, on that memorial day" of April 19, 1775—"a day religiously to be regarded by all professed Christians." In holding this day in sacred memory, America's patriots were to remember those who sacrificed, "bled and died, in the cause of God and their country, by the sons of violence, and the hands of murderers" who committed such atrocities in the name of Britain.[26] Second, the patriots who were fighting in 1778 had to imitate those brave souls who held off the British attacks on that fateful day. Because of those courageous patriots who "manfully opposed the efforts of British pride, power and barbarity," those "barbarous savage enemies were put into fear; they were made to flee before us, and hastily to retreat (as wild beasts to their dens)," repelled by "a few scattered, undisciplined freedmen" who fought in the name of the Lord. In this revolution, "this unnatural war," American patriots must follow the courageous example of Lexington and Concord, serving "under God mighty in battle," using their "swords and instruments of righteousness," as God "calls us to the shocking, but necessary, important duty of shedding human blood." To the militia of the town, therefore, Cushing proclaimed the divine command of Moses and of God: "To arms! To action, and the battle of the warrior!" He commanded them to "cultivate" within them "a martial spirit," striving toward excellence "in the art of war" so that they might defeat "the enemies of God and this people" in America.[27]

As these sermons reveal, the Exodus did not just make sense of British conspiracies and political policy; it made sense of British atrocities in war. Patriotic ministers gathered strength from the militancy of divine intervention on behalf of the Israelites. In essence, the battlefields of the Revolutionary War prompted ministers to proclaim the Exodus a war story. The victory at the Red Sea became a providential model of divine militancy. Just as God was "a man of war," so must God's people be war-ready patriots.

Slavery and the Limits of Liberty

At its most basic level, the Exodus story is about liberation from slavery. From the passage of the Stamp Act on, when colonists read the Exodus story, they analogized it to their experience. They believed they were slaves, oppressed victims of British tyranny. In opposition to tyranny, they preached the political message of the revolutionary gospel—that equality was a mark of creation all people shared.

Even as they preached this message, though, founders and ministers alike sometimes acknowledged the grand hypocrisy of a people complaining of slavery while they enslaved thousands of Africans. This point was not lost on British ministers who castigated American patriots. John Wesley, founder of the Methodist movement, ridiculed American patriots' complaints that the British had "enslaved" them with taxes even as these same patriots held Africans in chains. "Look into America," Wesley wrote in 1775, "and you may easily see" the "negro, fainting under the load, bleeding under the lash" while his master "is screaming, 'Murder! Slavery!'" So the American master complains loudly of slavery while his slave "silently bleeds and dies!" The contradiction was also clear to some American patriots. Jacob Green, a Presbyterian minister from New Jersey, asked in 1778: "Can it be believed that a people contending for liberty should, at the same time, be promoting and supporting slavery?" This inconsistency could not stand, Green asserted. Even if Americans were victorious in their revolution against political "slavery," actual slavery in America would produce "inward convulsions, contentions, oppressions, and various calamites, so that our liberty will be uncomfortable, till we wash our hands from the guilt of negro slavery."[28]

After the Revolution, this grand contradiction between revolutionary ideals and slaveholding realities would of course become clearer than ever, and pose more challenges than many Revolutionary-era Americans could have imagined.[29] Not surprisingly, when African Americans encountered the Bible, they often followed the revolutionary pattern of identifying with the Exodus narrative. The crucial difference, of course, was their perception that actual slavery in America, not the political oppression the revolutionaries complained about, was the true parallel to the Israelite bondage in Egypt. African Americans reversed Revolutionary America's reading of the Exodus story: the United States was not the new Israel; it was the new Egypt. "Slavery" in the Exodus was not a mere metaphor for political oppression; it was a literal counterpart to slavery in America. This interpretation of the Exodus was widespread among slaves and abolitionists in the nineteenth century. Historian Albert J. Raboteau argued persuasively that "no single symbol captures more clearly the distinctiveness of Afro-American Christianity than the symbol of Exodus."[30]

Understandably, few slaves in the Revolutionary era voiced this interpretation of the Exodus openly. One who did dare to imply that slaves were
the true Israelites and slaveholders were the true Egyptians was David, a
preacher in Savannah, Georgia. In May of 1775, almost one month after
the Revolutionary War began, Georgia merchant James Habersham wrote
that David had preached on the Exodus to a congregation of whites and
blacks. Apparently David preached that "God would send Deliverance to
the Negroes, from the power of their Masters, as He freed the Children
of Israel from Egyptian Bondage." That was all some whites in the crowd
needed to hear. To them, David's sermon was no less than a threatened
slave revolt. Whether or not David actually had planned a true revolt or
knew about one, these white citizens intended to "hang him, if they can
lay hold of him," Habersham wrote. To save David's life, and to avoid
additional disruption, Habersham arranged for David to be shipped off
to England.[31]

David's case was exceptional. More often, those who drew connections
between American slavery and the Exodus in Revolutionary America were
subtler. We find an example in one of the few Revolutionary War sermons by an African American, *A Sermon on the Evacuation of Charlestown*,
from 1783. The preacher, described only as "An Aethiopian," dedicated
the discourse to Thomas Heyward, South Carolina representative to the
Continental Congress and signer of the Declaration of Independence.
Early in the sermon, the preacher argued that the Revolutionary War had
been a story of divine deliverance best compared to the Exodus. Anyone
who read "the sacred writings, cannot fail of seeing deliverance on every
page," beginning with the Exodus, in which God "delivered Israel from
the hand of Pharaoh, when he had them in bondage, in the cruel land of
Egypt" by calling "his servant Moses to speak in the ears of this tyrannical monarch these awful words—*If you will not let my son go, even Israel
my first-born, I will slay thy son even thy first-born*" (Exodus 4:22–23). But
Pharaoh, "this haughty Monarch, like Britain's present King, hardened
his heart against the Lord, and it ended in his utter destruction." In this
way, God had delivered Israel, and, as "he is the God of America," this God
delivered America.[32]

In this preacher's view, God had delivered America, quite miraculously,
in many battles. The war was over. And, much to the patriots' delight,
the British had finally evacuated Charleston. Note here that this African
American writer applied Exodus to the Revolution in the same way that
many white ministers had: the revolutionary story was, primarily, the story

of miraculous deliverance, as "an infant country, no men, no money, no allies, no disciplined troops" rose up "to meet a veteran army commanded by able generals." The British generals were able but not civilized. They commanded a "savage" force that created martyrs everywhere they wielded their weapons against the American faithful. The British had embraced "savage soldiery and [the] ruthless sword wantonly and barbarously," and, for Britain "there is wrath in store," a divine "sword of justice for him that delighted in blood."[33]

This preacher was following the standard revolutionary interpretation of Exodus, but he did not stop there. He made another significant point: this American story of liberation, this revolutionary Exodus, owed its success in part to patriotic slaves and free blacks who had fought against the British. He hinted at this argument early in the sermon, pointing out the witness of that famous African American patriot, Crispus Attucks, who had died courageously at the Boston Massacre.[34] By invoking Attucks's patriotism, the preacher was no doubt arguing that most African Americans were patriots—a case that needed to be made at a time when many slaves faced retribution for aligning with the British to liberate themselves from slavery.[35]

The legacy of African American patriots was important for African Americans and abolitionists in the nineteenth century. Significantly, this legacy was the subject of one of the first scholarly histories written by an African American, William C. Nell's The Colored Patriots of the American Revolution, published in 1855. In the book's preface, Harriet Beecher Stowe, the famous author of Uncle Tom's Cabin, underscored the importance of African Americans' patriotic service in the Revolution. Nell's book, she argued, would "redeem the character" of African Americans from accusations that they were "deficient in energy and courage." Moreover, African Americans' service in the Revolution was all the more impressive, given that they had sacrificed their lives for a nation that "enslaved them." Stowe concluded, "bravery, under such circumstances, has a peculiar beauty and merit."[36]

Understandably, the African American preacher of Evacuation of Charlestown made this point less directly. But he was no less clear about the irreconcilability of slavery with the ideals of the American Revolution. As he expounded on British barbarities and American virtues in courage, he used the common image of slavery to describe the British treatment of the colonies. "Be no more her slaves," the minister implored. And, in this drive for freedom, "make our states independent states indeed, by gradually abolishing slavery, and making the Aethiopian race comfortable amongst us."[37] So this anonymous African American author from South Carolina asserted that the spirit of '76 opposed the spirit of tyranny, whether that of a British monarch or an American slaveholder.

Even so, this preacher cited the Exodus in opposition to the British, but not in opposition to slavery. He did not envision American slaves as Israelites, nor did he call American slaveholders "pharaohs." This is understandable, given that the majority of his readers were white, and many would have supported slavery. He did connect slavery with British tyranny, but he did so subtlety. Calling slaveholding Americans contemporary pharaohs would have defeated that purpose.

In Revolutionary America, then, the biblical narrative of liberation in the Exodus mainly applied to the political "slavery" of British tyranny, and not the chattel slavery of African Americans. Even sermons and treatises that focused on the evils of African slavery did not often cite the Exodus story. Consider one of the few antislavery treatises written by an African American, Lemuel Haynes's "Liberty Further Extended: Or Free Thoughts on the Illegality of Slave-keeping." It is unfortunate that Haynes never published his treatise, because it is remarkable for several reasons. First, before Haynes became a noted preacher and theologian, he was a soldier from Massachusetts. He joined the ranks of the militia following the battles of Lexington and Concord, and later enlisted in the Continental Army, marching off to Fort Ticonderoga in 1776. Second, Haynes became well versed in New England Calvinist theology, republican political ideology, and enlightened moral concepts such as disinterested benevolence—all of which shaped his arguments for the Revolution and against African slavery. His title, "Liberty Further Extended," is revealing. He was arguing that liberty applied not only to the struggle against British tyranny but also to the struggle against slavery, since the two were intimately related. Others had made this argument, and Haynes was influenced by their works, notably New Divinity minister Samuel Hopkins's *Dialogue Concerning the Slavery of the Africans*, published in 1776.

Haynes began his treatise, likely written in 1776, by quoting in full the first sentence of the Declaration of Independence: "We hold these truths to be self-Evident, that all men are created Equal, that they are Endowed By their Creator with Certain unalienable rights, that among these are Life, Liberty and the pursuit of happyness."[38] The same drive against tyranny that empowered the Revolution should also empower opposition to slav-ery, Haynes argued. When it came to tyranny, Britain, though obviously the most visible culprit in the fiendish practice of oppression, was not its only perpetrator. As "we are Engaged in the important struggle"—namely, the Revolution—Haynes argued, "it cannot Be tho't impertinent for us to turn one Eye into our own Breast," to discover if "we Do not find the mon-ster Lurking in our own Bosom." Liberty applied to all people, Haynes stressed, not just to white British citizens. "Liberty is Equally as pre[c]ious to a *Black man,* as it is to a *white one,* and Bondage Equally as intolerable to the one as it is to the other." Further, "Shall a mans Couler Be the Decisive Criterion whereby to Judge of his natural right?" Slavery and the slave trade were as tyrannical as King George III and Parliament combined. Americans needed to battle tyranny in all its forms, to "be consistently Engaged in the Cause of Liberty!"[39]

Haynes took on the classic defense of race-based slavery using several texts from the Bible, not the least of which was the Sermon on the Mount. But he did not mention the Exodus. His main biblical argument cen-tered on God's vengeance against tyranny and all forms of oppression. Often, God's means of dealing with tyranny was to turn the tables on the oppressor, to allow the opponents to experience what it was like to be persecuted. Such was the case with "wicked Ahab, and Jezebel," who per-secuted and killed poor Naboth, but then reaped God's vengeance when the dogs licked the blood from their corpses. This pattern held strong throughout the Bible. It was "God's way of Dealing, by retaliating Back upon men the Same Evils that they unjustly Bring upon others." God was patient, to be sure, but not endlessly so. He eventually would seek ven-geance on the wicked. Haynes read the Revolution into this scenario. The tyranny of Britain was quite possibly God's way of heaping retribution on Americans for their tyrannical enslavement of Africans. No one knows, Haynes wrote, "how far that the unjust Oppression which hath abounded in this Land, may be the procuring cause of this very Judgment that now impends."[40]

Haynes's book indicated that the Exodus narrative had not yet become as clearly identified with slavery as it would in the nineteenth century. And yet, the beginnings of that parallel between chattel slavery and Exodus were emerging in Revolutionary America. One of Haynes's main influ-ences, Samuel Hopkins, did include the Exodus in his *Dialogue Concerning the Slavery of the Africans,* and he dedicated the *Dialogue* to the Continental Congress, which had adopted a resolution against the slave trade in 1774.

This statement against the slave trade was not a rejection of the institution of slavery altogether. But it was a step in the right direction, Hopkins believed. Encouraged by this stance, provisional though it was, Hopkins pushed forward to attack slavery itself. He called on the Continental Congress to use "the great influence you have in these colonies" to effect "a total abolition of slavery, in such a manner as shall greatly promote the happiness of those oppressed strangers and the best interest of the public."[41]

Here, the leading New Divinity theologian and minister used the example of Pharaoh to counter the claim that God had ordained slavery. That black people existed and were enslaved did not prove that God had cursed the black race into bondage, Hopkins argued. He opposed the common interpretation that people of the black race were "the children of Ham," whom God had cursed into perpetual slavery in Genesis 9. According to proponents of slavery, the curse of Ham was God's will: to free slaves would be to disobey God. Hopkins countered that, even if slavery did fulfill the scriptures, it did not excuse the slaveholders. Consider, he argued, that God knew that Pharaoh would enslave the Israelites in Egypt, and had allowed it. Did that mean that Pharaoh was innocent of enslaving the Israelites? Certainly not, for God judged Pharaoh harshly. God would also harshly judge the American slaveholder, Hopkins argued. Those who defended slavery were like "Pharaoh and the Egyptians," who likely "had as many weighty" arguments against freeing the Hebrews as Revolutionary-era slaveholders had "against freeing the slaves among us." Eventually, however, God drowned all Pharaoh's arguments for slavery in the Red Sea.[42]

That was an ominous thought for revolutionary Americans. Hopkins condemned the blatant hypocrisy of holding slaves in bondage while demanding freedom from British rule. In his dedication of his *Dialogue* to the Continental Congress in 1776, Hopkins asked that members be "deeply sensible of the inconsistence of promoting the slavery of the Africans, at the same time we are asserting our own civil liberty at the risk of our fortunes and lives." These "many hundreds of thousands of blacks in slavery...have an equal right to freedom with ourselves" even as "we are maintaining this struggle for our own and our children's liberty." He thought the Exodus story "well worthy" of "our serious consideration, whether we have not reason to fear the hand of God, which is now stretched out against us, will lie upon us, and the strokes grow heavier, unless we reform this iniquity."[43]

Hopkins argued that even if Americans did not care about the slaves, if they cared about the Revolution they should abolish slavery. To those who said that the issue of slavery would have to wait until the war ended, Hopkins responded that wartime was precisely the right time to oppose slavery. If slavery was "a very great and public sin," and if God punished sinful nations with multiple calamities, including war, then the colonies should reject slavery before they incurred God's wrath. For colonists to condone slavery was not just morally reprehensible and "unspeakably criminal," it was "awfully dangerous," Hopkins warned.[44]

Several other ministers agreed. In 1774, Nathaniel Niles of Newburyport, Massachusetts preached, "let us either cease to enslave our fellow-men, or else let us cease to complain of those that would enslave us. Let us either wash our hands from blood, or never hope to escape the avenger." Likewise, Baptist minister Elisha Rich expressed this sentiment in a poetic reflection on the battle of Bunker Hill in 1775.

> Would thou obtain thy liberty,
> Then break all bands of slavery,
> And do thou liberty proclaim
> To all that have a human frame.
> But if oppression here is found
> Can you with victory be crown'd,
> No, no, be sure this cannot be,
> While thou thy neighbours do not free.[45]

Hopkins argued that slavery was wrong because it violated the natural rights proclaimed in both the Declaration of Independence and the Bible. He remarked that the slaves saw the revolutionary "cry and struggle for liberty" but that they also "behold the sons of liberty oppressing and tyrannizing over many thousands of poor blacks who have as good a claim to liberty as" anyone. This obvious contradiction rightfully "shocked" the slaves, while white patriots seemed unaware that the tyranny they feared was "lighter than a feather compared to" the "heavy doom" inflicted on the slaves. For this contemptible situation, Hopkins blamed ministers who either supported slavery or stood silent, refusing to condemn it outright. True republicanism cried out for liberty against slavery. When the Exodus became the central narrative of liberation for slaves in the nineteenth century, therefore, this interpretation drew in part on arguments in favor of the Revolution.[46]

America's Moses

Moses was many things, but for the preachers of Revolutionary America his most important role was as God's prophetic leader and lawgiver, the man who led the Israelites out of Egypt and through the wilderness. Moses was entitled to the highest respect, earned through his heroic leadership and virtuous character.[47]

Ministers knew the power and relevance of Moses, and so did the founders.[48] In 1776, when John Adams wrote to Abigail about how the Revolution paralleled the Exodus story, he ruminated on what it must have been like to be Moses. "Is it not a Saying of Moses, who am I, that I should go in and out before this great People? When I consider the great Events which are passed, and those greater which are rapidly advancing, and that I may have been instrumental of touching some Springs, and turning some small Wheels, which have had and will have such Effects, I feel an Awe upon my Mind, which is not easily Described."[49] In this letter, Adams brought Moses to America, putting himself in Moses' position. If the American Revolution were the new Exodus, there had to be a new Moses. Adams seemed to be campaigning for the role.

At this point in the spring of 1776, no one had yet claimed the "title" of America's Moses—that is, the authoritative leader of the Revolution. Surely the leading candidate would have been George Washington. Granted, Benjamin Franklin had a greater international reputation than any other American, including Washington. But Franklin, who was twenty-six years older than Washington, was known mostly for his scientific discoveries, while Washington owed his emerging fame to his courage and leadership. Even so, at this point Washington had only recently assumed command of the Continental Army. Although he was widely admired for his courage during the French and Indian War, Washington was not yet the hero of the Revolution.[50]

Once independence had been secured and he was overwhelmingly selected as first president of the United States, it was clear that Washington was America's Moses. Everyone, including Adams, knew it. If anyone doubted Washington's heroism, ministers were happy to dispel them. In his much-reprinted sermon *The United States Elevated to Glory and Honor*, Yale president Ezra Stiles heaped plenty of glory and honor on Washington. Stiles preached this election sermon in Hartford, Connecticut, on May 8, 1783, less than a month after Congress declared the Revolutionary War to be over. "O Washington!" Stiles preached, "how do I love thy name! how have I often adored and blessed thy God for creating and forming thee the great ornament of human kind!" In these exuberant times just after the victory, Washington had earned such praise, Stiles believed, because he had "carried through one of the most arduous and most important wars in all history." Accordingly, "the sound of thy fame shall go out into all the earth, and extend to distant ages." Washington's greatest asset was his virtuous character. Washington had "convinced the world of the Beauty of Virtue" and "those who would not recognize any beauty in virtue in the world beside will yet reverence it in thee."[51]

Though most Americans assented to Washington's exalted status, his popularity was both exhilarating and disconcerting. Some ministers even worried that people might be tempted to worship Washington. In 1784, the year after the Treaty of Paris was signed, Thomas Brockway, a pastor in Lebanon, Connecticut, felt the need to caution Americans that "we are not, my hearers, to worship the man," George Washington. Instead, "we are to worship God for the man; for he is but a creature gift, a rich pledge of divine mercy; though great, he has been only to us, what God has made him." Keep your respect for Washington within appropriate bounds, Brockway warned, for "when the veneration is carried beyond this boundary, it is criminal."[52]

Washington's great popularity ushered in questions about the proper nature of republican leadership. Could a people, fresh from their rebellion against a king—and, at least theoretically, against monarchy itself—call for a powerful executive leader? How powerful could or should a president be?[53] These questions stirred much debate after the Revolution. There were many who still yearned for aspects of the monarchial style of leadership. They had known no other form of government, so it made sense that monarchy would die hard, even in a new nation founded on republican principles. In 1789 the Senate spent weeks arguing over whether the new office of the presidency should include a royal title. Certainly, the president needed to command authority, and a dignified title seemed to be in order. Before finally settling on calling the executive leader simply "Mr. President," the Senate considered such exalted titles as "His Highness, or . . . His Most Benign Highness." Even if the official title of the American president was up for debate, his identity was not—it would be Washington. For most Americans, only Washington could satisfy demands for an authoritative leader who would be self-sacrificing and virtuous instead of tyrannical and corrupt.[54]

Despite Washington's popularity, therefore, some Americans worried about giving too much authority to any individual. Also worrisome was the sheer magnitude of Washington's fame. Even John Adams, who admired Washington immensely, nurtured a longtime jealousy, not only of Washington, but of Benjamin Franklin as well. In 1790, after Washington had been elected president and just before Franklin died, Adams remarked, "The History of our Revolution will be one continued Lye from one end to the other. The essence of the whole will be that Dr. Franklin's electrical Rod, smote the Earth and out sprung General Washington. That Franklin electrified him with his rod—and thence forward these two conducted all the Policy, Negotiations, Legislatures and War."[55]

Even as Adams hoped that he would be credited with "touching some Springs, and turning some small Wheels" in America's founding, he knew that memories of his contributions would pale in comparison to those of Washington and Franklin.[56] Washington would always receive due accolades as the military leader of the Revolution, the first president, and the Father of his Country—all legacies that a significant number of ministers captured with the biblical title, "America's Moses."

Americans compared Washington to many biblical figures—Joshua, for instance, when praising his heroic leadership in battle.[57] When speaking of Washington's political leadership, however, they looked overwhelmingly to Moses. For a new nation that had sworn off monarchial tyranny but had not completely lost sight of some of monarchy's advantages, Moses seemed to be the Bible's answer to America's need for presidential leadership. Moses was not a warrior-king like King David but a warrior-legislator, making him a "safer" vessel for monarchial yearnings in republican society.

Comparisons of Washington to Moses reached their peak in numerous eulogies that followed his death in 1799, many of them preached by Federalist clergy who worried about what America would do without Washington.[58] The times were desperate, many Federalists believed, and the nation needed the kind of leadership that Washington favored—a strong, centralized national government—as a check against the chaotic forces unleashed by radical republicanism and the French Revolution. At first, Americans had hailed the French Revolution as a virtuous import from America. But it quickly lost its appeal when the French zeal for liberty degenerated into violence and disarray. At that point the main American defenders of French influence were radical Republicans. It was with them in mind that Cyprian Strong of Chatham, Connecticut, praised

Washington's legacy while warning of a "mock patriotism, which advocates foreign measures, concerted to divide and weaken us...under a specious zeal for liberty."[59]

In the years before his death, especially in the controversy surrounding the Jay Treaty in 1795, Washington had seen the advent of the kind of party politics he deplored, with Federalists and Republicans fuming against each other. And since Washington was the leader and symbol of Federalist power, much of the raging against Federalism focused on him.

Attacks came from various Republican fronts, including a vicious published letter from none other than revolutionary pamphleteer Thomas Paine, written from Paris in 1796. In it, one of the most radical advocates of the French Revolution spewed pure venom against the perceived corrupt English influence that many Republicans saw in Washington. From Paine's pen, nothing about Washington was sacred. Paine claimed to set the record straight on the so-called father of the country. "It is time, sir, to speak the undisguised language of historical truth," Paine proclaimed. Of Washington's administration, Paine declared, "I know it to have been deceitful, if not perfidious." Of Washington's seemingly unassailable courage and military leadership in the Revolution, Paine claimed, "had it not been for the aid received from France, in men, money and ships,...your cold and unmilitary conduct...would in all probability have lost America." Paine's diatribe included unfair, even ridiculous statements: "You slept away your time in the field, till the finances of the country were completely exhausted, and you have but little share in the glory of the final event." Not even Washington's famous reputation for self-sacrifice and disinterestedness was safe from Paine's attack. "Elevated to the chair of the Presidency, you assumed the merit of every thing to yourself, and the natural ingratitude of your constitution began to appear. You commenced your Presidential career by encouraging and swallowing the grossest adulation...You have as many addresses in your chest as James the II...if you are not great enough to have ambition you are little enough to have vanity."[60]

Paine's assault on Washington was extreme. Very few Republicans would have dared to launch such attacks against Washington publically, and not many more would have even entertained such vicious sentiments privately. Most readers of this open letter against Washington questioned Paine's views, and John Adams even questioned his sanity. Still, Paine was not completely alone in his opposition to Washington's influence. Republicans in general expressed substantial disagreements with Washington and his Federalist allies.[61]

Washington achieved his identity as America's Moses, therefore, through a hard fought contest—a battle waged between conflicting political ideas about the meaning of the Revolution and the nation it had founded. Upon Washington's death, some eulogists saw nearly perfect parallels between the two men. Just as "God qualified and raised up Moses" to lead the Israelites "through the stormy period of their national birth," God also "raised up a Washington," qualifying him to lead "the American armies, through the bloody and arduous contest for national independence," preached Cyprian Strong.[62] Washington's fortitude under fire was unassailable—his courage "was never doubted by friend or foe," David Barnes preached in Scituate, Massachusetts.[63] Like Moses, Washington exhibited "patriotism...of the virtuous kind," said Barnes, "if ever there was a man in the world, who discovered a truly patriotic spirit, who spent life for the good of his country and countrymen, who exposed his health, hazarded his life, and everything dear to him of a temporal nature, Washington was the man." But neither Moses nor Washington was a war hero only; they were legislative heroes as well, true founders of their Judaic and American republics. Just as "Moses was as much distinguished in the cabinet, as in the field" so "Washington was as much respected at the head of councils, as he had been at the head of our armies." He was, as was often stated, "first in war" and "first in peace."[64]

If Washington was the American Moses, he was also the American Cincinnatus. Like that champion of classical Rome, Washington did not attempt to capitalize on his status as a war hero to satisfy personal ambition. Just as Cincinnatus abandoned wartime fame for the humble life of a farmer, Washington shocked everyone by retiring from public life after the Revolutionary War. Such an amazing gesture of selflessness secured his reputation for republican virtue. Washington knew this, of course, and he self-consciously embodied disinterestedness and classical republican integrity. Given Washington's fame after the Revolution, he could have, in Gordon Wood's estimation, "become king or dictator," but he instead gave up his power, and that move only increased his fame.[65] As Garry Wills has observed, Washington "gained power from his readiness to give it up."[66] As King George III reportedly said, if Washington truly surrenders his victorious command and retires to Mount Vernon, "he will be the greatest man in the world."[67]

Washington may not have become the "greatest man in the world," but he was certainly the most respected man in America—and he remained so mainly because he nurtured a reputation for disinterested selflessness, even as he accepted the office of president of the United States. There had been no rival for the office. And though Washington was reluctant to assume the presidency, he knew, as most Americans did, that only he could give the new nation the prestige, leadership, and command that it needed to survive.

This reluctant willingness only fueled the comparisons to classical figures and to Moses. While the comparisons to classical figures were common, it was Washington's similarities to Moses that dominated the eulogies.[68] When eulogists occasionally associated Washington with classical figures, they often did so to assert Washington's virtuous superiority over the legendary classical heroes. "Should you search the records of ancient Greece, or the annals of mighty Rome, you search in vain" to find a virtuous character comparable to Washington, proclaimed Peter Folsom of Gilmanton, New Hampshire. "Alexander the Great" may have "conquered the world; but never conquered himself: his object was conquest, in order to glut a vain ambition."[69]

Although likenesses to classical antiquity were appropriate, therefore, there was really no contest: Washington exceeded all classical heroes in republican virtue. Only Moses, biblical "father of his country," could rival America's hero. Like Washington, Moses did not seize leadership of the people; he resisted it, only taking command when God demanded it. Moses's reticence appeared to exemplify republican virtue, a character of sacrificial leadership for the common good. In his extended comparison of Moses to Washington, for example, Thaddeus Fiske of Cambridge asserted that "power, in the hands of Washington, was safe," for Washington used power "only to the welfare of his country."[70] Catholic Bishop John Carroll echoed the Protestant clergy. "There existed not in the world a name so bright as his: no character stood on such lofty preeminence," preached Carroll. Like other ministers, Carroll could not resist equating the retiring Washington at Mount Vernon with the retiring Moses on Mt. Pisgah.[71] Many believed that Washington displayed his virtue most persuasively in his famous "Farewell Address," which at least one minister reprinted along with his eulogy to Washington.[72] As Fiske observed, Washington's "farewell was accompanied, like that of Moses to the Children of Israel, with the best legacy that 'the father of his country could leave.'"[73]

The clergy's identification of Washington with Moses helped to affirm Washington's religious credentials, which were not conspicuous. This was a tricky issue, as Washington was a nominal Anglican with somewhat veiled deistic beliefs. But one would never know that from the eulogies. Ministers unabashedly asserted Washington's firm religious convictions. "Moses was a man of piety, religion and morality. And so was Washington," David Barnes declared.[74] Likewise, Baptist minister Richard Furman of South Carolina unabashedly asserted Washington's firm religious convictions. Washington "possessed a high sense of the importance and excellency of religion," and insisted on "the necessity of religion, for the support of morality, virtue, and the true interests of civil society." Furman also observed that Washington regularly attended worship and encouraged others to worship. Regarding Washington's theological views, Furman asserted that he "was more fully acquainted with the sublime doctrines of Christianity, and their gracious, experimental influence on the heart, than" he often declared publically. Moreover, Washington "acknowledged the interposition of Heaven in the great events of the revolution, and pledged himself to supplicate the Almighty in behalf of his country, and of his companions in arms."[75]

Above all, the clergy overwhelming insisted that Washington "was no sophist, nor atheist."[76] This statement was both compelling and true. Although Washington was no evangelical, he had only positive things to say about religion, especially as a source of moral influence in society. In his beloved "Farewell Address," Washington wrote, "Of all the dispositions and habits which lead to political prosperity, Religion and Morality are indispensable supports." Both were "great pillars of human happiness," and it was only "in vain" that anyone could "claim the tribute of patriotism" without them. "Let it simply be asked," Washington wrote, "where is the security for property, for reputation, for life, if the sense of religious obligation desert the oaths which are the instruments of investigation in Courts of Justice?" Washington was also wary of any enlightened attempt to forgo religion in favor of a morality without religious supports—"let us with caution indulge the supposition, that morality can be maintained without religion."[77]

Religiously, therefore, George Washington was no George Whitefield, but neither was he Thomas Jefferson, who disliked evangelicalism and had to fend off charges that he was anti-Christian. Washington's religious convictions alone were neither substantial enough nor public enough to gain the approval of most American Christians. But his favorable comments about God's providence and religion's benefit to society made up for his few displays of piety and his reluctance to mention Christ. His respect for religion, together with his unrivaled status as the first among Americans, were more than enough to justify comparisons to Moses.

The need to assert Washington's dignity, righteousness, and authority led some to claim that Washington was superior to Moses. Incredibly,
revolutionary heroism superseded biblical heroism. While "some have
compared [Washington] to Moses," Peter Folsom observed, there was one
major distinction: "Moses conducted the Israelites in sight of the Promised
Land; but, Washington has done more, he has put the Americans in full
possession" of the new nation. Moses may have "led the Israelites through
the red sea," but " has not Washington conducted the Americans thro'
seas of blood?"[78]

Ministers not only noted the character traits that made Washington
superior, they also pointed out that Moses had certain advantages that
Washington did not, most importantly his direct relationship with God.
God communicated directly to Moses the prophet; he even revealed himself bodily to Moses. Moses thus had God's assurance that his people
would be victorious in the end. Washington had no such guarantees.
While he had faith, he had no God-given certainty that the Revolution
would succeed and that he would not be hanged for treason.[79] For several
of the eulogists, Washington was therefore not only more virtuous than
classical figures such as Cincinnatus; he even surpassed Moses. For some
Americans, even ministers such as Eli Forbes, Washington was no longer
the Moses of America; Moses was "the Washington of Israel."[80]

After the Exodus:
The Constitution of Moses in the New Nation

These celebrations show that revolutionary Americans endorsed a particular view of political leadership through biblical authority, one that offered
a biblical solution to the complex problem of what to do with the incomparable reputation of George Washington. By honoring Washington as
America's Moses, Americans insured themselves against any concerns
that he was really a monarch. It is significant that Americans called
Washington America's Moses and not America's David. Unlike King
David, Moses did not reign over a nation; he led a republic. He did so as
a military champion and as a legislator, deliverer, and enforcer of God's
republican laws. Moses's chief symbols were tablets filled with laws, not
thrones and palaces filled with harems.

By claiming Washington as America's Moses, ministers revealed their
admiration for biblical models of republican government. Republicanism
had existed since the sixteenth century and was especially prominent among

Reformed Protestants. It gained greater currency after the Revolution, when ministers and other colonists shifted their focus from biblical warfare to biblical politics. Above all, the tradition of Hebraic republicanism enabled Americans to use the Bible to combat monarchy. Thomas Paine used the argument to perfection in *Common Sense*. Only God should be a king, Paine argued, citing 1 Samuel 8, in which God, through Samuel, implores the people not to demand an earthly king. Paine drew on a tradition of republicanism that extended through the seventeenth-century English Civil War. Paine's case against monarchy based on the Old Testament was central to *Common Sense*.[81] Monarchy, Paine asserted, was sinful and unbiblical. He insisted "that the Almighty hath here entered his protest against monarchical government is true, or the scripture is false." Paine reasoned that the people's obedience to a king was disobedience to God, both in biblical times and in the eighteenth century.[82]

As a legislator, Moses also contributed to the conversation about the shape of government in the new nation. The republicanism of the Old Testament could serve not only to tear down monarchy; it could also build up a constitutional government grounded in the sacred legitimacy of scripture. John Adams wrote that "the government of the Hebrews, instituted by God, had a judge, the great Sanhedrim, and general assemblies of the people." Here Adams found biblical precedent for the three components of all "good government," namely, "monarchy, aristocracy, and democracy."[83]

The themes Adams cited were developed in sermons as the states were ratifying the federal Constitution, and Moses's influence was undeniable. Perhaps the best example is a sermon whose title captured the essence of Moses's constitutional influence: *The Republic of the Israelites an Example to the American States*, delivered by Samuel Langdon in New Hampshire on June 5, 1788. Langdon was a Congregationalist minister who had been president of Harvard through much of the Revolutionary War. The theme of Langdon's sermon was not just constitution but evolution. The Israelites' deliverance from Egypt, as miraculous as it was, would have come to nothing had not the people organized around a constitutional government under Moses's direction. After fleeing from Egypt, the people were a disordered "multitude," united as "a body under the conduct of Moses, without any proper national or military regulation." Yet mere months after their adventure at the Red Sea, the people had established order, electing "captains and rulers" from their tribes. Then, when Moses complained "that the burden of government was too heavy for him," God led the people in creating "a permanent constitution."[84] This progress from lawless multitude to godly constitution served as an example for the United States, which had to complete the miraculous delivery from the British by establishing a federal government on sound principles.

The Exodus is a biblical narrative with almost universal political appeal. Nearly everywhere that bondage and injustice have existed, oppressed people have recalled the Exodus and claimed it as their own. The American Revolution, therefore, is but one episode in an ongoing saga. Soon after the 2008 presidential election, a popular book appeared, with a provocative title: *America's Prophet: How the Story of Moses Shaped America.*[85] This book revealed the astounding pervasiveness of the story in contemporary politics. If Moses and the Exodus have remained prominent in America, the American Revolution is a major reason why. By making the Exodus story their own, especially by associating it so strongly with the republican ideals of liberty and the republican institutions of the new nation, the patriots set the parameters for later Americans, including nineteenth-century slaves, who saw the liberation of the Hebrews from Egypt as a model for their own struggles. After all, in calling America the new Egypt, slaves not only condemned slavery as an unjust institution; they also condemned the United States for not holding true to its revolutionary claim to resist Pharaoh in all his oppressive forms.

At the center of the Exodus narrative of liberation was a violent God. The dramatic statement from Exodus 15, "The Lord is a Man of War," filled colonial American sermons because it proclaimed that God liberated his people through war. Moreover, the Exodus story was effective in Revolutionary America because it showed how God's wartime deliverances defied expectations. Against all odds, God defeated the Egyptians just as it appeared that Pharaoh's forces had the Israelites trapped on the coast of the Red Sea. Although the Americans had confidence in their cause— perhaps too much confidence, some worried—they recognized that they were overmatched and underprepared to fight God's sacred battles. Only fervent discipline—both spiritual and martial—could steel American patriots for the battles ahead.

The divine "Man of War" was hardly confined to the Exodus. Wartime urgencies led ministers to call on various images of divine violence. And among all such images in scripture, none were more prevalent than those of courageous prophets and judges, the subjects of the next chapter.

3

"Cursed Be He that Keepeth
Back his Sword from Blood"

DEBORAH, JEREMIAH, AND PROPHETIC VIOLENCE

COLONIAL MINISTERS DID not shy away from biblical violence. They embraced it, almost celebrated it, even in its most graphic forms. And graphic violence abounded in scripture. The violent commands of the judges and prophets attracted the most attention. In terms of pulpit appeal, no prophet or judge rivaled Deborah. Technically, Deborah was a judge, though ministers often called her a prophet, and they certainly considered her commands to be prophetic. The Song of Deborah (Judges 5) was the most cited passage in over a century of colonial war sermons (1675–1800). What made this text so appealing? The famous "Curse of Meroz" (Judges 5:23) in which God, speaking through an angel, condemned the inhabitants of the mysterious Meroz because they refused to fight against his enemies was a popular war text in the English Civil War, and it was even more popular in America. But American preachers were also drawn to other elements of the story, including Deborah herself; general Barak, her military ally; and perhaps most interestingly, the tent-dwelling woman Jael, the song's ultimate hero, who killed the Canaanite general Sisera by driving a tent peg through his skull. As Jael's blessed homicide demonstrated, this was a bloody ballad, a song that praised sacrifice to the death in allegiance to God.[1]

Ministers often associated Deborah's story with an equally gruesome curse from the prophet Jeremiah: "cursed be he that keepeth back his sword from blood" (Jeremiah 48:10), a verse that appeared in several sermons during wartime. These graphic curses seemed to advocate holy war, and yet they were overwhelmingly popular among ministers who claimed to participate only in civilized "just" wars—wars fought with limited means and ends, wars that minimized violence rather than relishing in it.[2] Why, then, the fascination with the biblical blood and gore of Deborah, Jael, and Jeremiah? The answer had much to do with the realities of war, and especially the personal crises that many revolutionary soldiers—especially those who were Christians—had to overcome to do their duty as patriots. As good patriots, these soldiers had to answer two primary callings: they had to be willing to die, and they had to be willing to kill. Soldiers were typically more prepared for the former than the latter. After all, the essence of both Christianity and patriotism was self-sacrifice, even martyrdom. So giving one's life for a righteous cause seemed to fit with soldiers' view of the world. Death on the battlefield, though terrifying, promised eternal rewards in heaven and perhaps even renown at home. Killing was another matter. What historian Drew Gilpin Faust said of the American Civil War applies also to the Revolution: motivating soldiers to kill for their country was more difficult than inspiring them to die for it. It "required the more significant departure from soldiers' understandings of themselves as human beings and...as Christians."[3]

The crisis of conscience that soldiers faced when taking up the musket partially explains why preachers looked to scripture for inspiration. Colonial preachers shaped these violent curses into a militant form of the jeremiad, a call to arms that praised violence as virtuous and chastised nonviolence as sinful cowardice. In making such appeals to the violence in scripture, wartime preachers revealed the militant character of their faith and consecrated violence—even the most graphic violence—as obedience to God.[4]

Prophetic Violence in America before the Revolution

In times of crisis, people often look to the Bible's prophetic books. Prophets threatened judgment that would doom the people—even God's chosen people—if they did not obey God's urgent commands. Not surprisingly, therefore, revolutionary times were prophetic times. Even ministers, pledged to uphold spiritual virtue and to witness to the "prince of peace," could not get enough of these prophetic calls to war. It is no accident that one of the most virulent patriot sermons, Moses Mather's *America's Appeal to an Impartial World*, featured three prophetic texts on the title page—one from Isaiah, one from Samuel, and one, of course, from Jeremiah.[5]

Similarly, Presbyterian minister William Foster, preaching to a company of recruits on February 18, 1776, preached Jeremiah's curse: "Cursed be he that keepeth back his sword from blood in such a cause. There can, strictly speaking, be no neutrality in the present case—he that is not with us must be against us." What Foster most feared *was* fear: "I fear many will shrink back, and under some pretext desert the cause, when their assistance will be most needed." Anyone fearful of battle needed to be more fearful of Jeremiah's dreaded curse against any who refused to take up the sword. This war was "the cause of God and religion." Accordingly, Foster implored these Pennsylvania troops to "quit yourselves like men; stand ready to march into the field when God and your country call."[6]

As appropriate as these texts were for the 1770s, they were just as appealing to colonists in the 1740s and even earlier. So before we delve into the revolutionary reverence for these curses, we need to discover where they came from. What about them so interested colonists at war before the Revolution? And how did these pre-Revolutionary concepts of biblical violence resurface anew in the Revolution?

The curses of Deborah and Jeremiah echoed throughout the colonies in wartime decades before the American Revolution. We find a striking example in Virginia, where the Presbyterian minister Samuel Davies cited Jeremiah in *The Curse of Cowardice,* his impassioned plea to military recruits during the French and Indian War. Preached in Hanover County, Virginia, and published in both London and Boston, this sermon made a statement on war, frontier style, to win support for Britain's military efforts in America. Davies originally delivered the sermon on May 8, 1758, with the purpose of inspiring men to join Captain Samuel Meredith's militia. Davies's choice of Jeremiah's violent verse was strategic; he wanted all to know that war in Virginia was barbaric, the kind of war that called all men to bathe their swords in blood. Davies bemoaned the crisis in which "barbarous" and antichristian enemies "ravage our Frontiers" and "butcher our Fellow-Subjects." In this circumstance, Davies argued, "even the God of Peace proclaims by his Providence, 'To Arms!'" War was not merely a civil duty; it was a spiritual obligation. When the war raged against the popish Antichrist on earth and his Indian allies, "the Art of war becomes a Part of our Religion."[7]

Davies channeled all his revivalist skills to the military cause. His insistence that the military "Company to be made up this very Day before we leave this place" resembled the revivalist's call on the sinner to embrace the offer of salvation before death and damnation could steal away the soul. In this case, however, the threat was the sin of cowardice. So Davies called on potential soldiers to embrace "the Author of true Courage, and every heroic virtue, to fire you into Patriots and Soldiers at this Moment!" The crisis was imminent, Davies insisted, so "You that Love your Religion enlist: for your Religion is in Danger," threatened by "Heathen Savages and French Papists," an alliance that encompassed "the Powers of Hell."[8]

In describing the barbarity of the frontier, Davies drew heavily on monstrous images of French and Indian hostilities. The situation was dire. God's army—Protestant and British, of course—was not so much fighting a war against armies as it was lashing out desperately against the "Barbarities and Depredations [of] a mongrel Race of Indian Savages and French Papists" who had committed untold atrocities against non-combatants. Even as Davies preached, he guessed that "the savage Shouts and Whoops of Indians, and the Screams and Groans of some butchered Family" could be heard in the wilderness, and perhaps some poor woman was being raped—"suffering [an] involuntary prostitution to savage Lust; and perhaps debauched and murdered by the same Hand." Against such brutalities, God demanded war, calling all Virginians "to repel Force with Force," giving "them Blood to drink in their Turn, who have drunk ours." In the face of such a war, the most wicked sin was the scandal of an unbloodied sword.[9]

In calling on Virginians to take up the challenge, Davies stirred up colonial rivalry, noting that "the little colony of Massachusetts-Bay has raised no less than 7000 men" even though many of Virginia's fifty-three counties were larger than all of the Bay Colony. Here, Davies threatened Virginians with the Curse of Meroz—"Shall this Curse fall upon Virginia? No, fly from it by venturing your Lives for your Country: for this Curse is far more terrible than any thing that can befall you in the Field of Battle." This is a curse from God, after all, calling upon soldiers to embrace military combat "as the Work of the Lord."[10]

Many agreed with Davies that both Jeremiah's curse and the Curse of Meroz were warnings against sheer cowardice, though, in the case of Meroz, that identification was not explicit in the text. But if Deborah was silent on the motivations of Meroz, colonial preachers were ready to compensate with their own explanations, motivated by the military needs of the eighteenth century. Perhaps the inhabitants of Meroz were principled noncombatants—pacifists, equivalent to colonial-era Quakers, for instance. This was a sensitive issue, particularly in the middle colonies, and preachers enlisted the support of the Song of Deborah in staging a full assault on Christian pacifism.

A prime instance is Samuel Finley's sermon *The Curse of Meroz; or, The Danger of Neutrality, in the Cause of God, and our Country*, preached October 2, 1757, and later published in Philadelphia with a preface by the revivalist preacher Gilbert Tennent. Finley was a noted Presbyterian and a future president of the College of New Jersey, where he succeeded Samuel Davies. Against pacifists who contended that a "God of Love" would never support a violent opposition to evil, Finley asserted that God's love is "tempered with Justice," and justice sometimes requires war. Like the inhabitants of Meroz, the sin of such pacifists was a sin of "omission"—of failing to do what God required. They refused to fight when their country and liberty were threatened, and God cursed them for this failure. And even though they had sinned by failing to defend God's country rather than by directly attacking it, God considered them "as his Foes." In the universal war between good and evil, there was no neutral position. They who did not stand for God were against God, regardless of their qualms of conscience. Finley speculated that the inhabitants of Meroz, like the pacifists of his day, "were Conscience-bound against Fighting" and considered themselves "more peaceable than their Neighbors" because they "would have no cruel Hand in shedding Blood." But regardless of their arguments for peaceful purity, these tender-hearted pacifists of Meroz were cursed for "their criminal Neglect." They had failed to defend their God and had left their fellow subjects "in the Lurch" at a time of dire need. The real tragedy was that these pacifists professed a "Love to Peace," because their efforts toward peace only led to conflict. These inhabitants of Meroz failed to realize that "Love and Mercy are false, when partial," and self-defense in a justified war fulfilled the law of love rather than violating it.[11]

In Finley's view, these biblical challenges to pacifism were critical for Pennsylvania, a colony that had been wracked by attacks from Native Americans in the backcountry regions, partially because the Quaker-dominated colonial assembly had refused to support an adequate military defense. Much had been done to shore up Pennsylvania's defenses by 1757, thanks largely to non-pacifists such as Benjamin Franklin. Still, Finley called out legislators who had let party politics interfere with colonial security by refusing to support a militia. The Curse of Meroz, Finley argued, was a terrifying text for "those who prefer private, or party Interest...to the public Weal," and "refuse to exert themselves for the Defense of their Country" against "the Enemies of our Religion and Liberty." Those "of the Legislature" who opposed "just and impartial Laws, necessary for our Defense" were like traitors. The colony trusted them for its defense, but they betrayed that trust. These legislators, "by an effeminate Delicacy," violated the commands of both Deborah and Jeremiah. That is, they "act the Coward, and keep back their Swords from Blood."[12]

Although many sermons focused on these curses, the ultimate hero of the Song of Deborah was its most violent combatant: Jael. In Judges 4, Jael, a tent-dwelling woman, killed Sisera, the mighty captain of Jabin's army. Sisera, on the run after Barak's army, aided by the Lord, had defeated Sisera's forces, was looking for a place to hide. Sisera came to Jael, expecting a friendly reception, and he received one—or so it seemed. Jael took Sisera in, gave him milk to drink and hid him in the tent. But while Sisera slept Jael approached him quietly, took a hammer in hand and drove a tent peg through his head, pinning his temple to the ground. Then Jael went to Barak and brought him to see Sisera's body. The Song of Deborah from Judges 5 included a slightly different description of Jael's violent conquest in which Jael drove a nail through Sisera's temple while he was standing, making her even more courageous (Judges 5:24–27). To honor these heroic efforts, Deborah praised Jael as a victor for the Lord, concluding with the hope that all God's enemies would encounter humiliating defeats like that of Sisera.

Jael's gender was an important aspect of the story. Preaching in Philadelphia in 1756, Presbyterian revivalist Gilbert Tennent called Jael's killing of Sisera a "famous Instance of Female Fortitude." Tennent, who in 1740 had ignited revival controversy with his famous sermon *The Danger of an Unconverted Ministry*, warned here against the danger of an unconverted and cowardly military. From Tennent's pulpit, the story of Jael served as a rebuke of cowardice in any form. Though Jael was a woman, Tennent proclaimed that her "martial Bravery exalted Jael above her Sex." Her courageous homicide of Sisera earned her great renown and exalted her well above the spineless men of Meroz, who, in contrast to Jael, backed away from divinely ordained violence and dishonored themselves and disgraced their gender. Such cowards forfeited "the Character of Men," and were "weaker than Women" in general and much weaker than courageous heroines such as Jael and Deborah.[13]

Colonial preachers usually attributed the surprising "female fortitude" of Deborah and Jael more to the miraculous power of God than to the women themselves. In his sermon to New Yorkers in 1759, Presbyterian minister Ebenezer Prime asserted that Deborah's victory was a classic instance in which God empowered the weak to defeat the mighty. In the heat of battle God chose to reverse the usual power dynamics. Although, as the Apostle Paul noted, the man was the head of the woman, in this case God "put the Head upon the Woman's shoulders." Deborah was courageous—even more so than general Barak, who would not go into battle without her. And it was Jael, rather than Barak, who was able to kill Sisera. But the most important facet of Jael's act was its humiliating, grotesquely violent nature, which demonstrated what would befall all of God's enemies.[14]

The story of Jael was critical in part because it strengthened the text's emphasis on God's agency in victory. How else could a woman overpower a military captain? asked colonial ministers, unable to transcend their patriarchal assumptions about male power and female weakness. Still, Jael's story also supported the even more important lesson for preachers: victory came only to those who risked themselves for it and depended on God. So this story of courageous risk was, in Ebenezer Prime's view, strikingly similar to "our Exercises in the present day." The message was "that when a General and his Forces" can be "well assured of the divine Presence," then "they may take Courage, and ought to improve every advantageous Opportunity against the Enemy, with Vigor and Resolution."[15]

Such violent texts were shocking but, in wartime, necessary, preachers believed. Soldiers needed to be inspired, not only to sacrifice their lives, but also to kill.[16] Wartime killing needed biblical motivation, and preachers needed the curses of Deborah and Jeremiah and stories like Jael's slaying of Sisera. But this kind of violent preaching was delicate business, and preachers were well aware of their complicated position as spiritual guardians who preached violence in war. In a sermon published in both London and Boston in 1756, George Whitefield acknowledged the potential awkwardness of a godly minister calling for bloody warfare. "Far be it from me, who profess myself a Disciple and Minister of the Prince of Peace, to sound a Trumpet for War," Whitefield stated. But of course he followed with the inevitable qualification: "But when the Trumpet is already sounded by a perfidious Enemy, and our King, our Country, our civil and religious Liberties are all…at Stake," then only two options remain: either pursue warfare or "justly incur that Curse" uttered by "an inspired Deborah." As a revival preacher like Whitefield knew well, there was often a vast difference between pious conversation and holy action. Such was the case in times of godly warfare: "the greatest Talkers are not always the greatest Doers." The best test of character was the violent trial of battle, a fight in which the brave were victorious and the cowardly were damned. To support his case for the seriousness of the curse, Whitefield asserted that Britain faced diabolical threats at "the hands of savage Indians, instigated thereto by more than savage Popish priests." As Whitefield graphically described, even though Rome was already "glutted" with the blood of

Protestants, "popish Priests [had] only grown more voracious, and (like so many hungry and ravenous Wolves, pursuing the harmless and innocent Flocks of Sheep) with double Eagerness will pursue after, seize upon, and devour their wish'd-for Protestant Prey."[17]

Soldiers should kill, therefore, because their cause was not only just, but sacred—God approved the war, and commanded true Christians to fight it. Preachers constantly felt the need to maintain the delicate balance between divine and human effort on the battlefield. It was this balance, preachers insisted, that was the key to the victory of Deborah and Barak.[18] As Samuel Finley preached from the Song of Deborah in 1757, success in war required "Helping the Lord" by "the vigorous use of all proper Means," including the weapons of war. Of course, success in battle ultimately depended on God, but God worked through military might.

In this way, military warfare was like spiritual warfare. In both, God worked through human effort and the proper means. As Finley asserted, "if Christians would obtain Grace, they must seek it earnestly, in the Use of all appointed Means," including Bible reading and prayer. Clearly, therefore, "they who expect divine knowledge without studying the Scriptures; the Holy Spirit, without Prayer; saving blessings, without attending on gospel ordinances; or *Deliverance from temporal enemies, without Fighting against them*, discover their deep Ignorance of Scripture, of Reason, and the Whole scheme of the divine government."[19] This message, heard by Finley's Pennsylvania congregation in 1757, was virtually the same as that heard in Ebenezer Prime's Presbyterian church two years later. Above all, Prime asserted, the message of "that eminent Prophetess" Deborah was that dangerous times required spiritual "Repentance, Reformation and Prayer" but also "carnal Weapons."[20]

In pre-Revolutionary America, ministers mined the Song of Deborah— and, to a lesser extent, the famous curse of Jeremiah—to make three related points. First, they wanted to show how clearly Deborah's story defied the natural tendency of soldiers to resist dying, and especially killing, in war. War itself, even the violence of war, was spiritually redemptive if pursued with divine authority and direction. Second, the story of Deborah proved to them that victory depended on both providential guidance and military weapons, neither of which could be neglected without sacrificing the chance for victory. Third, and most important, both Deborah and Jeremiah were prophets of courage in battle. No victory could be won without sacrifice, and patriotic zeal in battle was as essential as spiritual zeal in salvation.

Prophetic Violence in Revolutionary America

When the Revolution began and the tyrannical enemy shifted from France to England, the threat of biblical curses assumed a different character. To be sure, preachers reaffirmed some familiar themes. They still asserted that spirituality reinforced patriotism and made soldiers better fighters. They still preached the need for heartfelt piety and virtuous republicanism in all Christians and in all good patriots. What changed, however, was at least as significant. In the Revolution, the curses of Deborah and Jeremiah became even more important because the obstacles to war became even more difficult to surmount. That is, patriotic ministers still had to overcome soldiers' natural aversion to dying and killing in battle, and they still had to contend with a minority of colonists who were principled pacifists. Now, however, these threats to the war effort had a new, powerful accomplice: loyalism. A divinely inspired war required a godly wrath that would trample all those who opposed the cause, either through willful opposition or through mere neglect. It is not surprising, therefore, that army chaplains such as the Baptist Hezekiah Smith proclaimed Jeremiah's curse against any who refused to bloody their swords.[21]

Revolutionary-era preachers noted the uncanny similarity between their predicament and that of Deborah, Barak, and Jael. We find a typical case in Samuel West, a pastor at Dartmouth. In his view, the Song of Deborah was a revolutionary ballad against tyranny. In good revolutionary form, West's sermon before the Massachusetts Bay House of Representatives on May 29, 1776, identified Deborah's situation as "a case similar to ours" because "the Israelites were struggling to deliver themselves from the tyranny of Jabin the king of Canaan." Jabin's contemporary equivalent was, of course, the British Empire of George III. In West's sermon, the British were "merciless tyrants," even barbarians. Though the British claimed to be Christians, West cited them for "barbarity" that exceeded that of "Turks and Mahometan infidels." The British would even "be abhor'd and detested by the savages of the wilderness." They were scandalous to all humanity: "Tyrannical monsters" who raged against "the sacred cause of liberty." To refuse to fight this tyrannical power was to reject both a civic responsibility and a sacred duty.[22]

Cowardice was a spiritual problem, a sign that one lacked "faith in God," though this spiritual malady had political repercussions. Citing the curses from Deborah and Jeremiah, West proclaimed that patriots should "defend our lives, and fortunes, even to the shedding the last drop of blood." This patriotic sacrifice was not only noble, it was required—a divine demand. "To be careless and remiss, or to neglect the cause of our country," West warned, would "expose us not only to the resentments of our fellow creatures, but to the displeasure of God Almighty." Those who refused God's patriotic command were "base wretches" to whom "we may apply with the utmost propriety" Jeremiah's warning: "Cursed be he that doeth the work of the Lord deceitfully, and cursed be he, that keepeth back his sword from blood." Given such dire warnings from God's prophets, West proclaimed that "to save our country from the hands of oppressors" was "a duty so sacred, that it cannot justly be dispensed with for the sake of our secular concerns: Doubtless for this reason God has been pleased, to manifest his anger against those who have refused to assist their country against its cruel oppressors."[23]

The sin of Meroz was even more serious, West argued, because it worked against God's providential plan for America's future. "I have abundant reason to conclude," West preached, "that the great sovereign of the universe, has planted a vine in this American wilderness, which he has caused to take deep root, and it has filled the land, and that he will never suffer it to be plucked up, or destroyed." Specifically, West believed that America would "be the asylum of liberty and true religion" in the world. West called on the Curse of Meroz against any who would refuse to fight for God's American cause.[24]

But who, exactly, were the revolutionary equivalents of the citizens of Meroz? Many patriots harbored suspicions that these foes lurked among them—not only as active and visible loyalists, but also as covert operators who deftly subverted the revolutionary cause. The title of Salem pastor Nathaniel Whitaker's sermon is a perfect example: *An Antidote Against Toryism. Or the Curse of Meroz*. Whitaker dedicated this sermon to George Washington because he wanted to encourage in others the heroism that Washington exemplified. More importantly, Whitaker's dedication was a direct response to Washington issuing his own "curse of Meroz."

On November 30, 1776, British admiral Lord Richard Howe issued a proclamation in which he vowed to protect Americans who came over to the British side of the conflict. Much to Washington's dismay, some Americans did abandon the Revolution, including the famous patriot Joseph Galloway, a former member of the Continental Congress. Washington countered with his own statement. The situation was urgent, Washington implied, for Howe's proclamation had made it "necessary to distinguish between the friends of America and those of Great-Britain."

The way to do that, Washington believed, was to command an outward show of allegiance to the Revolution. All citizens of all states had to stand up for the cause, or show themselves to be opponents of American liberty.[25]

Washington hoped that his proclamation would inspire patriotism. His words certainly inspired Nathaniel Whitaker, an ardent patriot and revivalist, a devotee of both Washington and George Whitefield. Whitaker praised Washington's proclamation and then expanded upon it, rendering it persuasive as only a sermon could. Whitaker hoped his sermon would be particularly useful to the American troops under Washington's command. "Should all your Soldiers be inspired with the sentiments of love and benevolence here recommended," Whitaker preached to Washington, "they, like their General would be Heroes indeed." Whitaker hoped to inspire Washington's troops to be warriors of "serene bravery" who could "wing their way through legions of opposing Tyrants, to victory and triumph, to glory and renown." And yet this heroic character was on the wane because of the influence of the inhabitants of Meroz—those who refused to battle tyranny.[26]

As a remedy for this aversion to war, Whitaker proclaimed the Song of Deborah in strong revolutionary fashion. His first doctrinal point was that "the cause of Liberty is the cause of God and truth." It followed that God was pleased when patriots joined forces to defend liberty and that he condemned any who refused to fight against tyranny. Opponents of the Revolution were God's opponents. Like West, Whitaker proclaimed that "our struggle with Great-Britain is very similar to that of Israel with Jabin." But Whitaker made the parallels more explicit. In fact, Whitaker found revolutionary parallels in nearly every character and event in the narrative of Deborah, Barak, and Jael. He saw George III perfectly reflected in the tyrannical Jabin, who "robbed" the Israelites "of their rights, and held them in slavery twenty years." Jabin was no more than "a cruel tyrant" who "provoked God." In retribution, God commanded Israel "to wage war on the tyrant," by assembling troops from their "various States to join them in the glorious conflict."[27]

How could a group of diverse "states" unite around a common cause? When it came to drumming up patriotic loyalty, division was as dangerous as outright disloyalty. But here again, the Song of Deborah fit revolutionary needs perfectly because it included an evaluation of Israel's tribes, judging them according to their patriotic loyalty. Had they heeded Deborah's call to war or not? That was the central question. Unity was critical.

Whitaker was not alone in drawing this theme from the Song of Deborah. In November, 1775, Congregationalist Robert Ross of Stratfield, Connecticut, used the Song of Deborah (verses 15–16) as the main text in a sermon devoted, as his title detailed, to *The Union of the Colonies... And the Sad Consequences of Divisions.* Preaching here on Deborah's praise for the tribes who joined the war and her condemnation of the negligent ones, Ross proclaimed "the righteousness of the United States," and "the great importance of maintaining" the unity of the states, along with "the bad consequences of breaking it by divisions among ourselves."

As Ross and other patriots knew, Britain had focused its forces on New England, believing that most of the opposition was there. If New England could be subdued, thought British officers, then the states in other regions would collapse. But the United States had proven the British wrong. Despite "all the artifices and industry of the enemy," and despite "a few male-contents scattered" among the states, the Continental Congress had brought the nation together and authorized the Continental Army. But the struggle was not over. The states must remain united, Ross asserted, for unity under God's authority would bring a victory similar to Deborah's. As Ross proclaimed, "the history of mankind does not afford any instance, wherein any kingdom or empire could keep such distant provinces, inhabited by such vast numbers of men of spirit in slavery, unless they divide among themselves. Divisions tend to reduce and enslave us, but let us remain united and firm; this will procure deliverance and freedom, through the blessing of heaven." If any state dared to break this "solemn" confederation of states, it would provoke "the vengeance" of the other states, "not to mention the curse of God."[28]

The Song of Deborah spoke directly to two of the most critical issues of the war: the need for unity among the states, and the need to recruit troops for the Continental Army. In 1777, the year of Whitaker's sermon, General Washington and the Continental Congress struggled to get states to commit the needed number of troops for the war. Could Barak and Deborah have made a similar effort? Probably so, Whitaker surmised. After all, no one knew all the details about the mysterious Meroz. It was conceivable that Meroz was a "State in Israel" that had the duty to supply troops and funding to support the war effort but had failed to do so.[29]

Whitaker went on to speculate that the state of Meroz lagged in supporting the war out of fear. The citizens of Meroz worried that Israel would lose the battle. Such a loss would surely bring fierce retribution from the tyrannical Jabin. Perhaps, then, the state of Meroz was hedging its bets,

hoping to stay out of the conflict so as to curry favor from the tyrannical government that would surely win in the end. No parallel could be
clearer than that between the state of Meroz and the unpatriotic segments
in the new American nation, Whitaker believed. Or perhaps more was
at play. It could be that the state of Meroz was secretly allied with Jabin.
Perhaps the citizens of Meroz were currying favor with the tyrant, or perhaps some other "sinister motive" was at work. This was an unpatriotic
state, populated by an unfaithful people. Whitaker devoted the balance of
his sermon to identifying the heresy of Meroz in the revolutionary period,
giving specific cues to aid patriots in reviving their courage and filtering
out nonpatriotic elements. Like Washington's proclamation, this sermon
aimed to expose the wartime negligence of the people. Like Washington,
Whitaker wanted to make it abundantly clear that all Americans had to
choose—they would either join the Revolution or join the British. There
was no neutral ground.[30]

Patriots feared inactivity as much as disloyalty—in part because inactivity sapped the needed support and zeal from the cause but also because
inactivity could be a cloak for covert loyalists. Many who opposed the
Revolution pretended to be its friends. They were not openly critical of the
Revolution, nor were they overt defenders of Britain. Instead, they were
like tares hidden among the wheat. Be on the lookout, Whitaker advised,
for any who either do not go to war themselves or do not encourage others
to go. Be aware also of those who preach fear rather than courage, warning
of Jabin's "nine hundred chariots of iron," or, in its modern parallel, "the
dreadful train of artillery, and the good discipline of the British troops."
One's guard should also be up, Whitaker warned, against any who "talk
much for liberty" but are "never zealous to execute any" effort to support
the war. The point was that in military warfare, as in spiritual warfare, talk
proved nothing. The Curse of Meroz, therefore, condemned both spiritual
and military sinners. Those guilty of the "crime of Meroz," those who "did
not join in the glorious cause," were doubly condemned. "Not only" would
they suffer "eternal wrath in the world to come," but they would also suffer
God's "vengeance on them in this world."[31]

Whitaker's *Antidote Against Toryism* was, therefore, not only an antidote against conniving and aggressive loyalists; it was also an antidote
against passive opponents of patriotism—Americans who wanted to
stay out of the conflict. And here the major opponent was fear: the idea
of a band of colonists taking on the mighty British Empire struck terror in the hearts of a number of Americans. If fear was the disease that

sapped patriotism's strength, then Whitaker found the remedy in the Bible, and especially in the Song of Deborah. Whitaker preached that the American troops were just like the ragtag army of Israelites. Just as the mighty British scoffed at the paltry American militias and the struggling Continental Army, surely "both Jabin and Sisera despised this small body of undisciplined, unarmed troops; and were confident" that they could "quickly reduce those rebels," defeat them soundly, and put them back under submission. But Jabin and Sisera had not counted on God taking the lead in the war, allowing the lowly band of Israelites to defeat the mighty warriors of Jabin. To be sure, God "not only gave the victory to Israel, but utterly destroyed the whole host of Jabin"—except for Sisera, "the Captain General." But even Sisera's escape was part of God's plan, and he was "slain by the hand of a woman." Like other ministers in other wars before him, Whitaker seized upon the gender of the victors in this text. Jael was an unlikely victor, to be sure, but she was able to execute the mighty Sisera because she had one major asset: God-inspired courage. Jael proved to American patriots that God could use "the weakest instruments" to "conquer the most powerful enemies."[32]

Even if American patriots *could* conquer the mighty British Empire, *should* they do it? In short, was the Revolution against Britain a just war? After all, just wars were necessary defensive wars. Did the infamous British policies, harsh as they were, justify violent opposition? Here again the Song of Deborah seemed to fit the cause perfectly. Technically, the war of Barak and Deborah against Jabin was not a defensive war. Jabin's army did not attack Israel—Israel's army, at God's command, attacked first. So the story of Deborah was attractive to the revolutionaries precisely because it seemed to endorse aggressive war and preemptive strikes against a tyrannical king. "God commanded Israel to make war," and pronounced a divine curse on any who abandoned God's call to arms. So any loyalist who wished to dispute the righteousness of the Revolution had to face the biblical narrative of Deborah. God "did not require Israel to wait till Jabin had invaded their country and struck the first blow." Instead, "while all was peace in his kingdom," God still commanded "Israel to raise an army, and invade the tyrant's dominions." Whitaker justified this preemptive strike by appealing to divine right to resist oppressive tyranny. In fact, Jabin and George III did engage in offensive war through the "wanton use of their power" in oppressing the people.[33]

Another issue was the spirit of the war itself. Standard protocol declared that just wars be fought to restore order, to repair a breach of injustice. What Whitaker found in Deborah's war was something more: a just war, to be sure, but also a war of vengeance—principled vengeance, commanded by God. Throughout its narrative, the story of Deborah and Barak taught patriots that God commanded them to exercise divine vengeance on British troops.

But how could Christians be tools of vengeance? Did this not contradict the teachings of Christ, the "prince of peace"? These were thorny questions, and Whitaker responded by defending the right—even the responsibility—of Christians to hate wickedness and reap vengeance on evildoers. Even God hates, Whitaker asserted, because it was in God's nature to hate evil. After all, love itself, the chief divine virtue, "implies hatred to malevolence." Anyone who did not hate evil must be an enemy of both God and humanity. Just as "God himself hates sin with a perfect hatred," so Christians may measure their closeness to God by the degree of their hatred of evil. These were common ideas in eighteenth-century moral theology. In applying them to the Revolution, however, Whitaker moved these concepts from moral theory to wartime reality. His reading of the violent Song of Deborah, combined with his need to fire patriotic zeal against the British, inspired Whitaker to focus these ideas in an argument for vengeance on the battlefield.[34]

Such vengeance was spiritual vengeance—biblically defensible, responsible, and virtuous. Revolutionary soldiers were in the best position to exercise this virtuous vengeance. In defending Washington and his troops, Whitaker lauded the ideal Christian soldier, the patriotic saint. Far from fighting out of hatred, the Christian patriot took the battlefield armed with Christ's compassion and benevolence. "True benevolence," Whitaker preached, required hatred of British tyranny. Accordingly, no one—especially not patriotic soldiers—could be accused of violating "the law of love" just "because they hate and oppose such as are injurious to happiness." In their characters, soldiers should be similar to "a minister of the Gospel of peace"—not immoral but virtuous, not cruel but compassionate, not revengeful but merciful. Even in the heat of "the fiercest battle," Christian soldiers should pray for the enemies they strove to kill. In effect, just as the Curse of Meroz condemned those who refuse to help "the Lord against the mighty," so did God's praise fall on those who took up arms against evil. Here, then, the victor in military war, like the crusader in spiritual war, delivered the oppressed, restored "peace and happiness" to the "miserable," and sought "glory and honor" only in the self-sacrificial battle against evil.[35]

In effect, Whitaker argued that exercising divine vengeance, even on the battlefield, was not the same as exercising human revenge. After all, the Curse of Meroz was not really Deborah's curse; it was the curse of God. The distinction was significant. This call for vengeance was a prophetic call, directly from God, and even "by the command of Jesus Christ, the meek and compassionate Savior." The Curse of Meroz was also a curse of the people. In cursing the "selfishness and indifference" of "the people of Meroz," God "not only cursed them himself, but commands all the people to curse them, and inflict his wrath on them in this world." This, then, was both a divine curse and a curse of the people. It was a republican curse.[36]

A republican curse had to be owned by a people who rightly hesitated to curse anyone. Certainly, vengeance was always God's prerogative. But here God had demanded the people execute his vengeance. So Barak, Deborah, and Jael carried out this grim duty, and even celebrated its violent successes. In the same way, even pious, just warriors of the Revolution needed to be "God's ministers, to execute his wrath" upon those who neglected or opposed the revolutionary cause. It was the responsibility of God's revolutionary soldiers "not to deal gingerly with them, nor palliate their offence." As in the case of those under the Curse of Meroz in Deborah's time, the Israelites were "to make no excuses for them, nor to plead 'that they were of a different opinion, that they thought it their duty not to take up arms against their king that ruled over them, but to submit to the higher powers.'" Nor were revolutionary patriots to make excuses for loyalists by claiming "that liberty of conscience ought to be allowed to every one, and that it would be hard to punish them for acting their own judgments." "No such pleas might be made for them," Whitaker warned, "nor one word spoken in their favor." Instead, all God's patriotic people "were to curse those cowardly, selfish cringing, lukewarm, half-way, two-faced people, and to treat them as out-casts, and unworthy the common protection or society of others."[37]

The language of cursing and vengeance clearly moved revolutionary rhetoric in the direction of holy war. As Whitaker preached, God never commands "his subjects to execute his curses on their fellow subjects" except "where the crime is highly aggravated," and "much less does he allow them to curse them bitterly, unless their guilt is exceeding great." Since God commanded the people to curse Meroz, their offense must have been a heinous sin "of a crimson dye, and most provoking to him and his people." Accordingly, the same devastation curse awaits those who are "guilty of the like conduct in our contest with Great Britain."[38]

As important as biblical curses were to the Revolution, the end of the war was not the end of Meroz in America. In May 1783, one month after the Revolution ended, Nathaniel Whitaker celebrated by preaching yet another sermon on the Curse of Meroz. This sermon, a sequel to his 1777 *Antidote Against Toryism*, was appropriately titled *The Reward of Toryism*. Times were good, Whitaker admitted. The mighty British had fallen. Freedom had defeated tyranny because patriotic courage had triumphed over cowardice. "Sisera is conquered: Jabin is reduced to reason: the oppressor is confounded: the haughty are humbled" and "America is Free!!" Whitaker even counted himself among the patriots who had won the victory. As he recalled, his sermon against Meroz in 1777 was a radical statement that "would doubtless have cost me my head" if England had won the war.[39]

Even so, the crisis had not passed. Toryism still threatened America. And, again, religion contributed to the threat, as preachers throughout the United States called for Americans to forgive the loyalists and allow them to rejoin the states. Here, Whitaker took a hard stand on a critical issue. How to treat loyalists was one of the most urgent questions after the war, and was it was one of the most difficult points of negotiation in the Treaty of Paris, negotiated by Benjamin Franklin, John Jay, and John Adams and signed on September 3, 1783.

The Treaty came down on the side of leniency for the loyalists. Congress promised to "earnestly recommend" that "the legislatures of the respective states" restore "all estates, rights, and properties which have been confiscated" from loyalists "who have not borne Arms against the said United States."[40] Also, Congress declared, "there shall be no future Confiscations made nor any Prosecutions commenced against" loyalists. Congress could not enforce these declarations, however, and many patriots opposed leniency for loyalists both before and after the treaty was signed. Such founders as George Washington, Alexander Hamilton, and Patrick Henry lobbied for leniency in the treatment of loyalists. Henry fought a losing battle as the Virginia legislature denied the loyalists' rights. He had made a strong case for allowing loyalists to return to Virginia unhindered. "I feel no objection to the return of those deluded people," Henry said. "Their king hath acknowledged our independence. The quarrel is over." Henry argued that the return of the loyalists could stimulate Virginia's economy. "Those are an enterprising, moneyed people," he said. Moreover, he had "no fear of any mischief that they can do us. Afraid of them? . . . shall we, who have laid the proud British lion at our feet, now be afraid of his whelps?"[41]

Whitaker could not have disagreed more. What was needed, he preached, was not forgiveness of former loyalists, but a renewed commitment to cursing Tory influence. Such harsh words, Whitaker knew, would draw condemnation. Many would call him "sanguine, cruel, revengeful, and the like," and he would face abuse for his uncharitable attitude. But it was worth the cost, Whitaker believed, if he could again awaken Americans to the internal threats from those who secretly conspired to support British schemes. America "cannot be safe while the Tories remain among us," Whitaker proclaimed. "They, like Judas, wish to return among us, and like him they will sell us for thirty pieces of silver." So "if we do not curse them, we shall curse the public," and America will fall victim to nefarious traitors. He reminded those who responded that he was being cruel and malicious of the seriousness of the biblical curses God inflicted. "The curse required is a serious, deliberate, religious act of justice, which God requires of us." Tories were no more than treasonous murderers, and to forgive them was "to be an abettor of their crimes, and partaker in their sins."[42]

Even though the shooting had stopped, the fight to secure a free and independent nation was far from over. Britain was still more enemy than ally, Whitaker believed. Besides the ongoing threats that Tories could pose to the new nation, Americans must also consider how the return of Tories to the states would divide the nation from within. How galling it would be for true patriots to have to live side by side with traitors. Should Tories, who had opposed liberty in 1776, enjoy the fruits of liberty in 1783? As for the plan to restore confiscated property, Whitaker attacked it as traitorous and disastrous. Why not just steal the private property of all Americans and hand it over "to the British soldiers who ravaged our country"? "We may as well hope for Satan's cordial friendship to mankind, as for that of the Tories to these states." Permitting the Tories to return, Whitaker preached, would be like inviting a Trojan horse into America. Once inside, Tories would "lay our country in ruins" and "reduce us to slavery."[43]

The question ultimately came down to the righteousness of the Revolution. If the Revolution was not a righteous cause, then the blood shed was on the hands of the patriots. If that was so, then "we ought to atone for it by the sacrifice of an Hancock, an Adams, a Washington, and other leaders in the horrid rebellion and bloody massacre." But if the Revolution had been a righteous cause, then the blood was on the hands of the Tories, and they should "atone for it, as being the chief authors, by a sacrifice of, at least, their property now among us, and an everlasting banishment from us." The Bible was clear, Whitaker preached, "the guilt of blood is not easily purged away." The great sacrifice of blood spilled in the Revolution needed to be honored. And honoring patriotic sacrifice required Americans to heed biblical curses against all enemies of freedom. The curses of Deborah and Jeremiah were politically significant, but not only politically expedient. They were biblical curses, and, as such, were liberating, spiritual, and eternal. The United States could not claim its full glory, even in victory, if true patriots neglected to stamp out enemies in their midst.[44]

These concerns show how American victory in the Revolution, glorious as it was, led to postwar anxieties. Postwar sermons often mixed jubilation with lamentation, and both sentiments drew comparisons between the American military victory and Deborah's victory song. If Whitaker assumed a cautious tone, and warned that the loyalist citizens of Meroz posed a real threat to the new nation, Thomas Brockway of Lebanon, Connecticut, looked past warnings of Meroz to embrace the victorious jubilation of Deborah and Barak. In his sermon from 1784, *America Saved, or Divine Glory Displayed, in the Late War with Great Britain,* Brockway preached that the song of "Deborah and Barak" was a "divine song" of victory, so similar to the American victory over the British that "where is the Christian? Or where is the friend to his country, who can this day refrain from joining the chorus" of Deborah and Barak in singing "O my soul thou hast trodden down strength"? (Judges 5:21).

And yet, though God had sided with the Americans in the war, Brockway flatly stated that the new nation was not a new Israel. America, unlike the Jews of the Old Testament, did not have a "national covenant" with God. In fact, England had just as much a right to the title of God's people as America, for the British "worship this same God and Savior, and like us, what of them profess, profess the same gospel covenant." Why, then, did God side with Americans in their Revolutionary War? Brockway's response was that Britain did not simply oppress Americans; they attacked "the natural rights of mankind," and this attack set God against them. God sided with Americans because "liberty is the birthright of human life, chartered by heaven to every rational creature," and "no one has a right to take it from another." To celebrate victory in the war was to celebrate God and freedom. This was the reason "Deborah and Barak, so melodiously sung"—"freedom and liberty to Israel was their theme, and Jehovah was the object of their praise." The American Revolution was, primarily, a victory for humanity on behalf of liberty, but the chief end of the victory was to glorify God. The war was one of those cases in which

God intervened in a most dramatic way to break "the chain of Deistical reasoning" and to confound "the bold Atheist," to show forth his mighty presence and his power to intervene in the world. This day was a day of American victory, therefore, "the day we have often anticipated with peculiar delight, while struggling with the pains of an eight years bloody war." This is a day that future Americans call "sacred," the beginning of "the long wished for period of American peace." Brockway could hardly withhold his excitement: "It is not imaginary—it is reality!—America is free!" But freedom was not granted for America's sake. "It was not for thy sake O America, that God has wrought these wonders: but it was to humble the pride of Britain" and to "defend the cause of justice and liberty" in God's providential design.[45]

Amid their celebrations, Brockway cautioned Americans to understand the true nature of their victory. It was a gracious victory, achieved by God's hand. But it would be lost if Americans neglected to remember the sacrifices of the "martyrs to liberty" who, like Deborah and Barak, obeyed God's call to war. The message of Deborah's song was, in part, a celebration of sacrifice, and a warning to any who failed to honor wartime sacrifices. In essence, Deborah and Barak were patriots, and their story warned against those who forgot the integrity of patriotism and neglected its gracious roots.[46]

In Revolutionary America, then, no texts were more versatile or more violent than the curses of Jeremiah and Meroz and the narrative of Deborah and Jael. Such violent texts pushed the limits of just war theory and gave patriots biblical license to endorse the atrocities of war. This was a valuable and yet mostly unrecognized function of scripture in general and of the prophets and judges in particular during the Revolution. When historians have discussed the prophets and judges at all, they have cited the Curse of Meroz as a warning against opposing the patriotic cause.[47] But his famous curse, as we have seen, was much more than a proof text against loyalism. It was part of a larger biblical narrative that had various wartime functions. Behind the Curse of Meroz were the incomparable Deborah and Jael, whose courage patriotic ministers celebrated in graphic detail, and Jeremiah's famous warning against any coward who dared to withdraw the sword in a righteous war. Deborah, Jael, and Jeremiah were not known only for their curses; they were known for their heroic lives. As William Tennent of Charleston, South Carolina, asserted, Jeremiah had a "patriotic Soul" and a "holy Patriot's Heart" that "glowed with an enthusiastic Love for his Country."[48]

This is yet another instance of how historians have overlooked the bloody details of biblical violence and how ministers used them in wartime. More attention needs to be paid to the judges and prophets, therefore, for their service on battlefields to overcome soldiers' natural fear of combat. This attention is needed because, as patriotic ministers like Zabdiel Adams recognized, the Revolution made it "necessary for the *humble* and *quiet*, the *meek* and *inoffensive* to turn their attention to the art of war; and while they breathe the pacific spirit of the gospel, to furnish themselves with the instruments of slaughter." Such was the case in the Revolution, when God commanded his people to fight, and, in the words of Jeremiah, God levied "a most tremendous *curse...against such as do this work of the Lord deceitfully, and keep back their swords from blood.*"[49]

4

"Teacheth My Hands to War, and My Fingers to Fight"

DAVID'S REVOLUTIONARY HEROISM

David was a Man after God's Heart; yet he was a Man of War, skill'd in the bloody Art, and furnished above the common Standard, with the Qualifications of War: in this Art, terrible as it is, he informs us that he was taught of God.

SILVANUS CONANT, April, 1759[1]

Let us, in every enterprize, look to him who teacheth the hands to war, and the fingers to fight.

TIMOTHY DWIGHT, December, 1777[2]

MINISTERS IN REVOLUTIONARY America believed that all wars created heroes, but wars fought for God also created saints—warriors who could meet the martial and spiritual standards of scripture. In many colonial American war sermons, King David was the epitome of this ideal: prophet, king, soldier, and most importantly "the man after God's own heart."[3] Ministers admired David as a spiritual warrior in a pious conflict against sin and as a military warrior in violent combat against the enemies of God's people. This was a crucial point for patriotic ministers, who struggled to identify the religious value of military service. It was a subject they returned to often because they had a difficult case to make to a skeptical public. Obviously, there were pacifists in their midst, and they needed to be answered by sermons that advocated just warfare. But more often preachers countered resistance from those who agreed, in principle, that wars sometimes needed to be fought, but doubted the justification for particular wars. Many people thought it contradictory to preach the Gospel of Christ while also preaching aggression on the battlefield. In facing these obstacles, patriotic ministers often turned to David. No other biblical hero so perfectly exemplified both spiritual character and military might. At the beginning of the Revolutionary War, Nathan Perkins of Hartford expressed the prevailing sentiment among patriotic ministers: "When David prays...it is not because he was a coward; for he was as distinguished a warrior as eminent [a] saint."[4]

Although historians have rarely noticed it, there is no doubt about David's importance to colonial American war sermons. Of the twenty most popular biblical texts cited in war sermons from the King Philips' War through the Revolutionary era (1675–1800), six refer directly to David. Of these, the most popular can be classified under three headings. First is the image of David the warrior, expressed most popularly in the story of David and Goliath (1 Samuel 17). Second, and closely related, is the image of David the Psalmist. Third, and most controversially in Revolutionary America, was the legacy of David as king.[5]

Warrior: The American David and the British Goliath

Of all the violent scenes in scripture, few rivaled the sheer drama of the showdown between David and Goliath. Although two armies faced off, they were primarily spectators. The real battle was man versus man— actually giant warrior versus boy with a sling. It is no wonder that this story has been perennially popular, and it was certainly popular in colonial America. In the century between King Philip's War and the American Revolution, sermons on war cited the story of David and Goliath more often than any other episode from David's life or even the psalms. We can attribute much of this story's appeal—then and now—to the attractiveness of the underdog hero who triumphed against all odds against a mighty opponent. As told in 1 Samuel 17, the humble shepherd boy David was visiting his older brothers, who were serving in the Israelite army, when he saw the haughty Philistine giant Goliath, who terrorized Israelite soldiers. None of the Israelites dared to accept Goliath's challenge to a one-on-one fight to the death. David, outraged that Goliath had insulted Israel, and by association Israel's God, accepted Goliath's challenge. In dramatic fashion, David killed the heavily armored Goliath with a stone hurled from a sling, and then beheaded Goliath with his own sword.[6]

In pre-revolutionary America, the story of David and Goliath was a tale of both inspiration and warning. It was an inspiring story of unexpected victory—young David vanquishing the mighty giant. It was also a warn-ing that wartime victories are God's alone, bestowed by providence, and are outside the realm of human control. Any soldiers, military officers, or even kings who attempt to wage war without God's blessing risk disaster on the battlefield.

This was the urgent message of many sermons, including an unprinted sermon preached by Jonathan Edwards in the summer of 1755. Edwards preached just as some 3500 English soldiers had joined with about 400 Native Americans to attack the French Fort Saint Frederick at Crown Point, New York, located on Lake Champlain. Edwards, at the time a missionary in the Massachusetts frontier post at Stockbridge, addressed this sermon primarily to a Native American congregation that included some who would fight alongside the English troops. Seeking to prepare these troops for battle, Edwards focused his sermon on David's challenge to Goliath: "Thou comest to me with a sword, and with a spear, and with a shield: but I come unto thee in the name of the Lord of hosts.... This day will the Lord deliver thee into mine hand; and I will smite thee, and take thine head from thee;... for the battle is the Lord's, and he will give you into our hands" (1 Samuel 17:45–46).

Here Edwards described David as a soldier who had the right approach to war: trust in God, not might: "For men to trust in themselves when they go to war is the way for 'em to be overcome by their enemies. [Neither] their strength, courage, [and] wisdom, [nor their] numbers, forts, [and] weapons of war [will be sufficient for their victory]. Such men as trust [in these things] take that upon them which belongs to God. He takes [it] upon him[self] to order all things that belong to the effect and events of war.... Men that trust in themselves make gods of themselves." Edwards concluded that the chief sin to avoid at all costs was pride, the sin of Goliath.[7]

Through sermons like this one, David became the ultimate biblical hero. But the ultimate biblical hero was not the typical war hero. That is, David was courageous, but his courage was not his own but God's. Certainly, David was a skilled warrior, but he was not skilled enough to win battles without God's blessing. As ministers recognized, there was a tension between trusting in God's deliverance and relying on martial prowess. In wartime, ministers struggled to maintain this tension. In their view, soldiers needed to be courageous but not arrogant, trusting in God and not in themselves. Pride spelled almost certain defeat, both spiritually and militarily. Pride led to irreverence and vice, and all preachers knew that vices ran rampant in military ranks. The colonies needed soldiers who would recognize that God's providence, not human effort, ensured victory and defeat. In driving home these points, preachers proclaimed David the ultimate hero, the undaunted warrior who had both military courage and fervent, even poetic piety.[8]

In the American Revolution, the moral of the David and Goliath story shifted.[9] David's adventure with Goliath was still a valuable lesson for individual soldiers, but the story also portrayed military realities, as anyone could see. In contrast to the regular British army, colonial soldiers were not professional military men. They were ordinary citizens, and most of them had very little experience in battle. To make matters worse, they were vastly outnumbered. Given these facts, New Hampshire Congregationalist and army chaplain Samuel McClintock preached that the military comparison between the British and the Americans was "as unequal as that between the stripling David and the giant of Gath; and the improbability of our success as great as that he with a sling and stone should overcome that proud and mighty enemy, clothed with armor from head to foot."[10]

It is no wonder, therefore, that the Continental Congress cited the showdown between David and Goliath to illustrate the revolutionary crisis. In an appeal to all Americans on May 26, 1779, Congress issued a statement declaring that "America, without arms, ammunition, discipline, revenue, government or ally, almost totally stript of commerce, and in the weakness of youth, as it were with a 'staff and a sling' only, dared 'in the name of the Lord of Hosts' to engage a gigantic adversary, prepared at all points, boasting of his strength, and of whom even mighty warriors 'were greatly afraid.'" With these quotations the Continental Congress reinforced three important points—the great odds against the American cause in the face of British strength, the courage that empowered colonial patriots to face off against the powerful British with God as their ally, and the contrast in virtue between this American David and the proud, corrupt British Goliath. Regardless of these long odds, the American David needed to remain supportive of the cause.

Here Congress appealed both for money and patriotism. The British remained evil, Goliath-like in their proud opposition to American freedom even in the face of seemingly miraculous American successes on the battlefield. "Foiled again, and stung with rage, embittered by envy," the British had used nefarious methods against the colonies, including arousing the Indians "to horrid massacres of women and children," and tempting slaves "to the murder of their masters." "Rouse yourselves therefore," the Congress implored, encouraged by the fact that no nation had overcome such disadvantages and yet had been so victorious. Then, in a closing flourish, the Congress encouraged Americans "to repel the incursions of your enemies—place your several quotas in the continental treasury—lend money for public uses...provide effectually for expediting the conveyance of supplies for your armies and fleets...prevent the produce of the country from being monopolized...promote piety, virtue, brotherly love, learning, frugality and moderation—and may you be approved before Almighty God worthy of those blessings we devoutly wish you to enjoy." As this statement revealed, no story better illustrated the overwhelming odds of the American war against Britain than the story of David and Goliath. For the Continental Congress, David's victory over Goliath inspired colonists not to trust in sheer numbers and long odds, but to trust instead the miraculous possibilities of a courageous people united around a righteous cause.[11]

In comparing their situation to David's, the congressmen may have taken a cue from popular sermons of the day. From the beginning of the revolutionary crisis, ministers had turned the Americans' underdog status into a virtue in both republican and spiritual terms. This was reinforced after the battles of Lexington and Concord on April 19, 1775. After the overmatched New England soldiers more than held their own against British regulars, thereby surprising nearly everyone from Boston to London, ministers like Samuel Baldwin of Hanover, Massachusetts, proclaimed the great contrast between the courageous and virtuous Americans and the arrogant British. According to Baldwin, April 19, 1775 was "a day memorable for giving victory to a few hundred Americans, brave and determined, armed and engaged in the best cause...over an army of British troops, who judged themselves invincible, especially by Americans, upon whom they had been taught and accustomed to look down with as much contempt and disdain, as Golia [Goliath] of Gath did upon David the stripling." After all, it was the British, Baldwin asserted, who had epitomized Goliath's arrogance as they "bragged and boasted, that one regiment or two, could at pleasure, march from one end of the Continent to the other, unmolested, spreading havoc and desolation" through America.

Baldwin preached this sermon in December, eight months after the battles of Lexington and Concord. By this time, the David versus Goliath image had been reinforced by the American victory at Ticonderoga, and even more by the Americans' courageous showing in defeat at Bunker Hill. Most importantly, the contrast here was not just that of an underdog's surprising victory over a stronger opponent—it was the victory of good versus evil. The Americans were the advocates of God and freedom, while the British had lost their souls, as evidenced by their despicable conduct. "Our enemies have been inglorious in arms," Baldwin asserted, and everyone had heard of "their violence, blood and murder," while "the brave sons of freedom" from the colonies formed a Continental Army in heroic opposition.[12]

The contrasting of the virtuous American soldiers and dishonorable British marauders continued. Sometimes patriots identified specific British Goliaths. Author, lawyer and military chaplain Hugh Henry Brackenridge saw an uncanny resemblance between the boastful Goliath and the British general John Burgoyne, who suffered a humiliating defeat at Saratoga in October 1777. Reminiscent of Goliath's blasphemous challenge to the Israelites, was a similar challenge from Burgoyne to New England patriots, which Brackenridge satirized as: "O ye saints and rebels of New-England, wherefore are ye come out against me with pitch-forks, and with pruning hooks? Am I a dog that you think to drive me into Lake Champlain, with staves and with broken bayonets? But if so, leave your prayers, and your fastings, and come along, that I may scalp your heads, and tomahawk your carcasses." Burgoyne, like Goliath, was all talk, no courageous action on the battlefield, Brackenridge wrote. "I am of [the] opinion that Goliah, notwithstanding his challenge to the host of Israel, was, as all bullies are, a coward at the bottom." And Burgoyne followed in Goliath's path, probably out of ignorance because, as Brackenridge quipped, "I am not certain that Burgoyne reads the scripture."[13]

Burgoyne may have been a defeated Goliath, but the American cause was far from secure. There was one major difference between the revolutionary crisis and the narrative of David and Goliath: in the biblical story, the outcome was known, while in the Revolutionary War, patriots knew that victory was far from guaranteed. They hoped that they would prove to be victorious, but the specter of the British Goliath loomed large. Understandably, therefore, many sermons struck an ominous tone. One of the best examples came from David Jones, a Baptist minister from New Jersey. Jones personified what many saw as the ideal revolutionary David—a faithful minister of God and a devoted patriot. In the early 1770s, Jones had been a missionary to Native Americans in the Ohio country, but he threw himself into the revolutionary cause as the crisis escalated. Evidently, Jones became such an outspoken patriot in loyalist-heavy Monmouth County that he had to flee New Jersey for Chester County,

Pennsylvania, just as the Revolutionary War erupted. From that point on, Jones took his preaching to the battlefield. He served as a chaplain under Colonel St. Clair, and delivered a sermon to invigorate the soldiers before battle at Ticonderoga. Later, he served as a chaplain with General Horatio Gates, reportedly gained the trust of General Washington, and endured the harsh winter at Valley Forge while preaching to the troops. Most influential, however, was Jones's sermon, *Defensive War in a just Cause Sinless*, which he preached in Chester County on a Continental Fast day in 1775. Here Jones called for courage in war in the face of two major obstacles—the fear that such a war against Britain was unjustified and unchristian, and the fear that even if the war were justified, the odds against the overmatched colonists were too long to overcome.[14]

Against both fears, Jones wielded David. This war, Jones preached, was "consistent with the purest religion," and no man better exemplified religious purity in military engagements than "David, a man eminent for pure religion, the sweet psalmist of Israel, David, a man after God's own heart, yet all his life is a scene of war." Jones recognized the realities—"we are comparably weak to Great Britain," he admitted, and no one could doubt it. All American patriots were in the perilous position of the youthful David. And yet, of all Americans, congressmen were most vulnerable. Jones worried that "our Congress is in eminent danger.... These worthy gentlemen have ventured all in the cause of liberty for our sakes." Should colonists abandon these good representatives "to the rage of a relentless" British foe? "How could we bear to see these worthy patriots hanged as criminals of the deepest dye?"[15]

Fears of hanging were justifiable. Members of the Continental Congress knew well the danger of taking on the powerful British nation, and the repercussions that would follow what seemed a likely defeat. The scenario David had faced was all too real for them. The next year, as the Continental Congress had approved the Declaration of Independence, John Hancock urged all the congressmen, "We must be unanimous ... there must be no pulling in different ways; we must all hang together." Benjamin Franklin then chimed in, "yes ... we must, indeed, all hang together, or most assuredly we shall all hang separately."[16]

A similar comment came from Virginia's Benjamin Harrison, who famously remarked to Massachusetts's Elbridge Gerry, "I shall have a great advantage over you, Mr. Gerry, when we are all hung for what we are now doing. From the size and weight of my body I shall die in a few minutes, but from the lightness of your body you will dance in the air an hour or two before you are dead." In his observation of this exchange, Benjamin Rush reported that it "procured a transient smile, but it was soon succeeded by the solemnity with which the whole business was conducted."[17] Truly, many colonists were vulnerable Davids.

If Americans struggled with the anxiety of being overmatched Davids, the British pondered what it meant to be Goliaths. From the British perspective, the narrative of David and Goliath held more threat than promise—it was a jeremiad, a righteous warning to the powerful British, cautioning them not to rest secure in military superiority. As the British Methodist John Fletcher cautioned in a sermon published in 1776, the Americans were wrongheaded Davids, but they were Davids nonetheless. That is, the Americans were "fasting and praying," calling on God for deliverance, while the British were "ridiculing" the Americans as "fanatics, and scoffing at religion" while "running wild after pleasure" instead of nurturing spiritual discipline.[18] The contrast was sharp, and the consequences of such British sins were dire, Fletcher argued. "If the Colonists throng the houses of God, while we throng playhouses, or houses of ill fame; if they crowd their communion tables, while we crowd the gaming table... if they pray, while we curse; if they fast, while we get drunk... if they shelter under the protection of heaven, while our chief attention is turned to our hired troops; we are in danger—in *great* danger."

The British, therefore, were virtual Goliaths, "trusting only in the apparent strength of an arm of flesh."[19] And yet, "a youth that believes and prays as David, is a match for a giant that swaggers and curses as Goliath," Fletcher warned. The British cause was just and the American cause was misguided, Fletcher believed. But even a just cause did not ensure victory; only God could do that. And, as scripture revealed on several occasions, God would side against his people to punish them for disobedience. "To disregard the king's righteous commands, as the colonists do, is bad; But to despise the... commandments of the King of kings, as we do, is still worse."[20] The British could depend neither on their military might nor on the justice of their cause, for a pious though misguided David could overcome an arrogant though right-minded Goliath.

Although they were on the opposite side, Patriotic ministers in America agreed with Fletcher's logic: the contest between David and Goliath was a divine war story that revealed how God chose sides in the battle. But more than that, it was a story about divine–human alliances in wartime and the mysteries of divine providence. David killed Goliath because David had God on his side. And David had God on his side because he faithfully obeyed and worshipped God. Even so, just as the British Methodist Fletcher worried about a haughty, Redcoated Goliath, American ministers worried about a corruptible David.

One of those expressing this concern was John Witherspoon, who was president of the College of New Jersey, where he was a favorite teacher of James Madison. Witherspoon was also a Presbyterian minister and a member of the Continental Congress, which made him the only member of the clergy to sign the Declaration of Independence. Witherspoon was nearly as well known for his patriotism as he was for his teaching and preaching. John Adams once called him "as high a son of liberty as any man in America." In his well-titled sermon, *The Dominion of Providence over the Passions of Men,* Witherspoon marveled at the providential favor of the American cause early in the war.[21]

Preaching in 1776, two months before he would join his congressional colleagues in finalizing the Declaration, Witherspoon observed that "it would be a criminal inattention not to observe the singular interposition of providence...in behalf of the American colonies....What surprising success has attended our encounters in almost every instance?" The war was far from over, Witherspoon knew, but early on a David-versus-Goliath scenario seemed to be emerging. "Has not the boasted discipline of regular and veteran soldiers been turned into confusion and dismay before the new and maiden courage of freedmen in defense of their property and right?" Speaking specifically of the British evacuation of Boston in March 1776, Witherspoon praised the ways in which God had confounded British designs but cautioned his fellow patriots against becoming prideful Goliaths, "trusting in, or boasting of an arm of flesh." He worried that this was already happening. He read with concern the prideful, "ostentatious, vaunting expressions in our newspapers," and he hoped that more humble, thankful attitudes would prevail. Cautioning that "every boaster is a coward," he then launched into a quote from Goliath, in which he cursed David, and then followed with David's response: "Thou comest to me with a sword and with a spear, and with a shield, but I come unto thee in the name of the Lord of hosts, the God of the armies of Israel." This story was, for Witherspoon, as for other patriotic ministers, both an encouragement and a note of caution. As the example of Goliath proved, "ostentation and confidence" was an "outrage upon providence, and when it becomes general, and infuses itself into the spirit of the people, it is a forerunner of destruction."[22] Cautions like Witherspoon's were well taken. The American David could lose divine favor if he began to trust exclusively in his own strength.

Psalmist: Spiritual Inspiration for Wartime Violence

David's claim to fame lay not only in his mighty battlefield conquests but also on the martial work of his pen. Patriots praised David as much for his eloquent war psalms as for his military might, reinforcing the central theme that David united military heroism and spiritual devotion. What could more affirm David's spirituality than heralding his divine inspiration as a psalmist? And yet we must attend to David's image as a patriotic psalmist, to not only recognize the martial yet spiritual image of David, but also to recognize the overwhelming popularity of the Psalms in Revolutionary America. Whereas historians have focused on patriotic uses of the Book of Revelation and other apocalyptic scriptures in Revolutionary America, for example, wartime preachers cited the Psalms five times more often than the Book of Revelation.[23]

There may be several reasons the book of Psalms was so popular. It is the longest book in the Bible, so there were more verses for preachers to choose from. And various Protestant liturgies featured psalms as a central part of worship, so nearly everyone was familiar with them. One of the first books printed in the colonies was the famous psalter of 1640 called *The Bay Psalm Book*.[24] But it also made sense for preachers to turn to the book of Psalms because many of the psalms addressed war. And since most colonists considered David to be the author of the psalms, they attributed the abundant martial themes in the psalms to David's inspired pen, and, obviously, to his heroic life.

Many psalms were popular in wartime because they commanded soldiers to do their primary duty: kill the enemy. In colonial America, no militant verse from the Psalms surpassed the popularity of Psalm 144:1: "Blessed be the LORD my strength which teacheth my hands to war, and my fingers to fight."[25] If the main lesson of the David and Goliath story was that victory in war came only though God's blessing, many war psalms reminded colonists that God would bless neither idle soldiers nor negligent nations. In their efforts to recruit and inspire soldiers, preachers stressed both divine, providential deliverance and human, martial expertise. Just as spiritual warfare against sin required the use of proper "means"—including devotional reading of scripture, worship and prayer—so also did military warfare require the use of proper tactics and weapons. Trusting in the means of war meant embracing the horrors of the battlefield, just as David had done. David was attractive to revolutionary patriots because he was not only pious but also lethal. His fierceness as a soldier was made sacred by uniting David the warrior with David the psalmist, the inspired poet of God. Here again ministers had to argue for consistency amid apparent contradiction. David the psalmist did not contradict David the warrior; in fact, David was never more militant than when he wrote psalms, including Psalm 144. Ministers used this psalm above all to assert the spiritual importance of war: religious men must be fighting men. Following David's example, soldiers were never more spiritually faithful than when engaged in armed combat for a righteous cause.

Like the story of David and Goliath, the revolutionary reputation of Psalm 144 has its origins in the Seven Years' War. This text was even featured in one of the first Jewish publications in New York City, a militant prayer written by Rabbi Joseph Yesurun Pinto and performed at a synagogue. This prayer service, held on October 23, 1760, to celebrate the British defeat of Canada, included Psalm 144 among other militant psalms. Above all, these psalms praised the "God of Battles" who blessed "the Armies of our Lord, and King, against his Enemies," and gave wisdom to his military leaders that enabled them "to conquer all the Country of Canada, and to reduce the same to the happy Dominion of his Sacred Majesty, King George the Second." The prayer also asked that "it be Thy sacred Pleasure, to confound, and destroy, all Combinations, Plots, or Designs, that may, at any Time, be entered into by any whatsoever Power, Prince, or Potentate, on Earth, against the Life or Dominions of our said Lord the King." Moreover, the prayer asked all "wicked Schemes prove abortive," and that God would bless George II, "his Counselors, his Servants, his High Court of Parliament, with thy blessed Spirit of Wisdom and Power."[26]

Numerous Protestant ministers agreed with this Jewish prayer that David's militant God stood with the English against the French, and served as a divine military instructor. This idea was clearly revealed in the skillfully-titled sermon, *The Art of War, the Gift of God*, preached by Sylvanus Conant, a Harvard graduate and pastor of First Church at Middleborough, Massachusetts. Conant preached *Art of War* on April 6, 1759, a decisive year in the war when the British gained a strong advantage over the French, thanks largely to the colonists' efforts. Such British and colonial successes, Conant knew, owed much to divinely inspired warfare, and he began his sermon with thanks to God for instilling "war-like Principles into our Hearts, at a Time, when the Cause of God, of Religion, and Liberty calls us to War."[27]

There were many who doubted that this martial call came from God, however. From the outset Conant recognized the atrocities of war, and he acknowledged that most people naturally resisted the image of God as a warrior. A natural response to the "Horror" of war was "to flinch, start back" and respond "that the God of Peace" would never participate in something so "shocking to human Nature" as war. And yet Psalm 144 corrected this common misunderstanding: as David asserted, God not only condoned military war, he empowered the soldier. God did not simply intervene in battle: he taught David to fight. In Conant's words, David's "martial Dexterity, Skill and Strength were the Fruit of divine Teaching and Impressions."[28]

Here Conant asserted that the biblical characterization of David as the "man after God's own heart" related directly to David's military character. As Conant preached to colonial soldiers, "David was a Man after God's Heart; yet he was a Man of War, skill'd in the bloody Art, and furnished above the common Standard, with the Qualifications of War: in this Art, terrible as it is, he informs us that he was taught of God."[29] Here, then, three points were clear, shocking though they were to most people who naturally avoided seeing God's hand in violence. First, the obvious point: war was "terrible." Yet there was an "art" to war, an expertise in killing that distinguished good soldiers from the rest. Finally, David was a master of this art because God had instructed him in it.

Conant reasoned that if God could equip David for the battlefield, strengthen him in battle, and secure his victory, then God could do the same for the British forces fighting against the "Fury of French and Indian Demoniacks," who were both "savage and antichristian." But colonial soldiers needed to imbibe David's zeal, to become men "after God's own heart" in their godly, martial characters. Like David, they needed to embrace their military goals emotionally, with passion for the God-given "art of war," which was "the Art of disputing for Life and Liberty at the Point of the Sword, using the fatal Weapons of War with keen Slight of Hand, and with intrepid Resolutions of Mind, pressing home every advantageous Blow, with full Determination."

In the hopes that God would grant to them this warlike spirit, Conant asked the company of soldiers who were at Middleborough preparing for a Canadian expedition: "Do not some of you already feel the laudable Fire of martial Zeal, kindling in your hearts, by the touch of a live coal from the altar of the living God?" Note here that God inspired *military*, not only *spiritual*, warfare; God ignited a "martial Zeal" in the troops. But Conant was not finished. He further implored the soldiers to "Nourish the sacred spark" ignited by the "coal" from God's altar—"nourish" it until "it blazes out into a manly, heroic, unquenchable Zeal." Conant further prayed "[t]hat the martial fire already begun in your breasts, may...glow with a more intense heat," and to that end the "martial fire" would need "the most sacred Fuel."[30]

Many people would object to such a militant view of God, Conant knew. So he marshaled ample biblical examples to prove that God provided soldiers with skill and enthusiasm for battle. It was God who blessed those, like David, who did the "terrible Work" of war successfully. And terrible work it was. To further place divine sanction on the most atrocious violence, Conant even quoted the infamous Psalm 137:5: "Happy shall he be, that taketh and dasheth thy little ones against the Stones." This divine command directly contradicted just war theory, which prohibited any intentional killing of noncombatants, not to mention children. But even this extremely violent text did not bother Conant. He quoted it unapologetically, endorsing it as God's "blessing" on "him that does" war's "terrible Work faithfully."[31]

This scripture just proved again that God sanctioned war and inspired violence for righteous causes. God could instruct English colonists in "the Art of War" by "inspiring into their Hearts" the "noble, heroic Principles" needed for success in combat, including the "Wisdom to force Dangers and escape them" and the "Dexterity" to fight "with Skill." All such abilities were "the inspired Gifts of God."[32] It was this kind of warrior—a Davidic warrior—that the colonists needed to enact God's vengeance against "merciless Indians, and faithless Frenchmen."[33] The enemies were ominous and the need was great, and Conant implored the colonial soldiers "to vindicate the Cause of Religion and Liberty" against their unrighteous foes, and encouraged them, in true Davidic fashion, to display "the greatest Bravery in the bloodiest Actions."[34]

Keeping in mind that Conant's main goal was to spur troops on to war with a divine cause, his authority to do so was primarily spiritual. As a minister, his wartime authority depended upon the alliance between spiritual and military warfare, a bond that could not be severed without dire consequences both eternally and temporally. As Conant insisted, "we are involv'd in a two-fold War, spiritual and literal, and we ought not to neglect either; if we neglect the former we lose our Souls; if the latter, we lose our

Lives, or Liberty which is no less dear."[35] In both realms of battle, courage and sacrifice defeated cowardice and vice.

There was no less enthusiasm for David's militant psalms in the American Revolution. In 1775 no message was more timely than David's poetic proclamation that God taught his "Fingers to Fight." It reminded American patriots that the destiny of the war rested partially on their weapons. There was no substitute for courage and zealous fighting on the battlefield. As Zabdiel Adams preached to a company of militia in New England on January 2, 1775, three months before the initial shots were fired at Lexington and Concord, David could charge into battle with confidence only because "he knew that he and his subjects were well provided with weapons of war: For what probability of success can there possibly be in an engagement, if to all the modern instruments of death, we have nothing to oppose but our naked bodies, or useless arms"? No, successful armies must possess "military skill," and be adept at "the art of war among civilized nations," for without such skill the colonists would be foolhardy "to face a veteran, well disciplined soldiery"; such would be "to sacrifice our lives and betray the cause" of liberty. Zabdiel Adams, a cousin of John Adams, made these remarks even before the war began because he, like everyone in the colonies, knew trouble was on the horizon. Britain, once "the nurse of our infancy, the guardian of our youth," seemed primed for war against the colonies.[36]

Likewise, William Stearns, in a sermon before the Provincial Congress in Massachusetts one month after the war began, heralded David's military successes because he had made good use of the military guides God had provided. God taught his "hands to war and his fingers to fight," and David, the "man of war from his youth," had been successful because he trusted God more than his sword and bow. And yet Stearns worried that some would use David's example to justify slothful trust in a victorious God. David's example did not "prove that we are to sit still; but we are, relying on His assistance, to make preparation for engaging in battle, and to exert ourselves to our utmost" because "God will not assist us, unless we use our own endeavors," including uniting all the colonies for the common cause against Britain. So, Stearns warned, "if we now relinquish our rights and privileges—if we desert our cause," then "we shall be guilty of sacrilege to God, and treachery to future generations." In the spirit of David's charge, therefore, Stearns proclaimed "Let our troops consist of a respectable number of able-bodied men—let them be well equipped with the habiliments of war, and to their arms let them stand." In making his point, Stearns combined David's command that God equipped his "fingers to fight" with a similar command from David's most trusted general, Joab: "Be of good courage, and let us play the men for our people, and for the cities of our God" (2 Samuel 10:12).[37]

In the American Revolution, therefore, just as in the Seven Years' War, preachers worried about too much reliance upon God to ensure victory. In the heat of the war, when everyone from General Washington to the Continental Congress struggled to recruit soldiers, ministers insisted that troops and weapons alone could not win the battle, but the battle could not be won without them. In Psalm 144, God may have taught David to fight, but David still had to do the fighting. As dangerous as it was to imitate Goliath, trusting too much in military power, it was equally dangerous to neglect military training and weapons. What if the American David trusted so much in God's favor that he neglected his own military preparation? David may have refused Saul's armor and heavy weapons, but he did not approach Goliath unarmed. He took with him his sling—not the latest in military technology, to be sure, but the weapon he was skilled in the use of.

With the sling and stone, David was a courageous and lethal soldier because he was also a spiritually faithful psalmist. As Presbyterian minister Robert Cooper preached to General Richard Montgomery's battalion in 1775, "to trust in means alone, and neglect seeking to God, is pride and atheism; to pretend to trust in God, and at the same time to neglect the use of proper means, is foolish presumption and wild enthusiasm." Cooper then charged the troops "to stand forth in the face of danger and death." To refuse to face the fires of battle, "to draw back, if you were even before the cannon's mouth, would fix both awful guilt and indelible disgrace upon you, would brand you with perpetual infamy." So, warned Cooper, "if then you would escape deep guilt before God, and lasting contempt among men, forward you must go, wheresoever the drum shall beat, and the trumpet sound for battle." Their only choice, as Cooper proclaimed, was "to run the hazard of dying like heroes, or be certain of living like cowards."[38]

Monarch:
The Revolutionary Fall of the House of David

In Revolutionary America, images of David as a righteous and spiritual warrior overshadowed another image of David, perhaps his most well-known persona both in scripture and in history: Israel's most favored king. After the battles at Lexington and Concord, as the colonists careened toward outright revolution, fervent patriots increasingly denounced not only George III but also the concept of monarchy itself. The Bible played a prominent role in making these arguments. But, whereas the Bible's evil kings, such as Ahab, and ineffective and corruptible kings, such as Saul, served revolutionary purposes well, good kings were problems to be solved. Even so, American patriots knew that any use of the Bible to denounce monarchy had to come to terms with the righteous kings from ancient Israel. And since scripture heralded David as Israel's greatest king, he became revolutionary patriots' ultimate obstacle to overcome in arguing against monarchy.

David's reputation as a good king had been an asset in the French and Indian War. Consider, for instance, the prominent place of kingship in Abraham Keteltas's *The Religious Soldier: or, the Military Character of King David*, printed in 1759. Keteltas, pastor of the First Presbyterian Church in Elizabethtown, New Jersey, published his sermon in New York, dedicating it to General Jeffrey Amherst, who had led the capture of the French fortress of Louisbourg the year before and was rewarded with the title of commander in chief of British forces in North America. As Keteltas preached his sermon, Amherst was preparing for a more extensive maneuver against French forces in Canada. Given Amherst's great responsibilities and the dire circumstances, Keteltas mustered the strongest biblical support he could find to inspire the general, his officers, and most importantly, his soldiers. Calling David "the greatest General in sacred History," Keteltas examined several aspects of David's heroism—virtues that he believed were vital for officers and soldiers in conflict with their French and Indian enemies. Among all David's other attributes and roles, he "was a glorious King," who was "under the immediate and unerring Direction of Heaven."[39]

Even before he became king David set the biblical standard for loyalty by remaining faithful to King Saul, even though he knew that Saul was trying to kill him. In 1759, the popular King George II was on the throne, and so David's loyalty to monarchy was seen as an admirable quality. Keteltas emphasized David's refusal "to rebel against his king," even while "Saul was pursuing after him, and thirsting for his blood." Despite all of King Saul's evil intentions, David declared that Saul was "my master, the Lord's anointed," and so David would do no harm to Saul (1 Samuel 24:6). After Saul died on Mt. Gilboa, David executed the man who claimed to have killed him. If David could be so loyal to a corrupt ruler such as Saul, then certainly the colonists should be loyal to King George II, whom Keteltas called "the best of Kings."[40]

David's loyalty to Saul, in fact, seemed to discourage rebellion against any monarch. Keteltas, in his sermon from October 1777, entitled *God arising and pleading his people's cause; or The American war in favor of liberty, against the measures and arms of Great Britain,* thus had to reinterpret David's attitude toward Saul during the revolutionary crisis. Here, Keteltas downplayed David's loyalty to Saul and instead preached that David confronted "the cruel tyrant." Certainly, David did not threaten Saul, but he called on God to "plead my cause" against Saul and to "deliver me out of" Saul's grasp (1 Samuel 24:12).[41]

When it came to making biblical arguments against monarchy, it was not a minister but pamphleteer Thomas Paine who led the way, at least in capturing the widest readership. We have observed how Paine, in his enormously popular *Common Sense,* argued that monarchy was unbiblical. The Old Testament in particular, Paine asserted, taught that God had instituted a republic for his people, and that they had sinned by demanding that God give them a king to rule them. But in making this strong claim for biblical republic over monarchy, Paine had to deal with King David. David may not have been a perfect king, but scripture described him as Israel's greatest ruler, and the Israelites achieved great heights under his rule. How could Paine's argument that the Bible forbade monarchy stand up against David? Here Paine claimed that "the high encomium given of David takes no notice of him *officially as a* king, but only as a *man* after God's own heart." (Note that the italics are Paine's.) He was relying on a technicality. "Man after God's own heart," Paine asserted, was not a royal title. It was, however, a military title, at least in the view of many wartime ministers. Here again, as in the French and Indian War, Revolutionary-era sermons proclaimed that it was David's military prowess, his courageous service in both military and spiritual conflict, that earned him the epithet "man after God's own heart."[42]

The republican arguments of Paine and others captured much attention in the 1770s, and this attention affected the revolutionary legacy of David. As long as David was heralded as the military hero, he was an unassailably revolutionary patriot. And yet, Revolutionary-era patriots argued, David's royal authority led to his corruption, as manifested in his adulterous relationship with Bathsheba. This famous narrative of adultery and murder began when David abandoned his soldierly virtue to assume the monarchial prerogatives of a king. The results were disastrous, because while David's military service reinforced virtue and piety, kingship bred corruption and laxity. So David stayed away from the battlefield and remained in the palace, where he lusted after a bathing Bathsheba while his army—including Bathsheba's husband Uriah—was off fighting David's wars. After Uriah refused to go home to his wife and insisted on staying on the battlefield, David had him placed in the most dangerous part of the field, effectively coordinating his death. In effect, David used Uriah's faithful service as a solider to have him killed, and then David took Bathsheba into his house (2 Samuel 11–12).

David suffered for his sin, but his monarchial legacy suffered more. The history of the house of David became a chaotic story of betrayal and civil war. But it was also a revolutionary story, which patriots and Tories alike believed had great relevance for the American Revolution.

Consider first the initial fallout from David's sin with Bathsheba—the revolution of Absalom, David's third son. Absalom was ambitious, courageous, and handsome—"in all Israel there was none to be so much praised as Absalom for his beauty: from the sole of his foot even to the crown of his head there was no blemish in him" (2 Samuel 14:25). Eventually Absalom's popularity rivaled that of his father—"Absalom stole the hearts of the men of Israel" (2 Samuel 15:6). And Absalom, sensing that the people would soon reject David, conspired against his father. Absalom recruited Ahithophel, his father's trusted advisor, and launched a revolt, expelling David from Jerusalem. However, Absalom's revolt was put down in an ensuing battle, in which David's military commander Joab killed Absalom, much to David's horror (2 Samuel 17–19).

This story of betrayal, conspiracy, and revolt played well in the American Revolution. One of the most compelling revolutionary interpretations of the Absalom story came not in a sermon or a treatise, but in the embroidery of Faith Robinson Trumbull of Lebanon, Connecticut. Both Trumbull and her husband, Governor Jonathan Trumbull, were deeply committed to the patriotic cause. By 1770, the year of the Boston Massacre, Trumbull expressed her patriotic commitments through art, embroidering a piece called "The Hanging of Absalom." In the scene, Absalom's famously thick hair had ensnared him in the branches of a tree, leaving him hanging and defenseless against Joab's attack.

Artistic representations of Absalom were not uncommon, both in visual art and poetry. They were often direct commentaries on political events, the most famous example being John Dryden's *Absalom and Achitophel*

(1681), which addressed the Exclusion crisis under the reign of Charles II. Although Dryden's David (Charles II) was no absolute tyrant, Charles's ineffective leadership had alienated his subjects, who were "Improverisht and depriv'd of all Command/Their Taxes doubled as they lost Their Land." The evil player in Dryden's satire was neither David (Charles II) nor Absalom (the Duke of Monmouth), but Ahithophel (the Earl of Shaftsbury), who engineered the revolt. In Dryden's famous telling, then, Absalom was patriotic, even if mistaken. "Never was a Patriot yet, but was a Fool," Dryden wrote. But Dryden's satire did point to a David who ineffectively ruled and alienated the people, and the tragedy of the story was that Absalom and David were not reunited.

Given the strong patriot views of Trumbull and her family, her artistic rendering of the Absalom story seems to be an indictment of David as George III, with Absalom playing the part of oppressed colonial patriots. And, since she embroidered her Absalom piece not later than 1770, it is possible that she hoped for a reform of British policies rather than outright revolution and independence from Britain.[43]

While the Absalom story certainly indicted David, Absalom was an ambiguous figure—a heroic patriot to some, but to those who defended the British cause, a betraying son and malevolent rebel. Far less ambiguous was the other chaotic episode that resulted from David's adultery with Bathsheba and his arranged killing of Uriah: the civil war prompted by the tyrannical rule of David's grandson, Rehoboam.[44]

American patriots found a striking similarity between the Israelites' suffering under Rehoboam and their own struggles with George III and Parliament. Several ministers made this case. Baptist John Allen accused George III of Rehoboam-like tyrannies as early as 1773, when very few colonists risked making such accusations against the throne.[45] Another minister preached on Rehoboam's tyrannies in relation to the famous "Boston Tea Party" of December, 1773.[46] A rare sermon from an African American author specifically linked revolutionary battles in the Carolinas to the Rehoboam story. This anonymous preacher implored Carolina patriots to lash out strongly against the tyrannies of George III, and then to lash out just as zealously against the tyrannical practice of slavery.[47]

One of the most comprehensive and compelling applications of Rehoboam to the Revolution came in a sermon by Peter Whitney entitled *American Independence Vindicated*, preached on September 12, 1776. Whitney, who pastored in Northborough, Massachusetts, took his inspiration for the sermon from the Declaration of Independence, and he dedicated it to John Hancock, President of the Continental Congress. Although Whitney's main intention was to defend the Declaration, he was just as influenced by Paine's *Common Sense*, and he related both to the revolt against Rehoboam.[48]

As Whitney described in detail, Rehoboam was a tyrant, especially in comparison to his father, the relatively just King Solomon, and his grandfather, David. Instead of listening to the older men who had advised Solomon, Rehoboam heeded the counsel of younger advisors who implored him to tell the people that "my little finger shall be thicker than my father's loins," meaning that "whereas my father did lade you with a heavy yoke, I will add to your yoke: my father hath chastised you with whips, but I will chastise you with scorpions." In response, the people revolted, saying, "What portion do we have in David? Neither have we inheritance in the son of Jesse: to your tents, O Israel: now see to thine own house, David" (1 Kings 12:16).

Peter Whitney found in this statement an apt biblical parallel to the Declaration of Independence. Just as the people of Israel had declared their independence from the House of David, the Continental Congress declared the colonies' independence from Britain, and the similarities between the two situations were striking. For instance, Rehoboam had been the third king in the Davidic line, just as George III was the third king in the House of Hanover. And, as with the House of David, the Hanoverian rulers before George III had been mostly good kings, or at least as good as could be expected.[49] But, just like Rehoboam, George III rejected "the counsel of the old men, and followed the impolitic advice of his young mates," especially his preceptor, "Lord Bute," along with "Hillsborough and North, with their detestable Junto." They counseled oppression and unfair taxation, passed in acts of Parliament and reinforced by the throne. In response, Adams, Jefferson, Hancock, and their congressional colleagues had responded just as the Israelites responded to Rehoboam: "What portion have we in George? Neither have we inheritance in the house of Hanover; to your tents O Americans, and now see to thine own house George."[50]

Thus Rehoboam was not just a bad king—scripture was littered with those—but he was a bad king from the House of David. The days of David's reign were the glory days of Israel, the time of Israel's greatest justice and happiness. In preaching about Israel's rebellion under Rehoboam, ministers called out the downfall of the righteous Davidic house—an apt analogy, ministers believed, to the downfall of Britain under George III.

While other British monarchs had been faithful in the exercises of liberty, George III had violated the basic rights of British subjects. As Whitney asserted, "We need not wonder that the ten tribes of Israel fall off from the house of David, if the house of David fall away from" the righteous governance for which God had long blessed them as "ministers of God, for the good to that people." If Rehoboam had listened to his father's advisers, the people would have remained faithful to him. The people had not abandoned the house of David; the house of David had abandoned them—the same was true, patriots believed, of Britain under George III. Colonial patriots insisted that they were not itching for rebellion, and they hardly set out to declare independence from Britain. "We have not raised armies with ambitious designs of separating from Great-Britain, and establishing independent states," and "we fight not for glory or for conquest." Instead, the colonists "exhibit to mankind the remarkable spectacle of a people attacked by unprovoked enemies, without any imputation, or even suspicion of offence," Whitney asserted. The Continental Congress only declared independence "after mature deliberation," made necessary "by the wanton, cruel, and unprovoked conduct of the king and parliament of Great-Britain."

Thus Whitney justified revolt, applying "the revolt of the ten tribes of Israel from Rehoboam...to the Thirteen Colonies of North-America." Like Israel's revolt against Rehoboam, "our revolt is, undoubtedly, of God," Whitney preached. "God has ever been the friend and patron of the American Israel, and he will continue so, if we act up to our character and obligation." Most importantly, the story of Rehoboam justified rebellion against a king, even a king in the most divinely ordained monarchial line. If any king or any government violated the precepts of God and liberty, the people were obligated to rebel.[51]

What have historians missed by neglecting David, other than another tragic story of a good king gone bad? First, historians have not stressed enough the crucial relationship between spiritual warfare and military warfare in Revolutionary America. Preachers constantly insisted that spiritual men were not timid men; they were warriors, and David was the prime biblical model of this spiritual and martial valor. Better than any other biblical hero, David proved that a "man after God's own heart" was a man of war. Second, David was a key example of how patriotic ministers creatively adapted the Bible to their political and martial situations. David was not only a patriot; he was a patriot for all occasions, even when patriotic loyalty shifted dramatically from England to America. The fortunes of David as they played out in the colonial era through the Revolution illustrated the interplay between republican thought and biblical tradition. Though monarchy and republican ideas coexisted quite well for at least a century, the radical republicanism that ignited the Revolution reshaped David's wartime legacy, and David became the American Revolution's most versatile biblical character. Even when he failed miserably, committing adultery with Bathsheba and murdering her husband, he supported the revolutionary cause by proving that monarchy would corrupt even the best of men.

5

"The Liberty wherewith Christ hath Made Us Free"

PETER, PAUL, AND APOSTOLIC PATRIOTISM

AS WE HAVE SEEN, the colonists looked to the Old Testament for war heroes, dramatic battle scenes, and images of a warrior God. The New Testament contains relatively few episodes of military warfare, apart from the Book of Revelation, which described the ultimate war at the end of time. Even so, three of the five most cited texts in Revolutionary America were from the epistles of Peter and Paul. No biblical texts were more controversial. Patriots and loyalists disagreed dramatically over their meaning.

Most often, the controversy centered on two main themes. First, the teachings of Peter and Paul in 1 Peter 2 and Romans 13, which seemingly commanded absolute allegiance to sovereign rulers, were hotly contested. From patriotic Congregationalists in Boston and Anglicans in Williamsburg to loyalist Methodists in London, preachers waged rhetorical battles over these passages. In all these exegetical conflicts, apostolic authority was a polemical weapon, and American patriots struggled to counter loyalist claims that Peter and Paul condemned rebellion in the strongest terms. If the apostles required loyalty even to the obviously corrupt Roman government that imprisoned them, did not Britain demand the same allegiance? Patriots read these passages through the prism of republican ideology, arguing that obedience was due only to just rulers who fostered liberty, not to evil tyrants.

Second, Paul's advocacy of "the liberty wherewith Christ hath made us free" (Galatians 5.1) was a patriotic slogan that secured Paul's credentials as an apostle of freedom. Inspired by Paul's command to "stand fast" for liberty, both spiritual and political, the question for many Americans was not whether patriotism could be Christian but whether there was any alternative. Preachers found in Peter and Paul a rationale for political revolution in obedience to divine authority and an argument for Christianity as the essence of American patriotism.[1]

The Apostles and Civil Authority
(Romans 13 and 1 Peter 2)

Did the teachings of the apostles of the New Testament support the American Revolution? This question, flatly stated, captivated many patriots and loyalists in the biblically literate societies of Revolutionary America. Even today some people find a deep-rooted connection between the American Revolution and the apostles. A recent internet search turned up numerous websites that discussed whether the American Revolution violated Paul's command to obey civil rulers in Romans 13.[2] This chapter was the most cited biblical text in Revolutionary America—a surprising fact, given that so much emphasis has been given to Old Testament texts and apocalyptic scriptures. Also very popular was 1 Peter 2, ranking fifth.[3] It is no wonder that these texts had so much revolutionary significance. These passages from Paul and Peter had been known throughout history for their grand claims for the religious importance of civil rulers.[4] Before we assess the revolutionary importance of these texts, however, we should examine them directly. First, consider the most cited text, Romans 13, especially verses 1–4, which set the terms of debate for loyalists and patriots:

> Let every soul be subject unto the higher powers. For there is no power but of God: the powers that be are ordained of God. Whosoever therefore resisteth the power, resisteth the ordinance of God: and they that resist shall receive to themselves damnation. For rulers are not a terror to good works, but to the evil. Wilt thou then not be afraid of the power? Do that which is good, and thou shalt have praise of the same: For he is the minister of God to thee for good. But if thou do that which is evil, be afraid; for he beareth not the sword in vain: for he is the minister of God, a revenger to execute wrath upon him that doeth evil.

Many patriots turned to these verses, which constituted what some revolutionaries called "the politics of St. Paul," because they directly addressed the issues at hand.[5]

Nearly as popular and certainly as important was the "politics of Peter," which revolutionaries and loyalists gleaned from 1 Peter 2:13–17:

> Submit yourselves to every ordinance of man for the Lord's sake, whether to the king as supreme, or to governors, as to those who are sent by him for the punishment of evildoers and for the praise of those who do good. For this is the will of God, that by doing good you may put to silence the ignorance of foolish men—as free, yet not using liberty as a cloak for vice, but as bondservants of God. Honor all people. Love the brotherhood. Fear God. Honor the king.

Any biblical text that ended with "honor the king" had to favor the British side of the struggle—or at least that was the case made strongly by loyalists. Often, both Peter and Paul entered revolutionary debates on the pens of loyalist ministers who called on apostolic support to quell an uncivil—and, they believed, unholy—rebellion.

Apostolic Loyalism

Some of the most scathing biblical attacks on American patriotism came from British Methodists. In 1775, John Wesley, the founder of the Methodist movement, published *A Calm Address to Our American Colonies*, which counseled tranquil deliberations instead of frenzied patriotism. The Revolution was a massive conspiracy, Wesley argued, orchestrated by the enemies of George III. Most American patriots were not evil; they were misled, stirred up by troublemakers' inflammatory rhetoric. Wesley pleaded with American patriots, "Brethren, open your eyes! Come to yourselves! Be no longer the dupes of designing men" who "love neither England nor America, but play one against the other." At the end of this path lay mutual destruction. Truth and peace could be restored, Wesley argued, only if so-called American patriots would repent of their sinful rebellion and follow the command of Peter, "fear God and honour the king."[6]

Wesley's *Calm Address* received an enthusiastic British response, with some 100,000 copies in circulation by 1776. In that year, a torrent of other publications defended the British position, including another important work by a Methodist, *The Bible and the Sword* by John Fletcher. Wesley admired Fletcher immensely, and once even said that Fletcher surpassed George Whitefield "in holy tempers and holiness of conversation."[7] No doubt Wesley believed Fletcher's politics to be equally admirable. Fletcher agreed substantially with Wesley's attack on American patriotism but went even further in employing the apostles to undermine the Revolution.

The Bible and the Sword was a strong defense of King George's right to wage war on American rebels. The Bible was clear on this point, Fletcher stated, and no text was clearer than Paul's warning that the ruler "beareth not the sword in vain: for he is the Minister of God, a Revenger to Execute wrath upon him that doeth evil" (Romans 13:4). Harsh words, Fletcher believed, for any patriot who tried to rebel against England. "St. Paul, who knew the gospel better than English mystics and American patriots, asserts the lawfulness of using the sword in order to maintain good government and execute justice." Here Fletcher found ample proof that "the king is entrusted with the sword" with the responsibility "to execute wrath upon criminals." If the king refused to wield the sword to punish rebels and to maintain order, he would be guilty of neglecting one of his main responsibilities. On this matter, Paul sounded the same authoritative command as St. Peter, who proclaimed that "governors are sent by God for the punishment of evil doers." (1 Peter 2:14).[8]

Fletcher argued that kings should use the sword "with the same tenderness, with which a surgeon uses his knife, when he cuts a mortified limb from the body of a beloved child. His heart bleeds, while the dreadful operation is performed; and yet his judicious, parental affection makes him consent to sacrifice a part of his son's body, in order to prevent the destruction of the whole." The message was clear: the British Empire, divided by civil war, must stand strong against the rebellion, even though it meant the painful amputation of wayward colonial patriots. Peter and Paul insisted that the ruler had to maintain order. Rebellion could not be tolerated. Continuing the medical analogy, Fletcher wrote, "Wo to the man, who, to show that he has the power to use a knife, wantonly cuts his own flesh! And wo to the ruler, who, to make it appear, that he bears the sword, butchers his loyal subjects, and wantonly cuts off the sound limbs of that political body, of which he is the head!"

Such crimes could not be blamed on "our mild sovereign" King George. Writing in reaction to the famous destruction of the tea—later called the Boston Tea Party, Fletcher blamed the bloodshed on those "sons of Belial, belonging to the city of Boston," who "beset a ship in the night, overpowered the crew, and feloniously destroyed her rich cargo." Later, by arming themselves against the king to protect the tea-plundering "felons," colonists became "guilty of both felony and high treason." Paul and Peter authorized the king to wage war to punish these "daring felons" and "the infatuated people who bear arms in their defense."[9]

And yet, despite the patriots' sinful rebellion, the British bore their share of the blame for the Revolution. Britain had been a sinful Empire, Fletcher preached, and God had used America's rebellion to punish it. One of its most glaring sins was slavery. The British had conspired to incite African tribes to wage wars on one another so that the war captors could be sold as slaves. In effect, the British had "turned Africa into a field of blood" and had transported Africans in horrid conditions to enslave them in British lands. Such treatment of "innocent negroes" called for divine "vengeance upon us." Granted, the Americans were no better—they were probably worse. So-called patriots were "hypocritical friends of liberty, who buy, and sell, and whip their fellow men as if they were brutes, and absurdly complain that *they* are enslaved, when it is they themselves, who deal in the liberties and bodies of men."[10]

To be sure, Fletcher averred, the British needed to reform their nation to regain God's favor. But they also needed to punish the colonies for their rebellion. As dangerous to the British as their sins was their negligence in prosecuting the war. Britain had a God-given responsibility to restore order to the Empire, and that meant that it must defeat the Americans decisively. God was a God of order. Accordingly, Fletcher preached against those who used scripture to deny warfare, especially civil war against their fellow British colonists in America. In response, Fletcher reiterated the theme communicated in his title: *The Bible and the Sword.* The Bible condoned the sword, even insisted on it, to wage just wars and to enforce godly and civil rule. Here again the advice of Peter and Paul must be heeded. The ruler was God's "minister," and his purpose was "to execute wrath"—even God's wrath—on rebels and criminals.[11] American patriots certainly fit that description.

While British ministers such as Wesley and Fletcher waged polemical warfare against the Revolution from a safe distance, one of the most influential critics of American patriotism, Charles Inglis, preached from the patriots' side of the Atlantic. Perhaps his most important sermon was *The Duty of Honouring the King,* delivered in New York on January 30, 1780, which was the anniversary of the execution of Charles I. Anglicans traditionally celebrated January 30 to honor his memory and to denigrate the revolt that ignited the English Civil War and ushered in the protectorate of Oliver Cromwell. Such condemnation of civil war had special importance for loyalists in the throes of the American Revolution, as Inglis recognized. "Need I tell you that the unnatural Rebellion which, at this Day, desolates and disgraces America, bears the strongest Resemblance to the former Rebellion" that became the English Civil War? "The one is an exact Counterpart of the other—begun on nearly the same Principles, and carried on by the very same Methods."[12]

The Revolution would have disastrous effects, Inglis believed, and he regretted the "Horrors of Rebellion" that so-called American patriots had wrought. These rebels were hardly true, virtuous patriots. They were "Sons of Rebellion," intoxicated by a "Phrenzy of Enthusiasm" and "Republican Ambition."[13] Inglis believed firmly that the republicanism espoused by American patriots was as religiously radical as it was politically radical. Not surprisingly, therefore, he centered his argument on Peter and Paul, and especially Peter's command, "Fear God. Honour the king" (1 Peter 2:17). What Peter meant, according to Inglis, was that one could not be antimonarchical without being anti-Christian. God was a king, the ultimate monarch, and there was an inseparable connection between obedience to earthly kings and reverence for the heavenly Lord.[14]

To espouse this idea during the American Revolution required a strong argument, and Inglis knew it. So he did much more than cite Peter's command. He gave it full attention, reviewing its historical context and relating its message to the American crisis. In Inglis's view, the key to understanding Peter's message for revolutionary America was to understand Peter's situation in ancient Rome. The condition of Christians was dire, Inglis reported, and much of the blame rested on the Jews. Here Inglis recited the traditional anti-Jewish interpretation of Christian beginnings. The Jews were "abandoned by Heaven" because they had abandoned Christ. More politically important was the Jews' abandonment of civil society. "They were persecuting and uncharitable towards others," Inglis claimed, adding that the Jews "were seditious also, frequently raising Insurrections," constantly provoking citizens to disobey their rulers, and generally "making Religion the Cloak of Disloyalty." This seditious reputation of the Jews unjustly marred the reputation of Christians in Roman society, Inglis argued. Many Roman citizens viewed Christians as merely a Jewish sect, and Christians often bore the blame for Jewish crimes. This was the situation that Peter encountered, and this was the reason that Peter so adamantly commanded Christians to obey the Roman government. Christians needed to renounce Jewish disloyalty by reaffirming their own virtuous loyalty; they needed to "distinguish themselves by those Virtues which were opposite to the Vices so frequently

practiced by the Jews." Those virtues included honesty, good works, giving glory to God, and, especially, fearing God and honoring "the King."
Although Inglis mainly treated Peter's text, he associated it with Paul's
Romans 13:1–7. The texts were different but the message was the same,
he said.[15]

Inglis anticipated the obvious patriotic response: what did Peter's and
Paul's demands for obedience to rulers have to do with Revolutionary
America? King George was, in the patriots' view, a tyrant unworthy of their
loyalty. This was an ignorant position, Inglis believed, adopted only by
those who did not know the crisis that Peter and Paul faced. They lived
under Roman rule, which was an increasingly hostile rule. Consider
St. Peter in particular. He wrote this letter during a time of great persecution. In fact, the Emperor of Rome was none other than Nero, the
most notorious tormenter of Christians in all history. And still, Peter
commanded his followers to "honor the king." Clearly, Peter meant for
Christians to obey all rulers, not only good ones. "The personal Character
of the Magistrate was not to interfere with the Civil Duty of the Subject."
Character mattered, of course, and good rulers were always easier to obey.
But the apostles specifically demanded obedience to corrupt kings. The
reason, in Inglis's view, was obvious in the advice from Peter and Paul:
rulers were God's ministers, God's chosen leaders. No matter what crimes
rulers may have committed, God had placed them in power and entrusted
them with authority. To disobey them was to revolt against God.[16]

Scripture found reinforcement in practice, Inglis believed, and he
listed ample evidence to show why people should honor their rulers. Much
of that evidence demonstrated that "Sedition and Rebellion" had shed
more blood, incited "greater Miseries and Calamities," and brought about
"more audacious Impieties...than perhaps through any other Cause."[17]
Rebellion, "even in its mildest Effects," was "dreadful," constantly "stained
with Blood," and caused "Distress and Misery." Rebellion made good government impossible and rendered good religion impracticable. More than
a political movement, rebellion had spiritual causes and consequences.
Rebellion aroused "all the dark, malevolent Passions of the Soul" and subdued the soul's "mild and amiable affections" and "virtuous Principles."
Using the revolution in seventeenth-century England as a cautionary
example for the raging revolution in America, Inglis asserted that "Civil
Wars are always more cruel and barbarous than foreign Wars, and more
destructive to Morals"; they "kindle up the Soul to tenfold Rage," incit-
ing "personal Revenge and Animosity." Ironically, rebellions, which often

began as irrational uprisings against tyranny, usually resulted in even more tyrannical governments.[18]

These grievous results and moral disasters began when misguided people disobeyed "St. Peter's Precept—'honour the King.'" Such disobedience was often hidden under the cover of righteous piety, however. In the English Revolution—as in the American crisis—"ambition" concealed itself "under the usual Mark of Patriotism," just as "Enthusiasm" disguised itself "in the Garb of Religion." Together, ambitious "patriotism" and enthusiastic religion "blew the Trumpet of Sedition." The result was "Open Violence," producing "a bloody, ruinous Rebellion."[19]

Religion and rebellion were a dangerous combination, Inglis surmised, a blend of zealous piety and radical politics that came not from the people but from so-called patriotic leaders who manipulated them. This was certainly the case with the American Revolution, Inglis claimed. American patriotism was aroused when "imaginary Dangers were pretended; the Passions of the Populace were inflamed to a Degree of Phrenzy; and every Engine was employed to carry on the Work of Sedition." America's declared independence was a "Foible of weak Minds," manipulated by "ambitious Leaders" who "sought their own Aggrandizement" much to the "Ruin" of America.[20]

Rather than listen to these manipulative, "patriotic" leaders, the people should have obeyed the clear teaching of the Apostles, especially Peter's command to "Honour the king." Inglis wondered at how "any one who fears God, or loves his Fellow Creatures, can disregard this Precept." And yet American revolutionaries did disregard Peter's command, and they did so because they had turned from scriptural teaching guided by "worldly Prudence" to rely instead on "the Feelings of the People," which were easily manipulated by "the artful Management of designing men."[21]

Pre-Revolutionary Apostolic Patriotism

While loyalists claimed Peter and Paul as defenders of the divine authority of kings, American patriots denied this interpretation in the strongest terms. In so doing, they drew on earlier ministers who preached from Romans 13 to deny that Paul gave kings the right to be tyrants. One of the clearest statements of this view before the Revolution was Jonathan Mayhew's *Discourse Concerning Unlimited Submission and Non-resistance to the Higher Powers.* Although Mayhew had preached this sermon twenty-five years before the Revolutionary War began, revolutionary patriots remembered it. As John Adams recalled, this sermon had a significant influence: "It was read by everybody; celebrated by friends, and abused by enemies." And for good reason. As Adams wrote, this sermon was "seasoned with wit and satire superior to any in Swift or Franklin." Mayhew, Adams wrote, "had great influence in the commencement of the Revolution."[22]

In more than one way, this sermon was a poignant counterpart to Inglis's *The Duty of Honouring the King*. Like Inglis, Mayhew preached his sermon near January 30, 1749, the centennial of the execution of Charles I. And yet, while Anglicans—including Inglis—set apart this day to commemorate the memory of King Charles, Mayhew celebrated the memory of his beheading. Mayhew believed, as did most colonial Protestants, that Charles I was neither a saint nor a martyr. He was a tyrant who got the execution that he deserved.[23]

To expose the "mysterious doctrine" of Charles's "Saintship and Martyrdom," Mayhew turned to Paul's endorsement of civil authority in Romans 13. Defenders of Charles I had cited this text not only to condemn his beheading but also to condemn any revolt against authorized rulers. This passage from Paul certainly endorsed submission to civil rulers, and rightly so, Mayhew believed. But submission was not necessarily *unlimited* submission. Mayhew argued that Paul demanded both obedience to just rulers and protest against unjust ones.

To make his case, Mayhew first turned to Paul's historical circumstances. In Romans, Paul was addressing Christians who had taken too literally the idea that the Christian life was "not of this world." It was true that Christianity concerned itself primarily with Christ's otherworldly kingdom, but it also taught responsibility in this world, which included obedience to civil authorities—monarchical, aristocratic, or republican.[24] But submission to rulers only extended so far. What if a king were unjust, for instance, or what if a parliament oppressed its people? Here Mayhew argued that the key to Paul's advice was that the ruler was "the minister of God to thee *for good.*" That is, the purpose of civil government was to support "the good of civil society."[25] If a ruler were doing just that, then disobedience was "not merely a *political sin,* but a heinous *offense against God* and *religion.*"[26] But if a ruler failed to serve as God's "minister...for good," then the command to obey that ruler did not apply. History was replete with tales of tyranny, from scripture to Caesar to Charles I. And in each case resistance was justified, even demanded, because these rulers were not doing what God required.

There was one major problem with this view, Mayhew realized. Paul clearly commanded Christians to obey their rulers, but he did not clearly say that they could rebel if their kings turned out to be tyrants. But, by way of comparison, Mayhew noted that the same was true for scripture's other commands, such as the command for wives to obey husbands and for children to obey parents. Who could suppose that there would not be exceptions to these commands?[27] God demanded that children obey their parents, for example, but certainly God would not command children to obey a parent who flew into a "mad fit" and tried "to cut all his children's throats."[28] Likewise, Christians were to obey their ministers, but certainly not to respect those who were lazy or corrupt. What about "Right Reverend Drones" who refused to work and "preached, perhaps, but once a year, and then, not the gospel of Jesus Christ," but instead demanded only "the divine right of tithes" from their people?[29] Certainly, God would not demand unlimited submission to such corrupt authorities, whether they were ministers or magistrates.

In effect, therefore, Christians should obey their rulers and respect them, not according to their titles, such as king or governor, but according to how justly they performed their duty "by exercising a reasonable and just authority, for the good of human society."[30] Paul was not commanding obedience to unjust rulers, for "it is blasphemy to call tyrants and oppressors, *God's ministers.*" Instead, "they are more properly the messengers of Satan" than the ministers of God.[31]

Mayhew's sermon is important in part because of his theological perspective. As he had clearly demonstrated in his book *Seven Sermons,* he endorsed liberal theological positions and rejected traditional ones such as the doctrine of Original Sin. Still, he was hardly radical. In linking republican ideas of civil liberty with anti-Catholicism and a Protestant drive for religious liberty, he was advocating ideas shared across theological boundaries.[32]

Apostolic Patriotism in the American Revolution

During the American Revolution, the patriotic character of Paul and Peter was a critical issue. If loyalists were to win the argument, many patriotic ministers knew that the biblical support for the Revolution would be severely damaged. Accordingly, the patriotism of Peter and Paul needed to be defended at all costs. Throngs of patriotic preachers agreed with Pembroke minister Gad Hitchcock's statement: "No man was ever more tender of his liberties, or more desirous to continue such rich blessings in the world than the apostle Paul."[33]

In making their case for apostolic patriotism, Revolutionary-era ministers echoed some of Mayhew's points, but they expanded on them to counter the imposing arguments of the loyalists. Unlike Mayhew, patriotic ministers in wartime faced much higher stakes. Loyalism was a major force of opposition with strong biblical support. So patriotic ministers could not merely mimic Mayhew's arguments and reprint his famous sermon. They had to refine their own interpretations of the apostles against the likes of John Fletcher and Charles Inglis, who argued that the Revolution ran against the apostolic refrain of loyalty to king, God, and country.

Patriotic ministers also had to counter the claims of those who were hesitant to enter a war against Britain even though they chafed at Britain's treatment of the colonies. Among them were many who believed that the fault lay with Parliament, not with George III. For them, loyalist arguments from Romans 13 and 1 Peter 2 resonated with their ingrained respect for the king. The case is even more complicated by the fact that many colonists raged in anger against British policies but stopped short of endorsing any colonial move toward independence. Protest for reform was one thing, armed rebellion another, but an outright separation from Britain and the establishment of a new nation was, for many, no less than treason—reckless, irreverent, and wrong. It was to these colonists that loyalists appealed with the biblical support of Peter and Paul.

In the face of this opposition, patriots claimed that loyalists joined a long tradition of kings who had used Peter and Paul to justify tyranny. Admittedly, this long-standing political distortion of Peter and Paul was difficult to overcome. As John Adams's cousin, Zabdiel, preached in a sermon dedicated to John Hancock, "priests and fawning sycophants" had long "flattered kings" by telling them that Paul supported "the absurd" idea that kings ruled "jure divino." Granted, Paul did write that "the powers which be are ordained of God," but he did not mean "that rulers are elevated to their places by the immediate agency of heaven," nor did he "mean that Peter, Richard, John, Charles, Henry or George are particularly designated to office." Instead, Paul only intended that God favored civil authority and just government. Scripture never taught any "doctrine of unreserved obedience" to a king.[34]

In taking on loyalist interpretations of Peter and Paul, patriotic ministers employed various strategies. One approach, endorsed by David Jones of Philadelphia in 1775, was to clarify what Paul meant when he declared that all "be subject to the higher powers." Loyalists assumed—wrongly, in Jones's view—that "higher powers" referred to monarchs. That was impossible, Jones argued, because it would contradict various places in scripture where God's people heroically defied evil kings. What of Daniel, who refused to obey the Persian King Darius's demand that all his subjects worship his statue? What of Shadrach, Meshach, and Abednego, who faced a fiery furnace rather than worship Nebuchadnezzar's golden image? What of midwives in Egypt who rejected Pharaoh's command to murder Jewish babies? These examples, Jones argued, proved that scripture could not call for an unlimited submission to any earthly ruler.

When Paul called for all to "be subject to the higher powers," therefore, he was referring to "the higher powers" of law—"the just, the good, the wholesome and constitutional laws of a land." It was only through just laws that civil peace and happiness flourished. As most of English history demonstrated, the constitution protected the rights of all, mainly because everyone, including kings, were subject to its laws—they were "as binding on princes as people." Such obedience to law was critical for Paul, because he firmly believed that "anarchy and tyranny are essentially the same, and equally to be dreaded." Jones argued that Peter also placed obedience to the law above submission to kings. Peter called for submission to "every ordinance of man," meaning the laws that "are good, and ordained of GOD" (1 Peter 2:13–14). These divinely ordained civil laws protected the people's rights, defending citizens against all forms of persecution and tyranny.[35]

Any claim that Peter and Paul demanded unlimited submission to civil rulers not only contradicted scripture, it refuted the best insights of recent history. In that view, Henry VIII and other Protestant rulers would have been wrong to disobey the pope. To accept this argument, therefore, would be to reject the Reformation. Likewise, one would have to condemn those English subjects who rightly rejected James II, a tyrant who, like all tyrants, refused to "be subject to the higher powers" of law and instead proclaimed himself above the constitution. Accordingly, the loyalist claim "would lead back to all the horrors of popery and despotism; nay, it would even condemn the blessed martyrs, who refused obedience to arbitrary and wicked laws."[36]

This tactic was one way to deny that Peter and Paul supported the loyalist side. Another approach was to shift attention from their words to their actions. That was the strategy used by several ministers, including David Griffith of Williamsburg, Virginia. Griffith was southern, Anglican, and patriotic. He preached one of the most famous Anglican revolutionary sermons, *Passive Obedience Considered*, before the Virginia Convention at Williamsburg on December 31, 1775.[37]

Griffith admitted that the commands of Peter and Paul seemed to support the "slavish" requirement that Christians obey their rulers no matter the circumstances.[38] But they could not have commanded obedience to tyrannical kings because it was not in their character to do so.[39] Think of how Peter and Paul related to tyrannical rulers, Griffith argued. Did these apostles submit passively to unjust kings? Hardly. The Book of Acts includes several accounts of both apostles standing firm against unjust rulers. When the Romans arrested Paul and threatened to scourge him, for instance, Paul did not submit to authority. Instead, "he condemned this conduct as unjust and tyrannical, and appealed to the Roman constitution," and won his freedom.[40] In a more famous incident, recorded in Acts 16, magistrates in Philippi arrested Paul and Silas, stripped and beat them, and threw them into prison. Late that night, an earthquake broke open the prison doors and ripped off their chains. They could easily have escaped under the cover of darkness, but they defiantly refused to do so. The next morning, the magistrates realized their mistake and sent a message that Paul and Silas should be released. But the prisoners refused to go quietly, demanding that the magistrates meet them face to face and admit their unjust imprisonment. "Here is, beyond contradiction," Griffith preached, "an instance where this very Paul, who is said to have recommended passive obedience to Christians, absolutely refused to obey the command of magistrates. The reason...is obvious; he meant to reprove them for the unjust punishment, inflicted on him and Silas; and for exercising their authority in a tyrannical manner."[41]

Loyalist claims that Paul advocated passive obedience, therefore, were false, clearly inconsistent with Paul's consistent protests against tyranny. Paul was neither a coward nor a sycophant. He never hesitated to stand up for his rights. Given Paul's own conflicts with rulers in his day, it was "hardly to be imagined" that Paul would have demanded that Christians obey "every dictate of power, however unjust and oppressive, and however contrary to the divine will and intentions."[42]

The same was true of Peter. Though he commanded that Christians submit to the king, this command could not simply be torn from the Bible and cited in defense of civil authority. Peter hardly submitted to authority when he stood defiantly against the high priest who had thrown him and John into prison for preaching the Gospel. When the priest and other elders warned Peter and John to stop preaching, Peter boldly replied that they would obey God rather than human authorities. This was, for Griffith, plainly applicable to Revolutionary America. Certainly, Peter and Paul, unlike American patriots, had been directly commanded by God to revolt against civil power. But the situations were not entirely different. "Whenever oppression and injustice are exercised by the ruling powers, the commands of God are broken," whether in Imperial Rome or revolutionary Virginia.[43]

Griffith claimed that the apostles bore a strong resemblance to American patriots. Paul, for instance, was a Roman citizen, but he had to assert his rights against tyrants who denied them. Similarly, the colonists were British citizens, but the British government had denied them their rights, including the right to be represented in government. "In my opinion," Griffith preached, "the doctrine of transubstantiation is not a greater absurdity than the notion of America's being represented in the British parliament."[44]

Griffith's audience, as anti-Catholic as it was patriotic, would have agreed. "Though not born in Britain," the colonists were "as much entitled to the privileges of Englishmen, as St. Paul was to those of a Roman citizen, though born at Tarsus." In addition, like Paul, American colonists "have asserted their claim and appealed to the constitution of their country for relief from the arbitrary will" of tyrannical government.[45] Far from being supporters of loyalism, therefore, Peter and Paul had impeccable patriotic credentials.

The Apostle Paul's "American Motto" (Galatians 5:1)

The apostles' patriotic credentials were even more strongly confirmed by Paul's inspiring proclamation, "Stand fast, therefore, in the liberty wherewith Christ hath made us free" (Galatians 5:1). Above all, this verse meant, as Presbyterian John Zubly of Georgia preached in 1775 (before he became a loyalist), that "Freedom is the very spirit and temper of the gospel."[46] And yet, neither "freedom" nor "liberty" was a common word in scripture, so Paul's admonition was a rare commodity: a clear, biblical endorsement of liberty. Not surprisingly, this passage became the third most popular of the Revolutionary era. It was, as historian Harry Stout observed, "an American motto" that filled sermons and speeches throughout the war.[47]

In his enormously influential essays from 1768, *Letters from a Farmer in Pennsylvania*, the affluent Philadelphia lawyer John Dickinson made much of this verse. Dickinson viewed Paul's statement as biblical proof that freedom was the design of creation. God "hath made us free," meaning that freedom was a "birthright" ordained by heaven. "Divine providence" allowed him to live in "a land of freedom," Dickinson wrote, so he would defend that freedom against any tyrannical attempt to take it away. Later, Dickinson did defend American independence, but he was at first hesitant to do so, as he held out hope for reconciliation with Britain.[48]

The Continental Congress heard a sermon on this text on July 7, 1775, Jacob Duché's aptly titled *The Duty of Standing Fast in our Spiritual and Temporal Liberties*. Duché preached that Paul was an apostle of liberty who "was jealous of the least attempt to destroy or even obstruct" the blessings of freedom.[49] Duché dedicated his sermon to General George Washington, expressing great admiration for Washington's "many amiable virtues" both public and private. The admiration was evidently mutual, to the point that Washington was shocked when Duché sided with the British two years later. Duché even wrote to Washington at Valley Forge, calling on him to abandon the revolutionary cause. In reacting, Washington wrote that he "had entertained the most favorable opinion" of Duché, and so he was "not more surprised than concerned at receiving so extraordinary a letter from" him.[50] Not surprisingly, Duché's reputation never recovered. From a patriotic perspective, he was a disgrace because he did not practice the command from Paul that he preached—to "stand fast" for liberty.

An even more famous sermon on Paul's patriotic motto came from a much-celebrated patriot of the pulpit, Judah Champion of Litchfield, Connecticut. Like Duché's sermon, Champion's *Christian and Civil Liberty and Freedom Considered and Recommended* portrayed Paul as the apostle of revolutionary liberty and dwelt extensively on Galatians 5:1 as its main text. Champion's patriotic reputation expanded beyond the notoriety of this sermon, however. He was also well known for a prayer he delivered in a church service attended by Major Benjamin Tallmadge and his cavalry regiment. Here Champion explicitly called on God to fight against the British troops. "O Lord," Champion prayed, "wilt thou send storm and tempest to toss them upon the sea, to overwhelm them in the mighty deep, or scatter them to the utmost parts of the earth." Further, "should they escape thy vengeance, collect them together again, O Lord, . . . and let thy lightenings play upon them." Champion also called on God to equip the American troops with "swords terrible as that of thy destroying angel, that they may cleave [the British] down."[51] Champion's patriotic credentials were unquestioned. He was one of many clergy who moved from the pulpit to the battlefield, serving as a chaplain in battles at Ticonderoga and Saratoga.

Given his involvement in the war, no one knew better than Champion the patriotic authority of Paul's "American motto." Champion selected this verse as the main text for *Christian and Civil Liberty and Freedom Considered*, because he believed that "the liberty wherewith Christ hath made us free" was both religious and civil, and both types of liberty were mutually reinforcing. Even a cursory glance at history told colonial Americans how important civil liberty was to maintaining a Christian influence in society. Tyrants such as Charles I imperiled both kinds of liberty, which is why opposition to his tyranny was a Christian duty. Charles I, by his "lawless endeavors," ignited "a civil war, which raged until his blood quenched the flame."[52]

That "flame" needed to be "quenched" again in Revolutionary America, Champion argued. As threatening as the English Civil War had been, the revolution in America imperiled freedom even more severely. "Our privileges, civil and sacred, are imminently endangered," he preached.[53] The previous years had seen Parliament impose "cruel edicts" that violated "our essential rights." Among such violations, Champion mentioned the Quebec Act of 1774, in which Britain explicitly welcomed the practice of Catholicism in Canada. This move stirred fears among many colonists, who were predominantly anti-Catholic. "Is not the King of Great-Britain, by the Quebec bill, set at the head of the Romish church in Canada?" This was just one of many clear threats to "our sacred as well as civil privileges," Champion asserted.[54] These unjust policies had no righteous or reasonable defense; they could only be enforced by unlawful war. "Fleets and armies have been sent over, compelling us either to disobey" Paul's "divine precept" in defense of liberty, or to wage war. The choice of war, while terrible, was also noble. It was the colonists' only way to honor Paul's command to "stand fast" for freedom. The price was heavy, however. From Lexington and Concord on, the British proved themselves to be "inhuman murderers," fully "inglorious to the British arms."[55]

In coping with "the horrors of a civil war," patriots could turn to Paul as a biblical witness that liberty was worth the sacrifice. Liberty was "one of heaven's choicest blessings," Champion preached. It "inspires the human breast with noblest sentiments—dilates the heart—expands the soul, and is the source of almost every thing excellent and desirable on earth." In contrast, "slavery" was an incalculable evil that "debases the mind—clogs the finest movements of the soul," and promotes "universal misery."[56]

It was for this liberty that their Puritan forbears had come to America, Champion reminded the colonists. And "the ghosts of" these Puritan witnesses had critical advice for Revolutionary America: follow Paul's command. Just as Christ purchased this freedom "at the inestimable price of his blood," that freedom, both "civil and sacred," had been fought for and won "through rivers of blood." Patriots could not cast away their "civil and sacred" liberties "without incurring JEHOVAH'S most tremendous indignation and curse." The revolutionary cause was "glorious," admired in heaven, where "GOD, Angels and Saints in glory are looking on." As Champion asserted, "Heaven demands your most vigorous exertions." In fighting the war, patriots should "let the blood of CHRIST animate you." If patriots did as God commanded, then "Zion's GOD will support his cause in America."[57]

Champion knew the importance of the Bible, and particularly of Paul, to the cause. His main purpose was to prove that the "servile doctrines of indefeasible right, passive obedience, and non-resistance, are not the doctrines of reason, good policy or revelation. An attempt to vindicate them from scripture is highly criminal."

Other ministers read Paul's command to "stand fast" for liberty as a warning against loyalism, pacifism, sloth, or any other vice that prevented Americans from arming themselves against the British. No minister better communicated this than Nathaniel Whitaker in his often-quoted sermon from 1777 *An antidote against Toryism*. Whitaker, a Presbyterian minister from Salem, Massachusetts, dedicated his sermon to George Washington, "his Excellency" and "Commander and chief of the Forces of the United States of America." Whitaker wanted to uphold Washington's example as a heroic leader of a "band of Heroes" in the Continental Army. Their heroism derived from their selfless benevolence—they loved the cause of liberty more than they valued their lives. It was their benevolence and their "serene bravery" that inspired them to "wing their way through legions of opposing Tyrants, to victory and triumph." The crisis they faced, however, was all the more grave because of the legions of Americans who had not taken up the patriotic cause. Instead of being fired by benevolent zeal for liberty and self-sacrifice, they sought self-preservation. Instead of fighting against tyranny, they lusted after profit. Such unpatriotic people threatened not only the revolution, but the cause of Christ. After all, as Whitaker asserted, Washington and his army were not only fighting political enemies, they were fighting "enemies of God and man that invade our rights." In searching the scriptures to find support for his avid patriotism, Whitaker found many texts from the Old Testament, but Paul's command to "stand fast" for liberty was the ultimate proof that freedom's cause was God's cause. To refuse to join the patriotic drive against British tyranny, was no less than "a sin against the express command of God."[58]

From the patriots' perspective, Paul's command to "stand fast" for liberty was above all a martial command. Paul called for courage, and in the 1770s courage meant war. In his sermon to a militia company in Lunenburg on January 2, 1775, Zabdiel Adams called on patriots to "stand fast" for the liberty won by Christ's blood against the machinations of sinful people and tyrannical nations. To defend this liberty, patriots would need to unite around the cause of liberty, "a virtuous character," a real appreciation of their rights, and, above all, expertise in "the arts and instruments of war."[59] It was military zeal above all else that safeguarded liberty. "So much depends on the military character of a people," Adams asserted, well aware of the ominous signs of war in early 1775. Unfortunately, as Adams knew, the colonies were not yet ready "to meet the enemy in the gate," so they needed to rectify that situation immediately by strengthening their military capacities. They needed to follow Paul's call to defend the liberty granted by Christ. Failure was a realistic threat, but only through weakness in either character or "in military skill"—and the two were intimately related.[60]

More clearly than any other text from the New Testament, Paul's letter to the Galatians gushed with liberty—nearly unbounded liberty, liberty that was both civil and Christian. Clearly, many patriots believed they had a religious duty to battle the British. Both nature and scripture called on them to defend their rights against political tyranny.

The republican enthusiasm that rendered Paul so supportive of civil liberty caused problems when it came to religious liberty. How far did Paul's enthusiasm for liberty go? For many patriots, religious liberty meant, primarily, the obligation to oppose Catholic tyranny. Colonies were free to support Protestant churches as they chose, without foreign interference. For other colonial patriots, however, religious liberty meant that the colonies had no authority to force citizens to pay taxes to support an official church. If Christians were to "stand fast" for liberty against both civil and spiritual tyranny, what were the implications for church and state?

Some colonists discovered that Paul's endorsement of liberty could not only help patriots to fight the British; it also could combat tax-supported, established churches. In New England, Separates and Baptists claimed that patriotism required opposition to religious tyranny as much as civil tyranny. One sermon that was especially deft in making this connection was Jonathan Parsons's *Freedom from Civil and Ecclesiastical Slavery*. Parsons's sermon was overtly patriotic: He preached from Newburyport, Massachusetts, on March 5, 1774, the fourth anniversary of the famous Boston Massacre, and dedicated the sermon to John Hancock. Although it was over a year before the war would begin, it was three months after the destruction of the tea in Boston harbor, and New England was seething with outrage against British policies. So Parsons selected Paul's admonition to "stand fast" for freedom as the basis for his sermon to commemorate "the bloody Massacre, the barbarous butchery at Boston four years ago."[61] Recalling "the awful catastrophe," Parsons condemned the British in no uncertain terms. They were "sons of violence and blood" and were "worse than butchering Soldiers!" Parsons hoped that the memory of that bloody evening "be ever deeply engraven upon our hearts as it is this day!" Those memories of past atrocities would inspire future resistance, Parsons hoped, and that resistance promised to be both violent and God-inspired. He hoped that the "spirit of Christian benevolence would animate us to fill our streets with blood, rather than suffer others to rob us of our rights."[62]

As a Separate, however, Parsons was at least as focused on the religious tyranny in Massachusetts as he was on the civil crimes of Britain. Separates such as Parsons were Congregationalists whose support of revivalism compelled them to separate from the established church. Although not all revivalists were patriotic, most were, and Parsons was one of those who believed that evangelicalism and patriotism reinforced each other completely. It is appropriate, therefore, that Parsons preached this patriotic sermon from a church that also held the crypt of George Whitefield.[63] This mutually reinforcing zeal for revivalism and patriotism inspired Parsons to call on patriotic Christians in the established churches to account for their own tyranny. He called on patriots to be as zealous for liberty in church governance as they had been in civil matters. He hoped to harness the patriotic zeal for civil freedom and apply it to the church. Speaking of Massachusetts, he admitted that "it looks odd to me" that a colony could be so opposed to civil tyranny and yet so supportive of "ecclesiastical tyranny."[64] For Parsons, therefore, Paul's command to "stand fast" for liberty was spiritual and political. Religious liberty was not only a rejection of Catholic tyranny but opposition to colonial taxes that forced Separates to support churches from which they had departed.

The Baptists were even more radical than the Separates. One famous Baptist was John Leland, who hailed from Massachusetts but spent much of his preaching career in Virginia. Leland, an outspoken defender of religious liberty, famously stated the radical view that "government has no more to do with the religious opinions of men, than it has with the principles of mathematics."[65]

The leading Baptist advocate for religious liberty was Isaac Backus, a New England farmer turned revivalist who followed the path from Congregationalist to Separate and finally to Baptist. Believing as he did that Baptists were the most faithful practitioners of true revivalism and the authentic liberty of conscience, he was savvy in his use of republican language to argue for religious liberty. He was also biblically savvy, which explains why he turned to Paul's teaching on liberty in Galatians 5 as the main text for his most important treatise, *Appeal to the Public for Religious Liberty*, published in 1773.[66]

Backus condemned the vast hypocrisy of demanding civil liberty while enforcing spiritual tyranny. "Where is the officer that will dare to come in the name of the Lord to demand, and forcibly to take, a tax which is imposed by the civil state!" Moreover, what kind of minister is not satisfied "with all that Christ's name and influence will procure for him, but will have recourse to the kings of the earth, to force money from the people" in the name of God? Such practice, in Backus's view, seemed more like spiritual slaveholding than Christian ministry. Baptists could not obey the command "to stand fast in the liberty wherewith he has made us free" unless they refuse to obey "some laws about religious affairs that are laid upon us."[67] Such religious taxes were no more than taxation without representation, the very complaint patriots rightly made against the British.[68] In a final flourish, Backus asserted that patriots could not call on God to "turn the heart" of George III "to hear" patriotic "pleas for liberty" if these same patriots did not "hear the cries of their fellow-subjects" for religious liberty. In effect, as Backus asserted, "it is impossible for any one to tyrannize over others, without thereby becoming a miserable slave himself."[69]

No Americans were more patriotic than the Baptists, in Backus's view, because Baptists embraced complete patriotism, along with both civil and religious liberty. The opponents of the Baptists claimed otherwise, however. When Backus argued against disestablishment before the Continental Congress in 1774, John Adams and Samuel Adams dismissed the Baptists' claims as unimportant and meddlesome. Supporters of church establishments saw them as the natural order of things, so much so that, as Backus later commented, changing such establishments was comparable to altering "the solar system."[70] Despite their avowed dedication to the most thorough ideas of liberty, Baptists gained a reputation for loyalism. Such claims were mostly false, though there were notable exceptions, including the well-known Baptist historian Morgan Edwards. Backus defended Baptists as true patriots overall.[71] Most of all, however, Backus demonstrated that Baptists could adeptly shape republicanism to address ecclesial grievances. He did so by leading with Paul's admonition on liberty.

French Connections: Post-Revolutionary Apostolic Patriotism

Even the most zealous patriot knew that liberty, once unleashed, could be impossible to control. Some patriots saw this fact reconfirmed when Baptists like Backus marshaled republican arguments to deny all church establishments. This was an extreme move, many patriots believed, especially in New England, but it was a predictable one—a logical though worrisome extension of republicanism. Clearly, liberty needed to be rightly understood and properly focused. Even the most sincere desire for freedom from oppression could, if improperly controlled, lead to disaster. So patriots sought to define freedom, to channel it in productive ways, and no force was more important in this effort than the Bible. Furthermore, of all biblical texts, none was more helpful in defining the limits of liberty than the letters of Peter and Paul, especially the texts that had been so important to loyalists, Romans 13 and 1 Peter 2.

As the Revolution ended, therefore, the heady appeals to rebellion and Paul's zeal for liberty in Galatians 5 gave way to renewed appreciation for Paul's and Peter's calls for submission to government. In the Revolution, patriotic ministers had interpreted Romans 13 with careful qualifiers: Paul had commanded obedience only to just rulers and not tyrants. And yet the post-revolutionary need to bring people together into a "United States" caused ministers to refer back to Paul's endorsement of good rulers and just governments. Many Americans worried that no government could contain republicanism, once unleashed.

In these times, many feared anarchy as much as they had feared tyranny in 1776. So in May, 1783, one month after Congress officially declared the Revolutionary War to be over, Henry Cumings of Billerica, Massachusetts, called on Paul's calming endorsement of civil authority in Romans 13. "While civil rulers are to be cautioned against an abuse of authority, and exhorted to employ their powers for the good of the public; people are to be put in mind to honour and obey magistrates; to be subject unto the higher powers, and to submit themselves to every ordinance of man, for the Lord's sake." "When people give way to a refractory temper" and oppose government and disrespect their rulers, Cumings preached, political stability dissolved. "Let people be vigilant and guarded against the encroachments of arbitrary power; but let them, at the same time, take heed, that they deprive not themselves of the blessings of good government, and plunge themselves into all the disorders and mischiefs of anarchy, in order to secure themselves against tyranny." Running to either extreme would be disaster. What was needed, therefore, was "the middle course" advocated by Paul.[72]

In the hands of revolutionary patriots, therefore, Romans 13 was a biblical safeguard against unbridled liberty and radical republicanism. In the few years after 1776, Thomas Paine's classic statements in *Common Sense* still resonated with many Americans. "Society," Paine wrote, "is produced by our wants, and government by our wickedness; the former promotes our happiness positively by uniting our affections, the latter negatively by restraining our vices." "Society" is always "a blessing" while "Government even in its best state is but a necessary evil; in its worst state an intolerable one."[73] Government may have been "a necessary evil," but all governments were not necessarily evil, and post-revolutionary patriots would do well to recognize the distinction. Both ministers and governors alike worried that this distinction would be lost, so ministers employed Romans 13 to provide biblical support for the state.

It is no wonder, then, that Zabdiel Adams generously expounded on Romans 13 in his sermon dedicated to John Hancock in May of 1782. If any think that government is "unnecessary," Adams preached, then "Let them try; let them live without government if they can." Those present-day "enthusiasts" who deny the godly role of government were merely ignorant. Paine may have been right to value society over government, but without government there can be no society. To reinforce his point, Adams quoted both Paul and Peter, asserting that government was "an *appointment* of heaven, the *ordination* of God, who is a God *of order and not of confusion.*" Enemies of good government were enemies of God, therefore, doomed to die by the magistrate's sword. For, as Paul had made clear, the ruler was "the minister of God, a revenger to execute wrath upon him that doth evil." Leaning heavily on both apostles, Adams the patriot was as pro-government as any loyalist: "From these passages it appears, not only that government is an ordinance of heaven, but also that obedience to it is a duty enjoined under the highest penalty." Moreover, "rebellion against such authority is as the sin of witchcraft, and stubbornness as the iniquity of idolatry." And yet, ever the patriot, Adams asserted the necessary qualifier: the rulers deserving of such respect were those who were "introduced into office by the choice of the people, and are upright and faithful in their stations." These rulers had the right to ultimate rule. The people should even treat them "as the Dictator, when he marched thro' the streets of Rome, preceded by Lictors, bearing axes and rods."[74]

Patriotic endorsements of dictators were striking in Revolutionary America, but they reveal the concern that many patriots had for good government and republican society. In making these arguments, post-revolutionary patriots wrested Peter's and Paul's pro-government texts from loyalist control. In so doing, they reinterpreted Paul and Peter as a biblical means of coming to terms with the legacy of the Revolution.

This revolutionary legacy was never debated more furiously than in American reactions to the French Revolution. In the minds of many Americans, the French Revolution was a republican dream that had quickly morphed into a riotous nightmare. The Revolution in France broke out just as the United States was taking shape under its new Constitution. As Americans heard the news of France's revolution, most of them celebrated the spread of liberty around the world. France, the nation that had helped Americans defeat British tyranny in the American Revolution, seemed to be following the pattern set by American patriots. When the French defeated invasions from Austria and Prussia in September 1792, Americans celebrated. Songs from the French Revolution became popular in America, and the French made honorary citizens of several American founders, including George Washington and Thomas Paine.

The widespread American celebration of the French Revolution did not last long, however. When the revolution turned radical, some Americans, especially Federalists—who were horrified by the anarchy in France, and were even more concerned with French influence in America—worried about republican liberty run amuck. These anxieties peaked when Americans learned that the French had executed King Louis XVI in January 1793. This regicide seemed rash to Americans who remembered Louis XVI as the king who supported their Revolutionary War. Then, just weeks after executing Louis XVI, France launched a war against England. Not all Americans were apprehensive about these events, however. Thomas Jefferson firmly believed that Louis XVI had gotten what he deserved for being the tyrant that he was, regardless of his former aid to Americans. So Americans were divided in their reactions to the French Revolution, and these divisions reflected the political divisions that had been developing between Federalists and Republicans.[75]

The turmoil of the French Revolution brought the patriotic reputation of the apostles to the forefront once again. For those who feared that French anarchy and intrigue would spread to America, Romans 13 seemed to be a biblical antidote to anarchy. This text, along with a few others from Paul, provided the main biblical support for Salem minister John Prince's sermon against French revolutionary influence, delivered on May 9, 1798. President Adams had proclaimed this to be a national fast day, set aside for Americans to pray about "the difficulties subsisting between the United States and France."[76]

Prince, a liberal minister and quasi-scientist, chose the declared fast day to preach a sermon that was about France, though it was decidedly for America. The United States needed to be warned, Prince believed, that French influences were infiltrating the new nation with disastrous results. It was this danger that had prompted President Adams to declare a national day of prayer. The French menace threatened America first by dividing the people among themselves—the very party spirit that split the nation into political factions arose in part from French designs. In addition to planting this discord among Americans, French radical thought entrenched an even subtler and more dangerous force: luring Americans to reject government's virtuous and just authority. The French threat was so powerful because it began with liberty, an ideal that Americans valued. But French radicalism turned America's desire for freedom to evil purposes. Certainly, "every true patriot" had to agree with the principles that ignited the French Revolution, Prince said. But these principles did not reign supreme in France, as the revolution took a violent and radical turn and became a tyrannical enemy of liberty. In France, liberty was no more than a decoy. The story of the French Revolution was "the imposition of tyranny under the name of liberty."[77]

No authority, no matter how sacred, was safe from attack by French radicals, Prince warned. Under French influence, radical republicans had the audacity to attack President Adams and even His Excellency, George Washington. Adams and Washington had been providentially proven moral and trustworthy—God had favored them. Consider especially Washington, Prince said. "In the early stage of our struggle for liberty, when the enemy bore down all opposition, and spread himself like a torrent through the country," recall how God "inspired the illustrious Washington to attempt the scene at Trenton, and turn the scale of victory in our favor, with a few men." To be sure, if the radical, French-inspired Republicans were right in their attacks on Adams and Washington, "we are hopeless indeed." Undoubtedly, Prince argued, if Americans cannot trust Washington and Adams, they can trust no one, and the cause is lost.[78]

Religion was a major element in the French plan. Though Prince did not mention him here, Thomas Paine may well have been much on his mind. Paine's *Age of Reason,* an overt attack on traditional Christianity, had burst upon the American scene in the mid-1790s, much to the horror of Christians throughout the United States. As Paine's book became a bestseller—the best-selling book about religion of its time—Paine's reputation suffered immensely, and many Americans associated his deistic attack on Christian theology with his radical endorsement of the French Revolution. Not only Paine, but other French radicals knew the value of religion as a persuasive force. So Prince, who was no theological conservative, warned against "political intriguers, who have long since discarded a belief" in God's "agency in the affairs of the world, well know how to make use of that zeal and political ignorance to carry on their views against the government."[79]

In response, Prince turned to the apostles. Nearly every biblical reference in Prince's sermon came from Paul. Prince especially called on Americans to read Paul's Romans 13 and to be reminded that Christianity was not antigovernment. Instead, Christianity, as the apostles taught it, favored stability over anarchy, and respect for civil rulers as long as they ruled justly.[80] Revolutions were sometimes necessary, of course, but revolutionaries must always claim their rights "in such a cool, deliberate and wise manner" as to "remove the evils they suffer" without plunging into "the evils of anarchy." The French Revolution had gone awry because it had abandoned the necessary safeguards of liberty—authentic virtue and Protestant Christianity, both of which Prince found revealed clearly in the apostles, and especially in Paul.[81]

When Jonathan Mayhew stepped in to the pulpit to celebrate the repeal of the Stamp Act in May 1766, it was only natural for him to call on Peter's command to "fear God" and "honor the king." After all, King George III and his government had averted disaster by putting aside the Stamp Act, so Mayhew waxed eloquent on the colonists' longtime loyalty to the king. But even as he praised and called on his American colleagues to honor his majesty, Mayhew carefully stipulated his reasons. The king was to be praised not simply because he was the British monarch. Instead, the king was to be praised for the character of his rule. So Peter's command was not unqualified: one was to "honor the king," but only if the king merited the honor in the sight of God and good British citizens. As Mayhew described, George III had given "proof of his Majesty's moderation" in that he had shown concern for "the welfare of his people." The King had also proven himself ready "to redress" the "grievances" of the colonists, who had been "reasonable and humble" in their protests against the Stamp Act.

One could argue, and many did, that some of the American protests against the Stamp Act were neither "reasonable" nor "humble." But Mayhew had made his point: the Stamp Act deserved condemnation; American colonists rightly hated it, and, thankfully, the British government had relented. Of course, it soon would be clear that Mayhew's optimism was unfounded. The repeal of the Stamp Act was not the end of hostilities between Britain and the colonies; it was merely the beginning. Moreover, if the revolutionary struggle in America can be dated to the Stamp Act, it can also be supported by the revolutionary patriotism of Peter and Paul. So Mayhew appropriately called on the apostles, naming Peter in particular, to qualify Peter's apparently unqualified claim for absolute allegiance to the king.[82]

In the view of Revolutionary-era patriots, Peter and Paul located republicanism at the center of the New Testament, and, consequently, at the center of Christianity. Appeals to Old Testament wars in Revolutionary America could be contested, and they were. Nearly everyone believed that much of the Old Testament was typological— that is, the Old Testament was filled with dimly revealed symbols that found fulfillment and greater clarity in the New Testament. Conceivably, God's endorsement of wars, even wars fought for liberty such as the Revolution, could have been an antiquated relic of the Hebrew past that had no relevance either to the New Testament or the eighteenth century. Accordingly, no biblical argument from the Revolution could be convincing without claiming the support of the New Testament. And no revolutionary argument from the New Testament was complete without the support of Peter and Paul.

It is not surprising, therefore, that specific texts from Peter and Paul were the most controversial biblical texts in the American Revolution. Their commands to obey civil authorities became linchpins in the loyalist Bible, so patriots needed to answer these commands with revised, republican readings. For them, the spirit of the apostolic mission had to cohere with the spirit of '76.

6

"The Fierceness and Wrath of Almighty God"

REVELATION IN THE REVOLUTION

AMERICANS HAVE LONG been fascinated by apocalyptic ideas. The book of Revelation, the only apocalyptic book in the New Testament, has captivated and confused Americans from the colonial era to today. In Revelation, Americans have pondered images of Antichrist—which one historian called "an American obsession." Although the term "Antichrist" is nowhere to be found in Revelation, Americans have found the power of Antichrist in its pages—in mysterious numbers, images of a dragon, a whore, and wild beasts with multiple horns. In addition, Americans have used Revelation to support vivid speculations about the end of the world and Christ's thousand-year (millennial) reign. Overall, drawing on apocalyptic ideas, Americans have waged wars, pursued peace and health, founded new movements, supported and refuted slavery, advocated and opposed religious liberty, and launched terrorist attacks.

One prominent American who did not share this American apocalyptic interest was Thomas Jefferson. In 1825, Jefferson wrote that he had not read the book of Revelation in about sixty years, and for good reason. Revelation, in Jefferson's opinion, was "merely the ravings of a Maniac, no more worthy, nor capable of explanation than the incoherences of our own nightly dreams."[1]

Jefferson notwithstanding, if apocalyptic and millennial ideas have been an American obsession, they have been an obsession of historians as well. For years, when historians thought of the Bible in the American Revolution, they thought almost exclusively of apocalyptic ideas, and usually focused on millennialism. So many historians have examined millennialism in the American Revolution that, as Gordon Wood observed in 1997, the "historical literature on Revolutionary millennialism is approaching in complexity and sophistication the finespun discussions eighteenth-century clergymen themselves had on the subject."[2] Historians drew on several prominent sermons about the millennial destiny of America. One of the most cited of these was one we have already discussed, Samuel Sherwood's *Church's Flight into the Wilderness* from January, 1776, which included the stirring lines that few historians could resist: "God Almighty, with all the powers of heaven, are on our side. Great numbers of angels, no doubt, are encamping round our coast, for our defense and protection. Michael [a mighty angel of God] stands ready; with all the artillery of heaven, to encounter the dragon, and to vanquish this black host." Impressed by this kind of dramatic, apocalyptic rhetoric, historians have concluded that patriotic ministers combined their expectations for Christ's millennial reign on earth with republican political ideology to create a "civil millennialism," in which the Revolutionary War would launch the millennium, and the American republic would play a vital role in redeeming the world.[3]

Since the mid-1980s, some historians have been eager to deny millennialism's dominance in the Revolutionary era.[4] They have granted that millennialism was an important religious view in colonial America but denied that it dominated religious arguments for the Revolution. According to these historians, Samuel Sherwood was one of the few ministers to predict when and how the millennium would begin—a risky venture in any age—and he was one of even fewer who predicted that the Revolution could signal the crowning glory of history and the inauguration of the millennium.[5]

Moreover, these historians point out that the few ministers who made such grand millennial predictions for America often acknowledged that they were controversial. Sherwood certainly did, and so did Connecticut minister Ebenezer Baldwin in another often-cited sermon from 1776, *Duty of Rejoicing under Calamities*. Here Baldwin famously predicted that the colonies would "be the principal Seat of that glorious Kingdom, which Christ shall erect upon Earth in the latter Days." But even as he made this grand claim, Baldwin cautioned that it was "a Conjecture," and he added a footnote, acknowledging that "I had Thoughts of suppressing this Conjecture in the Publication of the Sermon, fearful lest it should appear whimsical and Enthusiastical."[6] Baldwin's sermon fit a common pattern— grand, millennial predictions often included obligatory disclaimers.

The question of millennialism's influence in Revolutionary America largely turns on how patriots applied the Bible to the war. And yet this is the problem because, as this book has shown, historians have lacked accurate and comprehensive information on this very question. Equipped with the new research that forms the basis of this book, we now know more than ever about how the Bible was actually interpreted in colonial American wars, particularly the Revolution, so we are in a position to reassess the primary question: Was millennialism really the key to religious patriotism in the Revolution?

The evidence indicates that the revisionist historians are primarily correct: millennialism did not dominate patriotic appeals to scripture in revolutionary America. If ministers were as focused on an American millennium as some historians have claimed, we would expect to find the book of Revelation listed among the most cited scriptures in Revolutionary America. Yet wartime ministers rarely preached on Revelation, or on the apocalyptic scriptures from the Old Testament. In the ranking of most popular biblical texts that ministers preached on when addressing war, we do not find an apocalyptic text in the top ten or even the top twenty-five. Instead, the most cited apocalyptic text in wartime is only the forty-first most-cited biblical text during the period 1674–1800. If we restrict our view to the Revolutionary era, apocalyptic texts were more popular. Still, the top-cited text ranked twenty-ninth.[7]

To be sure, ministers found millennial teachings throughout the Bible, not only in apocalyptic scriptures. Overall, however, apocalyptic scriptures were most important for shaping millennial ideas. Millennialism is, after all, an apocalyptic concept, drawn largely from apocalyptic scriptures. Strictly defined, millennialism is "the belief that there will be a period of peace and righteousness on the earth associated with the Second coming of Christ," and it is based primarily on Revelation 20:1–10.[8] So the fact that apocalyptic scriptures did not dominate revolutionary-era preaching is one significant indicator that ministers may not have focused on millennialism.[9]

If most ministers were not focused unduly on the millennium, how *did* they use the Bible to support their patriotic views? Previous chapters have answered this question to a large extent by examining the many biblical texts that outranked apocalyptic texts in colonial American war sermons. But what about the apocalyptic texts? Apocalyptic scriptures may not have been the most popular in wartime, but many preachers did use them. How, then, did apocalyptic scriptures, especially the Revelation, influence revolutionary patriots? Taking into account all varieties of wartime and military sermons, including many from outside New England, I argue that apocalyptic preaching focused less on America's millennial role in the future than it did on present, urgent needs in battle—especially the need to proclaim a militant Christianity that would recruit zealous patriots for a righteous cause.

The focus here is therefore on apocalyptic militancy, not an American millennium. Above all, revolutionary patriots read apocalyptic scriptures much as they read other biblical texts—as martial scriptures holding great relevance for American wars. That does not mean, however, that apocalyptic scriptures were not valuable for what they brought to wartime views. If we focus on Revelation, by far the most popular apocalyptic book in colonial America, we find that it had unique patriotic value. For some colonists, the book of Revelation supported patriotism as no other biblical book could. This apocalyptic patriotism took shape over time, in response to the challenges of colonial battles. These challenges came from several directions—from loyalists and pacifists, many of whom had biblical arguments of their own, and from the overmatched and ill-prepared colonial troops.

Previous chapters have assessed these wartime challenges, so this chapter reveals how ministers preached messages of Christian militancy from the most popular apocalyptic scriptures in Revolutionary America. Granted, these texts were not the only apocalyptic texts that were important to ministers as the colonies went to war. All the dramatic, violent images in Revelation—the beasts, dragons, martyrs, and more—gave patriotic ministers ample ammunition for the wartime pulpit, and they drew various messages from the sheer variety of apocalyptic images. In the hands of Revolutionary-era ministers, Revelation could support patriotism or loyalism; it could inspire an optimistic vision of future American glory, or it could warn of impending doom for the colonies. By examining these texts, we find that whether or not ministers made dramatic claims about America's millennial future, most of them agreed that wartime patriotism, as revealed in apocalyptic scripture, exemplified both selfless republican virtue and sacrificial Christian discipleship—following Christ, the ultimate patriot, who was courageous on the battlefield and on the cross.[10]

Patriotic Martyrdom in the Letters to the Seven Churches (Revelation 2)

In some ways the most popular apocalyptic text in colonial American wars is also the simplest. Unlike most apocalyptic scriptures, it has no strange symbols to decipher—no dramatic visions of beasts and dragons, no mysterious numbers, and no multicolored horses. Instead, the most popular apocalyptic chapter in wartime was Revelation 2, which contains the first of the letters that Christ directed John to write to seven churches in Asia. These letters included judgment and promise, mixed messages to be sure, but they focused above all on how the seven churches had witnessed for the faith (or not) during a harsh period of persecution. Colonial ministers found much of this material relevant to their own wars, but they specially seized upon Christ's command to the church in Smyrna: "Fear none of those things which thou shalt suffer: behold, the devil shall cast some of you into prison, that ye may be tried; and ye shall have tribulation ten days: be thou faithful unto death, and I will give thee a crown of life" (Revelation 2:10).

This command, ominous and encouraging at the same time, served colonial ministers well. Noticeably, the text said nothing of the millennium and offered no lofty view of national destiny; nor did it anticipate the outcome of war. What the passage did offer, however, was a message that ministers found essential in wartime: a pastoral way of coping with the real-life threat of death on the battlefield. To recruit soldiers for the war effort, ministers had to instill in men the courage to die and to kill. As we have seen, the courage to kill was considered the "harder courage."[11] But death was certainly much on the minds of soldiers. The courage to die, ministers believed, came only through the assurance of salvation, which soldiers could gain by waging "spiritual warfare" against sin. Ministers continuously reinforced the symbiotic relationship between soldiers' military battles against civil tyranny and their spiritual battles against the tyranny of sin. Soldiers needed to engage both types of wars zealously, because God only rewarded those who were "faithful unto death," both spiritually and militarily. As colonial ministers saw it, soldiers had to be faithful Christians, worthy of being rewarded with "a crown of life" if the battle required their deaths. Moreover, soldiers had to be faithful in battle, courageous soldiers, fighting for the cause.

This message was virtually the same in the Revolutionary War as it had been in previous American wars. One of the most practical invocations of Revelation 2:10 appeared in Ebenezer Prime's sermon from New York, *The Importance of the Divine Presence with the Armies of God's People.* Prime, a Presbyterian pastor from Long Island, preached it to provincial troops in Suffolk county on May 7, 1759. At this point in the French and Indian

War, colonial patriotism was on an upswing. Secretary of State William Pitt had encouraged colonial soldiers and officers—through offering them increased military rank and increased financial support—to believe that they were truly partners in Britain's war against France, and not merely hired hands. By increasing the status of colonists, Pitt also increased the expectations that they would fight.[12]

In keeping with this ongoing effort, Prime's sermon to the New York provincial troops enlisted Revelation 2:10 to inspire courage in battle. Just as in biblical wars, "the same Magnanimity, Courage and Resolution, if assured of the divine Presence, may now fill and animate every Breast, from the most noble General of the first Rank, to the lowest Subaltern, and meanest Soldier, in the Campaign." Whether soldiers were "ranging the Woods after the Skulking Foe, encountering their Troops in the Field of Battle, or scaling the strongest Walls of their Towns and Garrisons," they can be "assured" of God's "Presence" in battle if they abide by his scriptural dictates, and they can know that "Success is as sure now to the martial Enterprises of his People, as ever it was of old." Even so, not all soldiers "shall escape the fatal Stroke of Death" delivered "by the roaring Cannon, the destructive Shell, the whistling Musket, the piercing Sword, or cruel Hatchet." And yet, "if God be theirs in Christ," death in battle will lead to eternal bliss. Dying soldiers will emerge from the "Horrors of War" and "Rivulets of bloody Gore" to heavenly "Peace and Security." Fear is incompatible with the character of a Christian soldier in military battle. As the Apocalyptic letter implores, such soldiers will be martyrs in death, and as martyrs they should "Fear none of those Things which thou shalt suffer" but should be "faithful unto Death" so that they will receive "a Crown of Life" in return.[13]

Three months before the Revolutionary War began, Zabdiel Adams made similar use of Revelation 2:10. To prepare a militia company in Lunenburg, Massachusetts, for battle, Adams implored soldiers to repent of their sins and to purge their consciences "through the blood of Christ." This spiritual assurance would "give you necessary courage," and "be the means of covering your heads in the day of battle." Adams called for patriots to embrace the "necessary courage" to sacrifice themselves, not thinking of their lives, recognizing that "precious in the sight of that Lord is the death of his saints." If they died in battle, they would "die in the bed of…honor," and their names would be remembered. Faithfulness in both spiritual and military warfare would bring both salvation and a heroic legacy.[14]

Few texts were as serviceable in wartime as the apocalyptic promise that those who were "faithful unto death" would receive "a crown of life" as a heavenly reward. This promise reinforced the courage of soldiers, to be sure, and this was an important task. Ministers as well as generals wanted a successful outcome, and that required soldiers who would serve courageously by calming their natural fear of death. By urging soldiers to be Christians, preachers were also urging them to be moral, which was also important to generals and preachers alike. In the army, temptations lurked everywhere—temptation to flee the fight, and temptation to engage in all forms of sin and vice. This apocalyptic promise urged fortitude against temptation. Above all, it reminded soldiers that their souls were more important than their bodies. Death on the battlefield paled in comparison to eternal death. Military soldiers who excelled in spiritual warfare not only won God's favor and protection in battle, they also gained God's blessings in the hereafter.

The Woman and the Dragon in the American Wilderness (Revelation 12: 14–17)

If the letters to the seven churches in Revelation 2 lacked bizarre, apocalyptic images, many other texts from Revelation that fascinated revolutionary patriots did not. One popular example was the vision of the woman and the dragon in Revelation 12. This vision had a variety of interpreters in the Revolution, and their views on it varied widely. There were few women preachers in America at the time, but this vision captured the attention of the two most prominent, Ann Lee, leader of the Shaker movement, and Jemima Wilkinson, founder of the Universal Friends. As Catherine Brekus has shown, both Lee and Wilkinson "claimed to be the apocalyptic woman in the wilderness who had been sent by God to prepare for the millennium." The fact that both Lee and Wilkinson came to this vision independently says something about the interest in this vision in Revolutionary America.[15]

This stirring vision also caught the attention of Samuel Sherwood and served as the basis for his famous sermon, *Church's Flight Into the Wilderness*. As we have observed, this was the sermon that historians often cited to claim that patriot ministers predicted a great millennial destiny for America. Sherwood's sermon deserves another look, however, giving close attention to this vision and how Sherwood applied it to the Revolution.

Revelation 12 is a graphic combination of birth and war. The scene opened in heaven with a woman, "clothed with the sun, and the moon under her feet," and wearing "a crown of twelve stars." The woman was in labor. Just as she was about to give birth, "a great red dragon" appeared alongside and prepared to "devour her child as soon as it was born." The woman then gave birth to the child, a boy, revealed as Christ, who "was to rule all nations." Before the dragon could devour him, the child was taken up to the throne of God. The woman, then, fled "into the wilderness," where God protected her. Next, a war broke out in heaven in which the archangel Michael, accompanied by his angels, fought "against the dragon," who had fighting angels of his own. The dragon lost the battle, and was thrown from heaven to earth. The dragon was revealed to be Satan, who worked to deceive the world. Satan's time was short, however, because Christ had defeated him. So Satan, described both as the dragon and as the serpent, "persecuted the woman" who fled to the wilderness. The dragon also waged war against the woman's children, namely, Christians who obeyed God's commandments and testified to their faith in Christ.

Reflecting on the threating, revolutionary turmoil of 1776, Sherwood thought of this vision of a woman being persecuted by a "great red dragon." Sherwood read the woman as a symbol for the church, and the dragon as Satan, the ultimate tyrant who spread the power of Antichrist throughout the world. Like most colonial Protestants, Sherwood believed that the power of Antichrist was centered in the Roman Catholic Church, but he saw this tyranny spreading to other nations, even Britain. The wilderness symbolized America, which was the church's refuge from antichristian tyranny. Since America protected the church, the patriotic cause of the colonies supported the holy cause of Christ.

The Revolutionary War was thus a righteous war, a defense of both civil and religious liberty. "If the enemies of the church, in the wars they set on foot," kill God's people with the sword, these enemies of God "must be killed with the sword." To defeat religious and political tyranny, God inspired a "martial, heroic spirit" that empowered those with the "skill" and "courage...to defend and protect his church." In Sherwood's reading, therefore, American patriots were the agents of this Christian war, as "the honorable Continental Congress" had "wisely adopted" the divine "law of retaliation" in warfare against God's enemies. Sherwood was not alone in drawing this militant message from Revelation 12. In May of 1773, Massachusetts minister Elisha Fish preached that this text depicted the church as a persecuted people at war against the satanic dragon. "This rage and combination of earth and hell against God's true people renders the art of war necessary for true Christians, as a means to preserve themselves from the persecuting fury of evil men, moved with the rage of the old dragon."[16]

Like most other patriotic sermons, Sherwood's asserted a militant message in the face of strong opposition. He dedicated the sermon "[t]o the Hon. John Hancock, Esq; President of the Continental Congress," along with Hancock's congressional colleagues and "the brave Generals of our armies, and patriotic Heroes, who are spirited by Heaven to exert their superior abilities" to defend America.[17] At this critical time, the British Redcoats were terrorizing the colonial population, and many colonists thought it irrational to declare independence and to wage war against such an awesome force. Sherwood warned these fearful colonists that patriotic zeal, even against all odds, would earn divine rewards, while prudent loyalism would reap damnation. "When the wicked persecuting tyrants of the earth, appear to have great power and strength, some of a selfish and timorous turn of mind, may inadvertently think it safest to pay worship and allegiance to them," but such cowardly, selfish people "are most artfully deluded and mistaken." They "shall be tormented with fire and brimstone" and "have no rest day nor night." The apocalyptic message for 1776 was clear. To defend the colonies and the church was virtuous, selfless, and divinely militant.[18]

Sherwood worried that other interpreters had not caught on to the spread of tyrannical popery, and, therefore, were not aware of the millennial importance of the American Revolution. This connection, he wrote, "has not been suitably noticed and attended to by expositors and divines." Accordingly, mistaken interpreters had been wrong in "limiting and confining these prophecies to so narrow a circle, as papal Rome." Sherwood argued that some of the prophecies of Revelation predicted the "glorious events in the womb of providence" that the Revolution "may...be the means of bringing to pass."

Even as he wrote these words, however, Sherwood acknowledged that this interpretation was "unlikely in the view of some," and that it was hardly the predominant view. Sherwood fully recognized—perhaps more clearly than some historians have—that his sermon was novel, even controversial, in predicting that the American Revolution could play a major role in fulfilling millennial destiny. When applying the millennial prophecies of Revelation to Revolutionary America, Sherwood preached, "we may conjecture at least, without a spirit of vanity and enthusiasm, that some of these prophecies of St. John may, not unaptly, be applied to our case, and receive their fulfillment in such providences as are passing over us." Note the qualifiers: applications of Revelation to the Revolution were not reliable interpretations but "conjecture," and such applications of biblical prophecy to America could be mistaken for "vanity and enthusiasm." As enthusiastic as Sherwood was in claiming that the Revolution had millennial significance, he recognized the pitfalls of making definitive claims about how Revelation applied to present times. "I do not mean to undertake a nice, exact calculation of the periods pointed out in this prophetic book," he cautioned. He further claimed that "I am not anxious to determine with mathematical certainty" when "this great conflict and war" described in Revelation will be fulfilled—"let it relate to what period of the church it will," he preached.[19]

So these applications of the Revelation to the Revolution were more informed hunch than reliable prediction. Even Sherwood recognized that his claims for America's millennial role were unusual, which likely explains why he spent much of the sermon arguing for the millennial importance of the American Revolution—he knew how speculative it was.[20]

Sherwood also wisely hedged his bets. He did not place the full value of the sermon on his prediction for the millennial reign of Christ in America. Above all millennial speculations about America's cosmic, even redemptive significance, Sherwood recognized that, fundamentally, the Revelation was a war text for wartime, and not just for the ultimate war at the end of history that would launch the millennium. The Revelation was "for the instruction, support, and consolation of God's saints, in the wars and conflicts they might have with their enemies, in every age and period of time."[21] Like most other preachers, therefore, Sherwood's interpretation of apocalyptic war was not exclusively future-oriented. Revelation did not apply only to "end times"; it was instruction for Christians in all times—"in every age and period of time" in which Christians were at war.

In sum, even though Sherwood's millennial vision for the church in America was exceptional, it was based on broader themes that supplied many preachers in Revolutionary America with the arsenal they needed to craft a patriotic message. Along with Sherwood's qualified predictions of American millennial glory, he repeated the more familiar, less controversial themes that other wartime ministers preached: martyrdom and Christ-like militancy.

Militancy, Pacifism, and the Two Beasts
(Revelation 13)

Another of the most popular apocalyptic texts in Revolutionary America was the vision of the two beasts in Revelation 13. The first beast was a blasphemous sea monster with seven heads and ten horns. All its power came from Satan, again described as a "great red dragon," whom the people worshiped. The dragon empowered the beast to wage war against the saints. Reflecting on this vision, John declared, those who kill "with the sword must be killed with the sword," and referred to "the patience and the faith of the saints." Then the second beast arose. This second beast forced all the people "to receive a mark in their right hand, or in their foreheads," and disallowed anyone from buying or selling unless they bore the mark. The vision concluded with a mysterious number: "Here is wisdom. Let him that hath understanding count the number of the beast: for it is the number of a man; and his number is Six hundred threescore and six."

This apocalyptic number, 666 (sometimes calculated as 606), has stimulated fascination and conjecture through history, and the Revolutionary era was no exception. An anonymous pamphlet from 1777 attempted to solve the mystery of the number by calculating the numerical values of Hebrew and Greek letters that added up to 666, which, the author determined, spelled out "Royal Supremacy in Great Britain."[22]

The most extensive revolutionary interpretation of Revelation 13 came from Samuel West, an army chaplain and Congregationalist pastor in Dartmouth, Massachusetts. West was known for his liberal theology and his patriotic politics. He spoke to the revolutionary significance of Revelation 13 in his sermon before the Massachusetts House of Representatives on May 29, 1776. West preached that this dramatic vision displayed "the cruel savage disposition of tyrants, and the idolatrous reverence that is paid them." West evoked John's vision of a "horrible wild beast" that arose from the sea with "seven heads and ten horns, and upon his heads the names of blasphemy." The heads, West surmised, symbolized "forms of government," and "blasphemy" referred to idolatry. The meaning, he argued, was that tyranny is idolatrous, because tyrants demanded more than their due respect and honor. In effect, they demanded to be worshiped as gods.[23]

Consider, West continued, the graphic images of the vision and what they intended to communicate. The first beast, was a "horrible monster possessed of the rage and fury of the lion, the fierceness of the bear, and the swiftness of the leopard to seize and devour its prey." There could be no stronger description of the "rage, fury and impetuosity of tyrants in their destroying and making havoc of mankind." Not only were tyrants horrific rulers, but they were empowered by hell. The devil himself, symbolized by the dragon, gave the beast his power, and by doing so "constituted him to be his vicegerent on earth." This means "tyrants are the ministers of Satan, ordained by him for the destruction of mankind."

Even more horrifying than this Satanic beast was the astounding fact that the people worshiped him and the dragon that gave him power. West was not implying that the people intentionally worshiped the Devil. By honoring tyrannical rulers such as George III, however, the people were adoring Satan, the tyrant of tyrants, who gave all earthly tyrants their power. So "those who pay an undue and sinful veneration to tyrants, are properly the servants of the devil, they are worshippers of the prince of darkness." That's why Revelation 13 so condemned those who honored the beast, worshiped the beast, and carried the mark of the beast. John meant to show "God's abhorrence of tyranny and tyrants, together with the idolatrous reverence, that their wretched subjects are wont to pay them, and the awful denunciation of divine wrath, against those who are guilty of this undue obedience to tyrants." West argued that there could be no better biblical image of the people's "gross stupidity and wicked-ness" in "giving up their just rights into the hands of tyrannical monsters, and in so readily paying them such an unlimited obedience, as is due to God alone."[24]

Instead of idolizing tyrannical rulers, West asserted, colonists should fight against tyranny in its most diabolical form: Great Britain. West com-manded his fellow colonists "to strive to get the victory over the beast and his image, over every species of tyranny. Let us look upon a freedom from the power of tyrants, as a blessing, that cannot be purchased too dear." He called on "every person in the community," especially the representatives of the people in the colonies, to defend "our liberties against British tyr-anny." Like the beasts of Revelation 13, the British were "tyrannical mon-sters," and patriots needed to be "animated with a noble zeal for the sacred cause of liberty."[25]

Here, over a month before the signing of the Declaration of Independence, West used this vision to argue strenuously for independ-ence. He had high hopes for the war and its aftermath. He thought "that providence has designed this continent for to be the asylum of liberty and true religion." As West saw it, "both religion and liberty seem to be expir-ing" in Europe, so America remained the only "refuge" for liberty.[26]

America's future as a refuge for liberty, however, would not be realized if the Revolution failed, so West condemned the war's opponents in the harshest terms. Above all, he attacked pacifists, those "who pretend that it is against their consciences to take up arms in defense of their country." Pacifism, West argued, was an extreme view, a violation of scripture and reason. Most offensive to West were the religious justifications for pacifism. Those who think "that they please God while they sit still, and quietly behold their friends and brethren killed by their unmerciful enemies," committed an act that was "criminal in the sight of heaven," a great violation "of the law of God."[27]

West was not alone in reading Revelation 13 as an endorsement of military service and an attack on pacifism. These notions were a major thrust of an artillery election sermon by Simeon Howard of Boston, preached on June 7, 1773. Howard countered the biblical arguments for pacifism, especially from "our Saviour's own words in his sermon on the mount," Matthew 5:38–39, and 5:43–44:

> Ye have heard that it hath been said, An eye for an eye, and a tooth for a tooth: But I say unto you, That ye resist not evil: but whosoever shall smite thee on thy right cheek, turn to him the other also.... Ye have heard that it hath been said, Thou shalt love thy neighbour, and hate thine enemy. But I say unto you, Love your enemies, bless them that curse you, do good to them that hate you, and pray for them which despitefully use you, and persecute you.[28]

To counter this, Howard turned to Revelation. "In the apocalypse of St. John," Howard preached, "there are several passages which intimate, that the saints of the Most High, will fight in their defense against their enemies; and that though they shall in various instances be overcome, yet that they shall at length, by an amazing slaughter of their persecutors, obtain for themselves the peaceable enjoyment of that liberty wherewith Christ hath made them free." Since Revelation was a book of war that described the saints as fighting for their freedom, Howard concluded that "it cannot reasonably be supposed that the spirit of God would have represented his faithful servants, as thus fighting against their enemies, and being so favored by divine providence, as finally to prevail over them, if defensive war was inconsistent with the spirit of the gospel."

For support of this martial reading of Revelation, Howard cited Revelation 13:7, which stated that the beast would "make war with the saints." To be a saint, therefore, was to be at war against evil. Just, defensive wars, such as the one the saints would wage against the beast, were commanded of Christians. While it was true that the Sermon on the Mount called for Christians not "to resist evil," here Jesus was referring to "only small injuries," such as turning the other cheek when struck, and not war. In Howard's view, therefore, Revelation 13 refuted the pacifist view of the Sermon on the Mount.[29]

Although West and Howard used Revelation 13 to attack pacifism, others used this same apocalyptic vision to support it. Anthony Benezet, the great Quaker abolitionist, cited Revelation 13 in two of his antiwar publications. In *Serious Considerations...on War and its Inconsistency with the Gospel* (1778), he cited Revelation 13:10: "He that leadeth into captivity shall go into captivity: he that killeth with the sword must be killed with the sword. Here is the patience and the faith of the saints." This was the command of Christ to his suffering saints, who were to follow in Christ's path of suffering, not the world's path of war. In this, that "awful book" of Revelation, Benezet found a "righteous judgment" on humans who had allowed their violent and selfish passions to take them over. Revelation called all humanity away from such violence, leading them to "seek after the God of peace and love, and live." Those who would follow Christ must suffer persecution nonviolently.[30]

In Revolutionary America, therefore, the vision of the two beasts was controversial. Patriots used this vision to support war, while pacifists used it to oppose the Revolution. Essentially, for both patriots and pacifists Revelation spoke to present, wartime needs and not future, millennial speculations. From the patriotic side, the Revelation fit an explicit wartime need in that it was a martial text from the New Testament. That is, though the Old Testament was filled with wars and warriors, the New Testament had fewer scenes of battle, and fewer endorsements of war, so patriots offered a martial reading of Revelation as a response to the pacifist reading of the Sermon on the Mount.

Christ the Militant Victor (Revelation 19)

Among its other wartime functions, Revelation glorified patriotic service on the battlefield. Soldiers could rest assured that their wartime service was not only blessed by God; it was an imitation of God—Jesus was a warrior, just like they were. This interpretation of Revelation counteracted claims that Christians followed a peaceful savior who prohibited military duty. When colonists preached Revelation, they often highlighted the militant nature of Christ. Revelation abounded with militant images of Jesus, and one in particular caught their attention more than others: the vision of Christ at war in Revelation 19, often referred to as the "Christus Victor" scene. This was the apocalyptic text that wartime ministers most often used to refute pacifists' claims that Jesus would never endorse war. This reading was prominent not only in Revolutionary America, but in pre-Revolutionary America as well.[31]

In Revelation 19, Jesus charged out of heaven on a white horse to wage righteous war against his enemies. Christ was militantly fierce, with eyes like "a flame of fire" and his body draped in a bloody "vesture," leading heavenly armies clothed in white linen and mounted upon white horses. This militant Christ was well armed, wielding from his mouth "a sharp sword" with which to "smite the nations" in judgment, laying down "the fierceness and wrath of Almighty God." In this vision, Christ, the "King of Kings, and Lord of Lords," defeated "the beast, and the kings of the earth, and their armies." In the heat of the battle, Christ threw the beast and "the false prophet," while still alive, "into a lake of fire burning with brimstone," and he killed the armies of the beast with his sword. The vision closed with a gory image of birds eating their flesh, a grisly meal that the angel of the vision called "the supper of the great God."

In the decades prior to the Revolution, wartime sermons most often featured the militant Christ when opposition to war was strongest. This was the situation in Pennsylvania in 1747, during King George's War, when Benjamin Franklin was deeply concerned about the survival of the colony, with its frontiers under constant threat of attack from the French and their Native American allies. Pennsylvania was particularly vulnerable, in part because most members of the colonial assembly were Quakers who opposed war for religious reasons. This pacifism, Franklin believed, was far too passive when what was needed was active engagement in preparation for war. Franklin responded by forming a voluntary militia, calling it the "Association for Defense." Franklin's militia received hearty support from Scots-Irish Presbyterians, none of whom had principled opposition to war and many of whom lived in the most threatened frontier areas. In drumming up support for the militia, Franklin found an ally in a notable evangelical, Presbyterian minister Gilbert Tennent. As the crisis intensified, Tennent enthusiastically supported Franklin's proposal from the pulpit, and Franklin applauded Tennent's efforts by publicizing his sermons in the *Pennsylvania Gazette*.[32]

Tennent preached with a keen sense that Pennsylvania was defenseless, totally lacking in "Arms and Ammunition," and most importantly lacking "martial Discipline," with "no Officers, no Fortress, no Ships of WAR to protect us!" If an attack came, what could "a Number of undiciplin'd, unarm'd Men do against a regular Force, but tempt them to greater Severities against themselves and others?" What Pennsylvania needed above all was unity around the cause of defense. Citizens needed to "let a generous love" of "Country" inspire them to heights of "heroic Bravery," which was above all "Great and Noble!"[33]

Most ominously of all, this military problem was also a ministerial problem, which also made it a biblical problem. Tennent's special worry was that the chief impediment to Pennsylvania's defense was religious, and he preached "to remove the Scruples of such, who by their Religious Principles, are hindered from joining" the war effort. Tragically and ironically, pacifist opposition to defensive war arose from the Bible. Even Benjamin Franklin recognized the importance of scripture to the crisis. Though certainly not known for his biblical expertise, Franklin turned to the conquest of the city of Laish in Judges 18 to convince Pennsylvanians of the need for a strong military defense. Like the ancient city of Laish, Franklin asserted, the inhabitants of Pennsylvania had grown prosperous, complacent, and defenseless—ripe targets for an invading army. Unless Pennsylvanians recognized their defenseless position and bolstered their military resolve, they would suffer Laish's fate. "As the Scriptures are given for our Reproof, Instruction and Warning, may we make a due Use of this Example, before it be too late!" Franklin advised. Moreover, Franklin closed his *Plain truth* with a prayer that "the Lord of the Armies of Israel, inspire us with Prudence in this Time of Danger."[34]

Tennent agreed. The Bible, rightly understood, did not endorse pacifism. But the Bible was open to misunderstanding, and one of the most tragic misunderstandings of scripture was that it opposed all war. Moreover, Tennent recognized that Old Testament arguments, such as Franklin's interpretation of Judges 18, were not sufficient. What of those who believed that Old Testament support for war was irrelevant to Christians? As Tennent acknowledged, many pacifists believed that Christ's kingdom was a spiritual kingdom that needed no military support. All Jesus's wars were spiritual wars, some argued. He fought all his battles for the salvation of souls and for the kingdom of God—battles that had nothing to do with the bloody devastation of earthly warfare.

Again, support for this view came from the Sermon on the Mount, where Jesus seemed to forbid violence, teaching that one should turn the other cheek, always responding peacefully to violent attacks (Matthew 5.39). A lot of colonists quoted this statement, making it one of the most cited texts in wartime. This view of Jesus was dangerous, Tennent believed. It was a misreading of Jesus's view of war, one that had perilous consequences. In response to the pacifist resistance in Pennsylvania, therefore, Tennent sensed the urgent need to defend the New Testament's—specifically Christ's—endorsement of righteous war. "War, my Brethren was lawful under the Old Testament Dispensation, and therefore it is lawful under the New," Tennent insisted.[35]

What impressed Tennent was a martial image of Jesus, a biblical response to the pacifist Jesus of the Sermon on the Mount, and Tennent found this martial Jesus displayed most clearly in Revelation. In making this claim, he first denied the exclusively futuristic reading of John's apocalyptic visions. True, Tennent granted, Revelation was a symbolic description of last things, including the last judgment. More fundamentally, however, Revelation centered on warfare, with battles galore, populated by heroes and villains. The wars of Revelation were not merely symbols of spiritual warfare, they had direct military relevance. Tennent insisted that "the Book of Revelation relates and proves various Wars of pious People, under the New-Testament-Dispensation; which the Circumstances of Places sufficiently evince, are not to be understood only of spiritual Conflicts, but also of external WAR and effusion of Blood." Revelation was about real battles and real blood. The wars of Revelation were neither exclusively futuristic nor exclusively spiritual. They were timely and relevant to military conflicts in the colonies.

Especially timely for Tennent was the militaristic Christ of Revelation 19. Tennent cited this vision of Jesus charging into battle as proof that "The Lord Jesus Christ is a Man of War." And with a warrior king such as Jesus to inspire them, Tennent pleaded with soldiers not to allow their swords to "rust in the Scabbard," but to be ready "to brandish it to the Terror of Transgressors!" He implored them to fight bravely, inspired by patriotic love of the nation, love of family, devotion to "civil and Religious" liberty. But above all they should fight under "God's Authority, the Imitation of his Example," an example displayed vividly in militant images of Christ.[36]

Tennent was certainly not alone in this martial reading of the Christ of Revelation. Other examples could be noted, including Samuel Davies of Virginia, another evangelical who lauded Christ's militaristic example.

For Tennent, Davies and others, Revelation portrayed a military Jesus who corrected the mistaken image of a pacifist Jesus. Revelation was a futuristic book, but it was also a bloody book of warfare, as relevant to contemporary wars against the French and their Native American allies as it was to the spiritual warfare of the soul and to apocalyptic warfare at the end of history.[37]

One could assume that Tennent and Davies preached in unique situations, and that their arguments for a militant Jesus would not have been needed in New England, where there were fewer Quakers or pacifists of any variety. Were martial images of Christ, such as the one on display in Revelation 19, needed in an already militant New England?

Evidently so. A striking example comes from a 1771 artillery sermon by Eli Forbes, pastor of Second Church in Brookfield, Massachusetts. The crisis of the day, as Forbes saw it, was an overall lack of military character, and an urgent need for more experienced, more zealous soldiers to protect colonial interests. On the topic of war, and especially on the liabilities of an ill-equipped army, Forbes spoke with the experience of a soldier. He had enlisted in the fight against the French in July of 1745, the same month news reached Boston of the dramatic victory of New England colonists over the French fortress of Louisbourg. Later, he served as a military chaplain. From his own war experience, Forbes knew the peril of an inexperienced and ill-equipped military. He recalled the harsh early days of the French and Indian War, when colonial soldiers saw their forts overtaken, their lands "depopulated and burnt," their "wives ravished and then butchered," their "daughters deflowered and led away captive," their "children confined in savage dens," and finally their "brethren slain" in battle, "and left scalped, mangled, unburied, food for savage beasts." These were "horrid scenes!" And much of the horror could have been avoided if their soldiers had been better acquainted with the arts of war.[38]

Such horrific images vividly portrayed the religious urgency of military service. Accordingly, in his artillery sermon of June 3, 1771, Forbes wanted to equip soldiers with ample knowledge of the divine nature of their military calling. These were rather calm days, before the Revolutionary crisis would erupt violently in New England. Still, trouble was on the horizon. Forbes preached over a year after the so-called Boston Massacre, and he positioned himself as a mediator, steering clear of "dividing names, or party distinctions of British and American," hoping instead to illumine what his title described as *The Dignity and Importance of the Military Character*. Forbes's main agenda was to "revive the true martial spirit" in the colonies, to "inspire" Massachusetts soldiers to "excel in the art military." He hoped that these soldiers from Massachusetts would transform themselves into "future heroes, who may vie not only with Greece and Rome, but even with Great-Britain."[39]

Although Forbes may have worried that colonial troops might quite literally "vie" with Britain someday, he placed his hope for peace on the character of a Christian army. And yet, like the other ministers, Forbes recognized that the main threat to the Christian army's strength was in scripture, specifically in a peace-loving Christ who rejected all war. Forbes recognized the discrepancy that many saw between the divine "man of war" of Exodus (15:3) and the peaceful Jesus of the Sermon on the Mount. Acknowledging that "the blessed Jesus" was "emphatically the 'prince of peace,'" Forbes asserted even more strongly that Christ and his followers often had to accomplish peace through war.[40] When it came to connecting the Exodus "man of war" with the New Testament, no text was more persuasive than Revelation 19, with its description of a militant Christ. Here, as in other visions from Revelation, Christ revealed himself "under the most magnificent titles of a victorious commander." Christ enters the scene "mounted on a war-horse, with his bow and with his crown, to denote his martial skill and royal dignity, and he rides on victorious, from one conquest to another." This "commander" Christ "raised the military character of the highest dignity" through his example. Through such texts as Revelation 19, therefore, Forbes launched an all-out rhetorical charge for Christ's endorsement of righteous military conflict.[41]

Even in leading this charge, however, Forbes recognized the shock value of any image of Jesus charging into battle, wielding a sword, and slaughtering his enemies. Thinking of this and other violent images in scripture, Forbes acknowledged that "I shudder" at such fierce expressions, and he "would not misrepresent the sacred text" nor would he "represent the Divine Being, as laying aside the amiable character of the God of love." Similarly, Forbes winced at the possibility that anyone would believe that "the compassionate Jesus, that friend of mankind, delighted in blood and slaughter." Even so, in desperate times, even Revolutionary times, God endorsed war, and military conflicts become sacred battles. In such times, God "consecrates the sword to religion, and his right hand takes hold on vengeance" to defend "his own honor," and to defend "his people's rights." Christ led the charge. God commissioned "his eternal son, to do all his dreadful work of judgment," and Christ, "as captain of the Lord's hosts, takes the field, and connects the man of *war*, with the

Christian *Hero*, and makes the fidelity of the good solider an essential part of that religion which is founded on the immoveable basis of moral virtue and Christian grace."

Although one could imitate Christ in a variety of ways, no vocation brought one closer to the character of Christ than military service. More strikingly, Forbes asserted that no soldier could reach his ultimate fighting potential without faith in Christ: "I would not intimate that every good Christian is of consequence a good soldier,—an accomplished man of war; but this I will venture to say, there cannot be a good soldier, an accomplished man of war, destitute of the principles and practice of Christianity."[42] Not only *could* Christians be soldiers, therefore, but good soldiers *must* be Christians. The most proficient fighters became so through martial training nurtured by Christian spirituality.

Revolutionary Millennialism Reconsidered

Predicting the future is always tricky, especially when such predictions involve apocalyptic speculations. In 1812, John Adams, weary of constant predictions of Antichrist and the end of the world, revealed to Thomas Jefferson his hope that "sober Christians" would condemn such prognostications, "for nothing is clearer from their Scriptures than that Their Prophecies were not intended to make Us Prophets."[43]

This was good advice, many ministers knew, and most of them heeded it. Although most ministers did not doubt the reality of antichristian tyranny, both civil and religious, and even though they did not doubt that the millennium would someday dawn, few followed Samuel Sherwood in predicting that the American Revolution might bring it about, and that a new American nation could be an agent of Christ's redemptive rule. Yet, if most ministers' apocalyptic claims were less precise about America's millennial destiny, they were no less patriotic, for they found in Revelation a relevant message for soldiers, a message that endowed their sacrifice with sacred significance, and ordained their martial prowess with Christ's blessing.

When patriotic ministers preached from apocalyptic scriptures, therefore, they often did so more to stress militant Christianity than an American millennium. Certainly, some patriots did envision a grand, millennial destiny for the newly conceived United States. But even these patriots usually interpreted their visions of millennial glory within a biblical framework that prioritized the martial relevance of scripture.

Even if some historians have overstated revolutionary millennialism, therefore, they have understated part of its appeal. Millennialism did resonate with republican ideology, endowing liberty with cosmic, universal significance. More fundamentally, however, millennialism, like all forms of apocalyptic thought, often resonated with war. In Revolutionary America, most patriots who looked forward to a millennial future were also preoccupied with the present responsibilities of war, the ugly basics of battle. When wartime morale faded and patriotic rhetoric rang hollow, ministers turned to the dramatic visions of Revelation. Through these apocalyptic visions, including the victorious charge of a militant Christ, ministers proclaimed a bellicose Christianity that endowed patriotic sacrifice with sacred martyrdom.

Epilogue

AN AMERICAN PATRIOT'S BIBLE

ON DECEMBER 18, 1777, the first national thanksgiving day, declared by the Continental Congress to honor the victory at Saratoga, chaplain David Avery called on Americans to remember that their Lord was a military man. Avery preached from Exodus 15, "the triumphant song of Moses at the Red-sea." In this scripture, Avery proclaimed, "the Almighty" put "his hand to the sword" and rendered "vengeance to his enemies." God was the supreme warrior. "What are the Hannibals, the Scipios, the Caesars, the Pompeys, the Alexanders of the world, when once compared to the LORD as a MAN of WAR?"¹ Avery, who had seen his share of battles, including Bunker Hill, preached at a critical juncture in the war. The next day General Washington and his troops would stagger into Valley Forge to endure the legendary harsh winter that would test the mettle of the Continental Army and the patriotic cause itself. Not long after preaching this sermon, Avery would join Washington at Valley Forge, where he would deliver sermons much like this one, rousing soldiers with verses from the Bible that would fill them with martial courage. Like many patriots, Avery believed that, to succeed, the Revolution needed the Bible for instruction, admonishment, and inspiration.

The Revolution may be the most important event in American history, and the Bible was arguably its most influential book. I do not claim that the Bible was the key to understanding the Revolution, or that the Bible was the main source for revolutionary politics. Still, patriots fought the Revolutionary War in a society in which the Bible was the most read and respected book in the colonies. Through the American Revolution, many British colonists became patriotically American—and so did their Bible.

What role, then, did the Bible play in the Revolution? Its primary purpose was to forge militant patriotism. We can see this, in several ways, from the most-cited scriptures during the Revolution. First, the Revolutionary

American Bible prioritized present needs over future aspirations. Certainly revolutionaries thought about their place in history, and patriots believed that the United States could be a great beacon of freedom throughout the world. Some even speculated that America had a role to play in the end times, although recent historians have questioned the dominance of millennial thought among revolutionaries—rightly so, because the most popular biblical texts in Revolutionary America functioned to address present needs, especially inspiring troops for battle while defending the Revolution against loyalists and pacifists.

Second, the Revolutionary American Bible drew from a diverse range of texts from across the scriptures. Previously, when historians referenced the Bible in Revolutionary America, two main themes rose to the forefront—civil millennialism (drawn mainly from Revelation and Daniel) and Hebraic republicanism (antimonarchial arguments from the Old Testament, especially 1 Samuel 8). While those texts was indeed important, a much broader range of biblical texts were important to the Revolution, including a variety of topics from both the Old and New Testaments. Republicanism in scripture knew few bounds. It was a common idea, expressed well by Reverend John Mellen of Hanover, that "liberty is the spirit and genius, not only of the gospel, but *of the whole of that revelation*, we have, first and last, received from God." The Bible and republicanism had a long history before the Revolution. Even the Puritans in New England spread republican ideas. So it's not surprising that revolutionaries had grown accustomed to finding examples of liberty throughout scripture.[2]

Third, in the Revolutionary American Bible, character mattered. Both republican and Christian traditions esteemed virtue above all. It makes sense, therefore, that patriots scoured the scriptures, looking for virtuous heroes. To revolutionaries, the Bible seemed to be full of patriots, but historians have overlooked most of the biblical heroes in Revolutionary America. Of primary importance was David, a complex hero. Also significant were prophets and judges. While historians have noted that the Curse of Meroz (Judges 5:23) in the Deborah story was an important verse in wartime, they have not evaluated what surrounded that famous verse, namely, the heroic exploits of Deborah and especially Jael with her lethal hammer and tent peg. These were women at war, and American patriots made much of their heroism. Even the New Testament had its share of revolutionary heroes. Patriots admired Peter and Paul not only for their teachings on civil authority and Christian freedom, but also for their heroism. Sermons made much of how Peter and Paul faced persecution as they vowed to obey God rather than tyrants. Perhaps most surprising was patriots' reading of the heroic character of Jesus. In Revelation, they found proof that Jesus was a warrior, not the pacifist that some colonists found in the Sermon on the Mount.

Sacred Scripture for Sacred War

These characteristics point toward the militant character of the Revolutionary American Bible. Patriotic ministers shaped a martial view of Christianity that inspired wartime zeal. In the process, the Revolution, which patriots defended as a just war, also became a sacred war, endowed by God and defended by scripture. As is often the case, in Revolutionary America as well as today, Bible reading in wartime usually involves choosing sides. And when battle lines are drawn through the lines of scripture, the war takes on religious significance.

For many patriots, Revolutionary War battles required spiritual preparation. This was certainly true for George Washington and other military and political leaders. God was the "God of battles" for a reason, they believed. Not only did divine providence hold the key to victory, but God favored obedient, moral, and spiritual soldiers. So both generals and military chaplains constantly warned against neglecting spiritual motives in battle.[3] In an unprinted sermon manuscript from 1777, Congregationalist minister Peter Thacher of Malden, Massachusetts, wrote that soldiers should "consider themselves as fighting under God's banner and as the champions of his cause." If they did, "how forcibly would this operate upon a pious mind, with what ardor would it inspire his breast and urge him to deeds of heroic valor! When men feel themselves [influenced] by *motives of religion as well as natural obligation they must be in a sense invincible.*" Indeed, Thacher insisted, "*we are fighting…for our religion*, that religion which *the word of God* hath instituted and appointed." So Thacher charged American soldiers to "fight to the last drop of your blood in this glorious cause."[4]

To be sure, most revolutionaries claimed to be fighting a just war, and not an outright holy war. But how successful were they in staying true to that rationale? Too often, as historian George Marsden has observed, the problem with just war theory is with the theory—"it is too theoretical" in that "it does not take into account how people actually behave." Because patriots believed that their cause of liberty had divine support, they fought a war that blended political and religious motivations rather seamlessly. They saw the conflict as a just war, fully defensible on those grounds, but they fought it with religious resolve, fully believing that God endorsed the cause and actually helped to fight the war. One can find key insights into how revolutionaries actually thought about the war by observing how they applied scripture to it. The Bible was so much a part of their vocabulary that it determined how they viewed themselves in relation to the Revolution. So, just war theory "does not take into account how people actually behave," nor does it account for how people read scripture in wartime.[5]

That was clearly the case in the Revolutionary War. The patriotic scripture shaped by the Revolution centered on a particular view of the Bible as a book of war. For many colonists, the Bible was a dramatic, often graphically violent, succession of war stories featuring heroic exemplars of spiritual faith and military prowess.

Patriotic ministers believed that the Bible inspired patriots to take to the battlefield while also igniting zeal for the Gospel. The scriptures that proved most popular were often those that best revealed the spiritual value of military service. The best soldiers were like David—true champions in both military and spiritual warfare. As Brooklyn pastor Josiah Whitney preached to an infantry regiment near the end of the Revolutionary era, "Religion gives not to the soldier a spirit of fear, but a spirit of power, of fortitude."[6] Ministers hoped that soldiers, inspired by the spiritual nature of patriotic duty, would overcome their natural aversions to dying—and especially to killing—in battle.[7]

Preachers did not blatantly assert that Americans would go to hell if they did not go to war—but they sometimes came close. Consider, for example, a list of "beatitudes" of the American Revolution that an unnamed chaplain preached before General St. Clair's brigade in October, 1776. "Blessed be that man who in the present dispute esteems not his life too good to fall a sacrifice in defense of his country.... Blessed be the man who is a friend to the United States of America" and "Blessed be that man who will use his utmost endeavor to oppose the tyranny of Great-Britain." True to biblical form, blessings often accompanied curses, and this chaplain proclaimed several "curses to him who deserts the noble cause," including "let him be abhorred by all the United States...let him be...a terror to himself and all around him...let him be cursed...'till his wretched head with dishonor is laid low in the dust."[8] Could such a coward in military war be a champion in spiritual warfare? The preacher did not say, but it seemed doubtful. Here this chaplain not only cited scripture; he emulated it, crafting a list of blessings and curses of his own.

Legacies

Today, some Americans believe that scripture inspired the Revolution and profoundly shaped American patriotism. In 2009, the publication of *The American Patriot's Bible*, an edition of the Bible framed within a patriotic narrative of American history, garnered national media attention. Not surprisingly, the Revolution played a leading role. The volume included full-color inserts on the founders and the Revolution, and it credited the churches as "the primary source that stirred the fires of liberty."[9]

The American Patriot's Bible is part of a long tradition of works Americans often reach for in wartime. During the Civil War, for example, several books appeared that glorified the image of the patriotic minister in the American Revolution, especially those who left the pulpit for the battlefield. J. T. Headley, the author of one such book, wrote that clerical patriotism was the highest form of patriotic witness most needed as the nation faced catastrophic division. In the face of these threatening days, Headley called on the romantic visions of patriotic ministers in Revolutionary America, hoping that their witness could again inspire the clergy, and, by doing so, inspire the nation to a righteous patriotism. "The Revolution would have been less sacred," Headley wrote, "if [ministers'] blood had not mingled in the costly sacrifice that was laid on the altar of freedom."[10] Through their own courageous service, both on the battlefield and in the pulpit, clergy forged an image of themselves as patriots who had the unique responsibility of arousing wartime zeal through a patriotic Bible.

This book has examined the beginnings of that long-standing relationship between patriotism and scripture, an alliance forged in wartime and refined by preachers and even presidents. Historians have neglected the symbiotic relationship between religion and American war, and have not appreciated how much America's "sacred wars" depended on the sacred violence in the Bible. This book has ventured into that biblical terrain, focusing on some of the scriptures that patriots found to be most persuasive in supporting the Revolutionary cause. In the American Revolution, when it came to making the case for war and ushering citizens to the battlefield, the Bible was a persuasive ally. The ramifications of this relationship would cascade throughout American history as the United States came to define itself and its destiny largely though the justice and sacredness of its wars.[11]

Methodology

This book began in an attempt to answer the question of how colonists used the Bible in wartime. The problem was that there was little information on which biblical texts colonists used most often and how they interpreted them. To assess patterns of biblical interpretation over time, I designed a relational database that allowed me to input biblical citations from primary sources that focused on war. Not surprisingly, most of the texts that cited scripture in addressing war were sermons, but I have included other texts that also made substantial use of the Bible to address, for example, pamphlets such as Thomas Paine's *Common Sense*. In my analysis of sermons, I did not concentrate only on the main biblical text (or texts) for each sermon. Instead, I read every page of each sermon and added each biblical citation to the database. Although concentrating only on the main texts would have been a quicker process, it would have missed most of the biblical citations in these sermons. I do not claim that the database includes every sermon on war, but I have tried to include as many as possible. The result is the most comprehensive database on the Bible in colonial America, including 17,148 biblical citations from 543 sources over more than a century (1674–1800).

Based on this database analysis, table 8.1 ranks the most-cited biblical chapters in sermons that addressed political and/or martial themes during the Revolutionary era (1763–1800). Since my purpose was to analyze how patriotic interpretations of the Bible developed over time, I did not restrict myself to these texts. As the chapters in this book demonstrate, I have attempted to show how the themes in these texts developed from previous interpretations in wartime, particularly the Seven Years' War. Just as we cannot understand the American Revolution apart from previous wars, neither can we understand biblical views on war apart from their larger biblical and historical contexts. For instance, the fall of the Davidic kingdom was an important biblical theme in the Revolution, evidenced by the sixth most-cited text, 1 Kings

12. And yet, we cannot understand the power of that theme without examining the change in the martial image of David over time.

The texts cited most frequently were not always well-developed by colonists. The main example here is Psalm 124. This psalm was mainly cited for its second and third verses: "If it had not been the Lord who was on our side, when men rose up against us: Then they had swallowed us up quick." Colonists cited this psalm as a reminder that God was on their side in wartime. In a similar way, colonists often cited Romans 8:28, "We know that all things work together for good to them that love God, to them who are called according to his purpose." In both texts, colonists found strength in the belief that they were God's people, so ministers cited these verses, often in the closing flourish of their sermons, but they did not extensively discuss or debate them. Accordingly, I have not given them much attention. Instead, I have focused on the texts and themes that the colonists themselves discursively focused on most often. That is, the chapters in this book examine the texts and themes that generated the most interpretation, discussion, and even debate in wartime.

Table 8.1 Most Cited Biblical Chapters (50 or more citations) in the Revolutionary Era (1763–1800)

Rank		Text	Citations
1	Paul on Obedience to Civil Rulers *(See discussion in chapter 5)*	Romans 13	96
2	Exodus—Moses and the Parting of the Red Sea *(See chapter 2)*	Exodus 14–15[1]	75
3	Paul on the Freedom of Christ *(See chapter 5)*	Galatians 5	67
4	Deborah, Jael, and the Curse of Meroz *(See chapter 3)*	Judges 4–5[2]	64
5	Peter on Obedience to Civil Rulers *(See chapter 5)*	1 Peter 2	63
6	Davidic Kingdom Divided (Rehoboam's Tyranny) *(See chapter 4)*	1 Kings 12	55
7	David's Thanksgiving for National Salvation	Psalm 124	54
8	Sermon on the Mount *(See chapter 6)*	Matthew 5	53

Notes

INTRODUCTION

1. Bernard Bailyn, *Faces of Revolution: Personalities and Themes in the Struggle for American Independence* (New York: Knopf, 1990), 67. All biblical citations in this book refer to the Authorized Version of the Bible (the King James Version), since it was by far the most popular version used in Revolutionary America.

2. For a recent interpretation of Paine's "Hebraic republicanism," see Nathan R. Perl-Rosenthal, "The 'Divine Right of Republics': Hebraic Republicanism and the Debate over Kingless Government in Revolutionary America," *William and Mary Quarterly*, 3rd ser., 66, no. 3 (July 2009): 535–564. See also Eran Shalev, "'A Perfect Republic': The Mosaic Constitution in Revolutionary New England, 1775–1788," *New England Quarterly* 82, no. 2 (June 2009): 235–263. Hebraic republicanism was a common theme in American sermons, both published and unpublished. A typical example is in the unpublished sermon by Ebenezer Chaplin, "Sermon on Isaiah 33:13, Feb. 4 and Feb. 18, 1776," in *Sermons, 1759–1794*, 2 octavo vols., I: American Antiquarian Society. On Paine and the Bible, Mark Noll acknowledged, "Paine's skill at marshaling biblical narratives for republican ends was masterful." However, Noll contended that Paine's biblical dexterity did not indicate that the Bible was central to his political theory. Instead, the Bible served rhetorical, persuasive ends. Mark A. Noll, *America's God: From Jonathan Edwards to Abraham Lincoln* (New York: Oxford University Press, 2002), 83–85. See also Noll, "The Bible in Revolutionary America," in *The Bible in American Law, Politics, and Political Rhetoric*, ed. J. T. Johnson, The Bible in American Culture Series (Philadelphia: Fortress, 1985), 39.

3. Samuel Sherwood, "The Church's Flight into the Wilderness: An Address on the Times," in *Political Sermons of the American Founding Era, 1730–1805*, 2nd ed., ed. Ellis Sandoz, (Indianapolis, IN: Liberty Fund, 1998), 523. Sherwood's sermon was atypical in its millennial claims. It was, as Harry Stout categorized it, "the most explicitly millennial sermon to appear in 1776." Harry S. Stout,

The New England Soul: Preaching and Religious Culture in Colonial New England, 25th anniversary ed. (New York: Oxford University Press, 2011), 318. Millennialism is a subcategory of apocalyptic thought, which originated in the Jewish apocalyptic literature of 250 BCE to 200 CE. Among the various biblical writings that contain apocalyptic ideas and forms, two biblical books are explicitly apocalyptic: Daniel, from the Hebrew Bible, and Revelation, from the New Testament. Millennialism is "the belief that there will be a period of peace and righteousness on the earth associated with the Second coming of Christ," and is based primarily on Revelation 20:1–10. Timothy P. Weber, "Millennialism," in *The Oxford Handbook of Eschatology*, ed. Jerry L Walls (Oxford: Oxford University Press, 2008), 365.

4. The literature on America's religious destiny is plentiful. The classic statement on "civil religion" is Robert Bellah, "Civil Religion in America," *Daedalus* 96, no. 1 (1967): 1–21. Among many other influential works is a helpful reader of primary sources with interpretative introductions: Conrad Cherry, ed., *God's New Israel: Religious Interpretations of American Destiny*, 2nd ed. (Chapel Hill: University of North Carolina Press, 1998). See also Ernest Lee Tuveson, *Redeemer Nation: The Idea of America's Millennial Role* (Chicago: University of Chicago Press, 1968); Nicholas Guyatt, *Providence and the Invention of the United States, 1607–1876* (New York: Cambridge University Press, 2007). A negative biblical image, America's image as the world's "Goliath," is referenced in Michael Mandelbaum, *The Case for Goliath: How America Acts as the World's Government in the 21st Century* (New York: Public Affairs, 2005). See also Anthony D. Smith, *Chosen Peoples* (New York: Oxford University Press, 2003); William R. Hutchison and Hartmut Lehmann, eds., *Many Are Chosen: Divine Election and Western Nationalism*, Harvard Theological Studies 38 (Minneapolis: Fortress Press, 1994); and Todd Gitlin, *The Chosen Peoples: America, Israel, and the Ordeals of Divine Election* (New York: Simon & Schuster, 2010).

5. Harry S. Stout, "Review Essay: Religion, War, and the Meaning of America," *Religion and American Culture: A Journal of Interpretation* 19, no. 2 (Summer 2009): 275. See also Jonathan H. Ebel, *Faith in the Fight: Religion and the American Solider in the Great War* (Princeton, NJ: Princeton University Press, 2010). Paul Gutjahr has well demonstrated that "the Bible was the most common and thus most accessible printed text for Americans" in the colonial period and beyond. Paul C. Gutjahr, *An American Bible: A History of the Good Book in the United States, 1777–1880* (Palo Alto, CA: Stanford University Press, 2002), 118. In an illuminating essay on the use—and misuse—of scripture in relation to the public life of the United States, see Mark A. Noll, "The Image of the United States as a Biblical Nation, 1776–1865," in *The Bible in America: Essays in Cultural History*, ed. Nathan O. Hatch and Mark A. Noll (New York: Oxford University Press, 1982): 39–58. Noll observed, "the Bible was not so much the truth above all truth" in American history "as it was the story above all stories."

Often "ministers preached as if the stories of Scripture were being repeated or could be repeated, in the unfolding life of the United States." Ibid., 43.

6. Bernard Bailyn, Gordon S. Wood, et al., *The Great Republic: A History of the American People*, 2nd ed. (Lexington, MA: D. C. Heath and Company, 1981), 1:291. Also on the importance of biblical ideas for everyday understandings of current events, including the Revolution, see Harry S. Stout, "Religion, Communications, and the Ideological Origins of the American Revolution," *William and Mary Quarterly: A Magazine of Early American History* 34, no. 4 (October 1977): 536–537. Defending the importance of religion to the Revolutionary age, Gordon Wood argued that "despite the growth of Enlightenment among elites in the eighteenth-century America, Protestantism...remained the principal means by which most common people ordered and explained the world....Not everyone could get emotional fulfillment from contemplating a declaration of rights or from participating in representative government...religion met personal and social needs not comprehended by rational philosophy or Whig ideology." Gordon S. Wood, "Religion and the American Revolution," in *New Directions in American Religious History*, ed. Harry S. Stout and D. G. Hart (New York: Oxford University Press, 1997), 175. Wood specifically mentions covenant theology, drawn primarily from the Puritan interpretations of the Old Testament, as an example of biblical influence on revolutionary thought. Gordon S. Wood, *The Creation of the American Republic, 1776–1787* (Chapel Hill: University of North Carolina Press, 1998), 7, 17, 114–118. Sacvan Bercovitch argued, relatedly, that New England "Puritans provided the scriptural basis for what we have come to call the myth of America...their influence appears most clearly in the extraordinary persistence of a rhetoric grounded in the Bible, and in the way that Americans keep returning to that rhetoric, especially in times of crisis." Bercovitch, "The Biblical Basis of the American Myth," in *The Bible and American Arts and Letters*, ed. G. Gunn (Philadelphia: Fortress, 1983), 219.

7. John Adams, *Diary and Autobiography of John Adams*, vol. 3, Diary, 1782–1804 and Autobiography, Part One to October 1776, in *The Adams Papers Digital Edition*, ed. C. James Taylor (Charlottesville: University of Virginia Press, Rotunda, 2008), 333. For Adams's view that "the Bible is the best book in the World," see Adams to Jefferson, December 25, 1813, in *The Founders on Religion: A Book of Quotations*, ed. James H. Hutson (Princeton, NJ: Princeton University Press, 2005), 23. Although Adams greatly respected scripture, he often complained that it was misunderstood.

8. Quotations from *Age of Reason* can be found in Thomas Paine, *The Writings of Thomas Paine* (London: G. P. Putnam's Sons, 1896), 34. For a perceptive analysis of Paine's *Age of Reason* in America, see Amanda Porterfield, *Conceived in Doubt: Religion and Politics in the New American Nation* (Chicago: University of Chicago Press, 2012), chapter 1. As Porterfield argues, "Reaction against Paine's *Age of Reason* contributed to a new understanding of the relationship between

religion and politics. Against Paine's effort to link the two by attacking unwarranted authority in both, evangelicals elevated religion above politics and censored religious skepticism." Ibid., 15.

9. Robert Middlekauff, *The Glorious Cause: The American Revolution, 1763–1789*, rev. ed. (New York: Oxford University Press, 2005), 3. Stout, *New England Soul*, 303. As Frank Lambert wrote, "perhaps the most influential sermon during the period came from outside the pulpit, not delivered by a minister but published by the Radical Whig Thomas Paine." *The Founding Fathers and the Place of Religion in America* (Princeton, NJ: Princeton University Press, 2003), 218. On the use of scripture among the founders, see D. L. Dreisbach, "The Bible in the Political Rhetoric of the American Founding," *Politics and Religion* 4, no. 3 (2011): 401–427; D. L. Dreisbach, "The 'Vine and Fig Tree' in George Washington's Letters: Reflections on a Biblical Motif in the Literature of the American Founding Era," *Anglican and Episcopal History* 76, no. 3 (2007): 299–326. Jeffry Morrison noted that Washington quoted the Bible more often than any other literary source. *The Political Philosophy of George Washington* (Baltimore: Johns Hopkins University Press, 2009), 91, 144–153. Sermons heavily influenced how colonists applied the Bible to their wars. As Harry S. Stout's authoritative study of colonial preaching in New England demonstrated, the sermon's "topical range and social influence were so powerful in shaping cultural values, meanings, and a sense of corporate purpose that even television pales in comparison." Stout, *New England Soul*, 3. After twenty-five years, the only dated part of Stout's statement is his reference to television in the age of the Internet and social media. His well-documented thesis remains as persuasive as ever. The sources for this book include both printed sermons and unprinted sermon manuscripts. For a cogent defense of the influence of printed sermons as nonelitist discourse that largely responded to the requests of the laity, see Nathan O. Hatch, *The Sacred Cause of Liberty: Republican Thought and the Millennium in Revolutionary New England* (New Haven, CT: Yale University Press, 1977), 176–182.

10. Christopher Hill, *The English Bible and the Seventeenth-Century Revolution* (London: Penguin, 1993), 31; Fania Oz-Salzberger, "The Political Thought of John Locke and the Significance of Political Hebraism," *Hebraic Political Studies* 1, no. 5 (2006): 568–592.

11. John E. Ferling, *Almost a Miracle: The American Victory in the War of Independence* (Oxford: Oxford University Press, 2007), Kindle edition, chap. 1.

12. Peter Thacher, "Sermon on 2 Samuel 10:12, Preached after Independence, 1777," Sermons Collection, box 2, folder 37, American Antiquarian Society, Worcester, MA, 9. Ezra Stiles, "2 Chronicles 20:6–7, 25 Sept 1760," ES Sermon Number 366, Stiles Sermons, Folder 41, Beinecke, New Haven, CT, 4, 15. Historian Fred Anderson observed that Indian hating reached new levels of intensity and secured a lasting legacy in America during the French and Indian War. *The Crucible of War: The Seven Years' War and the Fate of Empire in British North*

America, 1754–1766 (New York: Vintage, 2000), 199–200. See also Anderson, *The War That Made America: A Short History of the French and Indian War* (New York: Viking, 2005), vi–vii.

13. Drew Gilpin Faust, *This Republic of Suffering: Death and the American Civil War* (New York: Alfred A. Knopf, 2008), 32.

14. David Fanning, *The Narrative of Colonel David Fanning* (New York, 1865), xxiii. Fanning cited 1 Samuel 15.23, "For rebellion is as the sin of witchcraft, and stubbornness is as iniquity and idolatry. Because thou hast rejected the word of the LORD, he hath also rejected thee from being king." See Charles Royster, *A Revolutionary People at War: The Continental Army and American Character* (Chapel Hill: University of North Carolina Press, 1979), 13, 381.

15. John Fletcher, "The Bible and the Sword," in Sandoz, *Political Sermons*, 572, 577; John Wesley, "A Calm Address to Our American Colonies," in ibid., 409–420. As Thomas O'Beirne, British chaplain, preached in September 1776, the British cause was "the cause of peace, loyalty, and sound reason, exposed to the attempts of misguided men, whom he seems to have given over to a blindness of heart that hurries them into all the violence and artifice of sedition, frenzy, and rebellion." *A Sermon, Preached at St. Paul's, New York, September 22, 1776.* (New York: Hugh Gaine, 1776), 14.

16. Ferling, *Almost a Miracle*, location 503. Gordon Wood noted that, in contrast to the professional British soldiers, on the American side "there were innkeepers who were captains and shoemakers who were colonels." *The American Revolution: A History* (New York: Modern Library, 2002), 77. For statistics on the social and economic makeup of the Continental Army, see Royster, *Revolutionary People*, 373–378.

17. William Linn, *A Military Discourse, Delivered in Carlisle, March the 17th, 1776* (Philadelphia, 1776) 16, 22. See also Kidd, *God of Liberty: A Religious History of the American Revolution* (New York: Basic Books, 2010), 121.

18. Chaplains were important to George Washington throughout his military career. In 1777, Washington opposed the plan of Congress to get more service out of fewer chaplains by shifting from regimental chaplains to brigade chaplains. He worried that the move would overtax the chaplains and spread their work too thinly among too many soldiers. See George Washington to Governor Trumbull, December 15, 1775, in *The Writings of George Washington*, vol. 3, ed. Jared Sparks (Boston: Russell, Odiorne, and Metcalf, 1834), 198–199; Royster, *Revolutionary People*, 163, 167–168. In his history of the Continental Army, Charles Royster noted the importance of chaplains in maintaining revolutionary zeal among soldiers. He argued that "soldiers eager to feel love of America, pride in military service, and strength in combat responded to chaplains who could foster such ardor and gave short shrift to those who could not." As Royster demonstrated, not just ministers, but "most revolutionary spokesmen believed that service in the Continental Army had a clear religious meaning for the soldier."

Revolutionary People, 13, 16, 163. Estimates vary on the number of chaplains in the Continental Army, but there were at least 100 and perhaps as many as 196. For a roster of chaplains, see Eugene F. Williams, "Soldiers of God: The Chaplains of the Revolutionary War" (PhD diss., Texas Christian University, 1972), 133–133. See also Charles H. Metzger, "Chaplains in the American Revolution," *Catholic Historical Review* 31, no. 1 (1945): 31–79.

19. See Theodore Dwight Bozeman, *To Live Ancient Lives: The Primitivist Dimension in Puritanism* (Chapel Hill: University of North Carolina Press, 1988), 15–17, 33. Bozeman's analysis draws on Mircea Eliade's description of mythic presence in remembrance. See Mircea Eliade, *Myth and Reality* (New York: Trade, 1963), 19, 51. While Bozeman focused on seventeenth-century New England, his description of the primitivist approach to life through scripture also accurately reflected the majority of biblical interpretation in the eighteenth century in New England and beyond. As Mark Noll observed, "Hans Frei's description of earlier Bible reading as 'strongly realistic, i.e., at once literal and historical,' remained true for most Americans far into the nineteenth century." *America's God*, 371. See Hans W. Frei, *The Eclipse of Biblical Narrative: A Study in Eighteenth and Nineteenth Century Hermeneutics* (New Haven, CT: Yale University Press, 1974), 1. For an excellent application of Frei's analysis to America, including a defense of the persistence of pre-critical exegesis long into the nineteenth century, see Peter Johannes Thuesen, *In Discordance with the Scriptures: American Protestant Battles over Translating the Bible* (New York: Oxford University Press, 1999), 6–11. The transitions in biblical authority, both theological and cultural, through the latter eighteenth and early nineteenth centuries is well analyzed in Jonathan Sheehan, *The Enlightenment Bible: Translation, Scholarship, Culture* (Princeton, NJ: Princeton University Press, 2005).

20. Scores of sermons reflected a providential interpretation of the American Revolution. See, for example, David S. Rowland, *Historical Remarks, with Moral Reflections* (Providence: John Carter, 1779); Nathan Strong, *The Agency and Providence of God acknowledged, in the Preservation of the American States* (Hartford: Hudson and Goodwin, 1780). See also Guyatt, *Providence and the Invention of the United States.*

21. Jonathan Edwards, *Works of Jonathan Edwards* (hereafter WJE), vol. 2, *Religious Affections* [1754], ed. John Smith (New Haven, CT: Yale University Press, 1959), 140; Jonathan Edwards, "In The Name Of The Lord Of Hosts" [1755] in WJE, vol. 25, *Sermons and Discourses, 1743–1758*, ed. Wilson H. Kimnach (New Haven, CT: Yale University Press, 2006), 680–685. Some eighteenth-century ministers expanded typological interpretation beyond the Bible. Instead of Old Testament types being fulfilled in the New Testament, some interpreters believed that biblical types could relate to nonbiblical figures, events, or institutions. To cite one major example, Jonathan Edwards looked to the natural world to find types that illustrated biblical truths. For example, he wrote that "the silkworm is a

remarkable type of Christ" because, when the silkworm "dies, [it] yields us that of which we make such glorious clothing." WJE, vol. 11, *Typological Writings* [1744], ed. Wallace E. Anderson, Mason I. Lowance, Jr., and David H. Watters (New Haven, CT: Yale University Press, 1993), 59, 70, 75–76, 106.

22. As E. Brooks Holifield observed of early New England, no "second-generation" Puritans "assumed that New England was the antitype of ancient Israel." Instead, "Israel's antitype was the true church....The New Englanders still called New England a New Israel; they still found countless analogues between themselves and the ancient Jews; but they did not think that their society fulfilled the biblical types." E. Brooks Holifield, *Theology in America: Christian Thought from the Age of the Puritans to the Civil War* (New Haven, CT: Yale University Press, 2003), 77. See also Reiner Smolinski, "Israel Redivinus: The Eschatological Limits of Puritan Typology in New England," *New England Quarterly* 63 (1990): 357–395.

23. Cyprian Strong, *God's Care of the New-England Colonies* (Hartford, CT: Watson, 1777), 5. See also Nathan O. Hatch, *The Sacred Cause of Liberty: Republican Thought and the Millennium in Revolutionary New England* (New Haven, CT: Yale University Press, 1977), 60. In an unpublished sermon from September 1760, Ezra Stiles celebrated the fall of Montreal to the British by arguing that "there is a striking Analogy and similitude obviously established by the God we serve, I say an obvious Likeness between the circumstances of Israel's prospering...and of...British Protestants...[in] this American Canaan." Stiles, "2 Chronicles 20:6–7, 25 Sept 1760." For similar parallels, see Joseph Bean, *A Sermon Delivered at Wrentham, October 26, 1773, On Compleating the First Century Since the Town Was Incorporated* (Boston: John Boyle, 1774), 10–11, 24; Samuel E. McCorkle, *A Sermon, on the Comparative Happiness and Duty of the United States of America, Contrasted with Other Nations, Particularly the Israelites* (Halifax, MA: Abraham Hodge, 1795). This parallel between America and Israel was important, but most ministers were careful not to call America the equal to Israel or the direct fulfillment of Israel. In a sermon preached to celebrate the twentieth anniversary of the Declaration of Independence, Massachusetts minister John Cushing preached that "God dealt with no people as with Israel: but in the history of the United States, particularly New England, there is as great a similarity, perhaps, in the conduct of Providence to that of the Israelites, as is to be found in the history of any people." John Cushing, *A Discourse, Delivered at Ashburnham, July 4th, 1796* (Leominster, MA: Charles Prentiss, 1796), 6. Likewise, Timothy Dwight preached: "No land, that of Palestine excepted, hath in the same time experienced more extraordinary interpositions of Providence than this." *A Sermon, Preached at Stamford, in Connecticut, Upon the General Thanksgiving, December 18th, 1777* (Hartford, CT: Watson and Goodwin, 1778), 13. E. Brooks Holifield argued that types and biblical examples differed because "types pointed beyond themselves" to future spiritual truths, but "examples bore their meanings on the surface." Also, "the visible types were abolished

when they found fulfillment in their Christian antitypes," whereas "examples endured as perpetual models for Christian behavior." Holifield, *Era of Persuasion: American Thought and Culture 1521–1680*, Twayne's American Thought and Culture (Boston: Twayne Publishers, 1989), 46. On the distinction between biblical examples and types, see also Gerald T. Sheppard, "Christian Interpretation of the Old Testament between Reformation and Modernity," in William Perkins, *A Commentary on Hebrews 11 (1609 Edition)*, ed. John H. Augustine, Pilgrim Classic Commentaries (New York: Pilgrim Press, 1991), 62. On the use of biblical examples in the Revolutionary era, see Joseph Montgomery, *A Sermon Preached at Christiana Bridge* (Philadelphia: James Humhreys, 1775), 12.

24. For studies of biblical typology in America, see Morgan, "Miller's Williams," *New England Quarterly* 38, no. 4 (December 1965): 514; Sacvan Bercovitch, "Typology in Puritan New England: The Williams-Cotton Controversy Reassessed," *American Quarterly* 19 (1967): 163–191; Sacvan Bercovitch, *Typology and Early American Literature* (Amherst, MA: University of Massachusetts Press, 1972); Sacvan Bercovitch, *The Puritan Origins of the American Self* (New Haven, CT: Yale University Press, 1975); Sacvan Bercovitch, *The American Jeremiad* (Madison: University of Wisconsin Press, 1978); Ursula Brumm, *American Thought and Religious Typology* (New Brunswick, NJ: Rutgers University Press, 1970); Mason I. Lowance, "Typology and the New England Way: Cotton Mather and the Exegesis of Biblical Types," *Early American Literature* 4 (1969): 15–37; Mason I. Lowance, *The Language of Canaan: Metaphor and Symbol in New England from the Puritans to the Transcendentalists* (Cambridge: Harvard University Press, 1980); Thomas H. Luxon, *Literal Figures: Puritan Allegory and the Reformation Crisis of Representation* (Chicago: University of Chicago Press, 1995); Smolinski, "Israel Redivinus."

25. In a 1780 sermon commemorating the battle at Lexington, Isaac Morrill preached, "Our conditions in this world are often in scripture represented by a state of war," an idea that was commonplace. Isaac Morrill was a military chaplain and pastor in Wilmington, Massachusetts. See Isaac Morrill, *A Sermon Preached at Lexington, April 19, 1780* (Boston: John Gill, 1780), 11. In one key example from 1674, just a year before New England would be ripped apart by King Philip's War, Puritan minister Thomas Shepard asserted that war was so integral to scripture that the Bible could have been titled "The Book of the Wars of the Lord." Shepard then summarized the war between good and evil that encompassed scripture. Shepard's quotation, "Wars of the Lord," is a reference to Numbers 21.14, and is taken from his preface to Urian Oakes, *The unconquerable, all-conquering, & more-then-conquering souldier: or, The successful warre which a believer wageth with the enemies of his soul: as also the absolute and unparalleld victory that he obtains finally over them through the love of God in Jesus Christ,: as it was discoursed in a sermon preached at Boston in New-England, on the day of the artillery-election there, June 3d. 1672* (Cambridge: Samuel Green, 1674), A1.

26. Joyce Appleby, "The American Heritage: The Heirs and the Disinherited," *Journal of American History* 74, no. 3 (December 1, 1987): 809; Noll, *America's God*, 371; Gutjahr, *American Bible*, 2, 118. On the place of the classical world in America's founding, see Carl Richard, *The Golden Age of the Classics in America: Greece, Rome, and the Antebellum United States* (Cambridge, MA: Harvard University Press, 2009); Carl Richard, *The Founders and the Classics: Greece, Rome, and the American Enlightenment* (Cambridge, MA: Harvard University Press, 1995); Eran Shalev, *Rome Reborn Western Shores: Historical Imagination and the Creation of the American Republic* (Charlottesville: University of Virginia Press, 2009); Caroline Winterer, *Culture of Classicism: Ancient Greece and Rome in American Intellectual Life* (Baltimore, Johns Hopkins University Press, 2002); Paul A. Rahe, *Republics Ancient and Modern: Classical Republicanism and the American Revolution* (Chapel Hill: University of North Carolina Press, 1992).

27. Adams quoted in Gordon S. Wood, *The Radicalism of the American Revolution*, vol. 1 (New York: A.A. Knopf, 1992), 95–96; see also Noll, *America's God*, 56–57.

28. Levi Hart, *Liberty Described and Recommended* (Hartford, CT: Ebenezer Watson, 1775), 8. Hart was among a group of ministers called "New Divinity," who followed the theological agendas set by Jonathan Edwards. See also Massachusetts minister Isaac Story's sermon from December, 1774, in which he attributed the fall of ancient Rome "to the extinction of a public spirit"—an "inglorious degeneracy" that he hoped would "never be the fate of America!" Isaac Story, *Love of Country Recommended* (Boston: Boyle, 1775), 16.

29. See Samuel Langdon, *Government corrupted by Vice, and recovered by Righteousness* (Watertown, MA: Benjamin Edes, 1775). According to Mark Noll, "American republican language returned consistently to two main themes: fear of abuses from illegitimate power and a nearly messianic belief in the benefits of liberty." *America's God*, 56. See also J. G. A. Pocock, *The Machiavellian Moment: Florentine Political Thought and the Atlantic Republican Tradition* (Princeton, NJ: Princeton University Press, 2003), especially chap. 15.

30. John Adams to Benjamin Rush, February 2, 1807, in Hutson, *Founders on Religion*, 23.

31. See John Milton, *The Tenure of Kings and Magistrates* in Merritt Y. Hughes, ed., *John Milton: Complete Poems and Major Prose* (New York: Macmillan, 1957), 761–762.

32. Recently, Michael Winship has argued convincingly that Puritanism supported republican ideas in both church and civil governments. In the view of many Puritans, Winship argues, "Jesus had intended each of his congregations to be little republics, each governed by a collective elected body called a presbytery." Consequently, Massachusetts had "republican civil and church governments created in the early 1630s" and "the fear of tyrannical power...in large measure shaped them." Moreover, in the American Revolution, Joseph Galloway, a

famous loyalist, held the Puritans partially responsible for sowing the seeds of revolution and republican thought. Michael P. Winship, *Godly Republicanism: Puritans, Pilgrims, and a City on a Hill* (Cambridge, MA: Harvard University Press, 2012), 2, 4, 249. Gordon Wood argued that "the traditional covenant theology of Puritanism combined with the political science of the eighteenth century into an imperatively persuasive argument for revolution." Wood, *Creation of the American Republic*, 118. See Bernard Bailyn, *The Ideological Origins of the American Revolution* (Cambridge, MA: Belknap Press of Harvard University Press, 1992), 32; Perry Miller, "From the Covenant to the Revival," in *Nature's Nation* (Cambridge, MA: Harvard University Press, 1967); Stout, *New England Soul*, 7. Mark Noll argued that "the Bible's direct political influence was extremely limited" in Revolutionary America and that "the occasions when leaders turned to [the Bible] for assistance in political reasoning" were "extremely rare." Noll, "Bible in Revolutionary America," 52. See also Daniel Judah Elazar, *Covenant & Constitutionalism: The Great Frontier and the Matrix of Federal Democracy*, The Covenant Tradition in Politics 3 (New Brunswick, NJ: Transaction Publishers, 1998), chaps. 1–3.

33. It was a common idea, expressed well by Reverend John Mellen of Hanover, that "liberty is the spirit and genius, not only of the gospel, but of the whole of that revelation, we have, first and last, received from God." John Mellen, *The Great and Happy Doctrine of Liberty* (Boston: Hall, 1795), 9. Mark Noll made the case that "the Bible is not a stranger" to Real Whig political theory, "but it is equally evident that the Bible is not determinative." "Bible in Revolutionary America," 45. Noll argues further that "the Bible was everywhere (in the national consciousness) and nowhere (in explicit political theory) during the early years of American politics, that the politics of Revolutionary America were distinctly biblical (because articulated by leaders who found inspiration in scripture and because taken for granted as the basis for national values) while at the same time quite untouched by the messages of scripture (because worked out *as politics* with almost no reference to the sacred page)." The Bible, Noll argues, was interpreted in Revolutionary America and the early nineteenth century "as if its values and themes melded easily and without strain into the major commitments of Western civilization." The Bible was therefore part of Western civilization, so it did not stand apart as an independent influence. "Bible in Revolutionary America," 53–54.

34. Catherine A. Brekus, *Strangers & Pilgrims: Femal Preaching in America, 1740–1845* (Chapel Hill: University of North Carolina Press, 1998), 71.

35. Mark A. Noll, *America's God: From Jonathan Edwards to Abraham Lincoln* (New York: Oxford University Press, 2002), 497n.1. Noll credited an unpublished manuscript by Stephen A. Marini for some of these statistics. See also Edwin S. Gaustad, P. L. Barlow, and R. W Dishno, *New Historical Atlas of Religion in America* (New York: Oxford University Press, 2001), 7–8, 209.

36. The drive for religious liberty was a major reason why, despite much inflamed rhetoric that connected "popery" with "tyranny," most Catholics in Revolutionary America were patriots. In fact, Maura Jane Farrelly argues that American Catholics "saw that the anti-Catholicism was really not about them;" it was more about British tyrants, who were mostly Protestant. Even though Catholics were mostly patriots, they did not preach about it. "None of the sermons" that Maryland's Catholic priests "delivered between 1776 and 1783 even mentioned the war." Maura Jane Farrelly, *Papist Patriots: The Making of an American Catholic Identity* (New York: Oxford University Press, 2012), 18, 217, 242, 247. See also Robert M. Calhoon, "Loyalism and Neutrality," in Jack P. Greene and R. R. Pole, *A Companion to the American Revolution* (Malden, MA: Blackwell, 2000), 235.

37. Wood, *Radicalism*, 104–105.

38. Susan Juster, "What's Sacred About Violence in Early America," *Common-Place* 6, no. 1 (October 2005), www.common-place.org/vol-06/no-01/juster/. On Foxe's influence in America, see James West Davidson, *The Logic of Millennial Thought: Eighteenth-Century New England* (New Haven, CT: Yale University Press, 1977), 241; Francis J. Bremer, "Foxe in the Wilderness: The Book of Martyrs in Seventeenth-Century New England," in *John Foxe at Home and Abroad*, ed. David Loades (Burlington, VT: Ashgate Publishing, 2004), 105–116.

39. Thomas Brockway, *America Saved, or Divine Glory Displayed, in the Late War with Great Britain* (Hartford: Hudson and Goodwin, 1784), 19–20. This idea of wartime sacrifice as martyrdom filled sermons during the Revolution. "Every one that may die in this dispute, will be justly esteemed a *Martyr* to liberty," a chaplain preached to General St. Clair's brigade at Ticonderoga in October 1776. *An Address to General St. Clair's Brigade, at Ticonderoga, When the Enemy Were Hourly Expected, October 20, 1776* (Philadelphia: Steiner & Cist, 1777), 3. See also two sermons by Israel Evans, one of George Washington's favorite chaplains: *A Discourse Delivered Near York in Virginia, on the Memorable Occasion of the Surrender of the British Army to the Allied Forces of America and France* (Philadelphia: Francis Bailey, 1782), 24; *An Oration, Delivered at Hackingsack, On the Tenth of September, 1780. At the Interment of the Honorable Brigadier Enoch Poor, General of the New-Hampshire Brigade* (Newbury-Port, MA: John Mycall, 1781), 24. Likewise, see George Duffield, *A Sermon, Preached in the Third Presbyterian Church, in the City of Philadelphia, On Thursday, December 11, 1783* (Philadelphia: F. Bailey, 1784), 19–20, 23.

40. Israel Evans, *A Discourse Delivered Near York in Virginia, on the Memorable Occasion of the Surrender of the British Army to the Allied Forces of America and France* (Philadelphia: Francis Bailey, 1782), 24. See also Evans, *Oration, Delivered at Hackingsack*, 24; Israel Evans, *A Discourse, Delivered, on the 18th Day of December, 1777, the Day of Public Thanksgiving, Appointed by the Honourable Continental Congress* (Lancaster, PA: Francis Bailey, 1778), 16. George Duffield, *A Sermon, Preached in the Third Presbyterian Church, in the City of Philadelphia,*

On Thursday, December 11, 1783 (Philadelphia: Francis Bailey, 1784), 19–20, 23; See also Levi Frisbie, *An Oration, Delivered at Ipswich, On Account of the Happy Restoration of Peace Between Great-Britain and the United States of America* (Boston: E. Russell, 1783), 21. In an attack on Arnold, an anonymous poet wrote: "Sure none but Judas of the race of man E'er form'd a plot more dreadful or more vile." *The Fall of Lucifer, An Elegiac Poem on the Infamous Defection of the Late General Arnold* (Hartford, CT: Hudson and Goodwin, 1781), 15.

41. Stout, *New England Soul*, 82–83. As Portsmouth pastor Joshua Moodey preached in his 1675 sermon *Souldiery Spiritualized*, "While there is Flesh as well as Spirit in the new man, there will be Warrs within; and while there are carnal men as well as Spiritual in the World there will be Warrs without." *Souldiery Spiritualized, or The Christian Souldier Orderly, and Strenuously Engaged in the Spirirual Warre, and so Fighting the Good Fight: Represented in a Sermon Preached at Boston in New England on the Day of the Artillery Election There, June 1, 1674* (Cambridge, MA: Samuel Green, 1674), 39. Numerous wartime sermons asserted this theme throughout the eighteenth century. See, for example, Jehu Minor, *A Military Discourse* (New Haven, CT: Thomas and Samuel Green, 1774), 11–14. This idea of spiritual warfare was commonplace in English Protestantism and was exemplified by many books, including John Downame's expensive but influential *The Christian Warfare Against the Devil, World, and Flesh*, a book that was first published in seventeenth-century London. See *The Christian warfare against the Deuill world and flesh wherein is described their nature, the maner of their fight and meanes to obtaine victorye*, 2nd ed. (London: William Stansby, 1634). Spiritual warfare was just as prominent in the eighteenth century. What George Marsden wrote of Jonathan Edwards could be said of many colonists in the period: "All of life…was spiritual warfare." *Jonathan Edwards: A Life* (New Haven, CT: Yale University Press, 2004), 137.

42. Evans, *Discourse, Delivered, on the 18th Day of December, 1777*, 21. As Presbyterian minister John Murray of Newburyport preached, "the works of providence are done by means." Moreover, "though the cause is the Lord's he will have it affected by ordinary means—walls and towers—gates and bars—forts and armies are not less indispensible than temple and sacrifice." John Murray, *Nehemiah, Or the Struggle for Liberty Never in Vain, When Managed with Virtue and Perseverance* (Newbury, MA: John Mycall, 1779), 18, 36.

43. We find a vivid illustration in a 1759 sermon, skillfully titled *The Art of War, the Gift of God*, in which Silvanus Conant asked soldiers who were preparing for a Canadian expedition: "Do not some of you already feel the laudable Fire of martial Zeal, kindling in your hearts, by the touch of a live coal from the altar of the living God?" Note here that God inspired "a martial Zeal" within the soldiers, launching them onward to battle. Conant further implored the soldiers to "nourish the sacred spark" ignited by God until "it blazes out into a manly, heroic, unquenchable Zeal." But Conant warned the soldiers that heroism

needed divine inspiration—the fires of military courage could only burn when supplied with "the most sacred Fuel." Silvanus Conant, *The Art of War, the Gift of God* (Boston: Edes and Gill, 1759), 9–10. See also William Emerson, "Sermon on 2 Chronicles 13.12, March 13, 1775," in *Diaries and Letters of William Emerson, 1743–1776* (Boston: Thomas Todd Company, 1775), 64–65.

44. Eli Forbes, *The Dignity and Importance of the Military Character Illustrated* (Boston: Richard Draper, 1771), 20. As Brooklyn pastor Josiah Whitney preached to an infantry regiment near the end of the revolutionary era, "religion gives not to the soldier a spirit of fear, but a spirit of power, of fortitude." *A Sermon Addressed to a military company belonging to the 13th Regiment of the Infantry* (Windham, CT: John Byrne, 1800), 10. See also John Devotion, *The Duty and Interest of a People to Sanctify the Lord of Hosts* (Hartford, CT: Ebenezer Watson, 1777), 33.

45. Numerous biblical texts could be studied, including the story of Esther, which Bernard Bailyn cited as a biblical parallel that some revolutionaries applied to their situation. Bailyn, *Ideological Origins*, 126–127. Esther was a fine example of how revolutionaries used scripture, but it was not as popular in sermons over time as the texts discussed in this book. Specifically, there were seventeen citations of Esther in wartime sermons between 1763 and 1787, compared to 67 citations of Romans 13, and 48 citations of Judges 5. See Oliver Noble, *Some Strictures Upon the Sacred Story Recorded in the Book of Esther, Shewing The Power and Oppression of State Ministers Tending to the Ruin and Destruction of God's Peoples—And the Remarkable Interpositions of Divine Providence in Favour of the Oppressed* (Newburyport, MA: E. Lunt and H. W. Tinges, 1775).

CHAPTER 1

1. Nathan Perkins, *A Sermon, Preached to the Soldiers, Who Went from West-Hartford, in Defence of Their Country* (Hartford, CT: Ebenezer Watson, 1775), 13–14, 9.

2. Harry S. Stout, *The New England Soul: Preaching and Religious Culture in Colonial New England* (New York: Oxford University Press, 1986), 3; Emory Elliot, "The Dove and Serpent: The Clergy in the American Revolution," *American Quarterly* 31, no. 2 (July 1, 1979): 187–188, passim.

3. Stout, *New England Soul*, 303.

4. Ibid., 6–7. Several other historians have confirmed Stout's figures by documenting the influence of the sermon in Revolutionary America, in New England, and beyond. For instance, Ellis Sandoz determined that "over 80 percent of the politically relevant pamphlets published during the 1770s and 1780s are either reprinted sermons or essays written by ministers." *Political Sermons of the American Founding Era*, vol. 1, 2nd ed. (Indianapolis, IN: Liberty Fund, 1998), 369.

5. Mark A. Noll, *America's God: From Jonathan Edwards to Abraham Lincoln* (New York: Oxford University Press, 2002), 83–85; Nathan R. Perl-Rosenthal, "The

'divine right of republics': Hebraic Republicanism and the Debate over Kingless Government in Revolutionary America," *William and Mary Quarterly*, 3rd ser., 66, no. 3 (July 2009): 535–564; Thomas S. Kidd, *God of Liberty: A Religious History of the American Revolution* (New York: Basic Books, 2010), 24–25. As Bernard Bailyn argued, "the dominant tone of *Common Sense* is that of rage. It was written by an enraged man." He was not advocating against incorrect polices; he was attacking evil, a diabolical government. It was this enraged tone that set *Common Sense* apart from other pamphlets of its day. Other pamphlets, usually written by educated men in an educated style, sought a reasoned discourse and aimed at recommending new polices. In contrast, "Paine's aim was to tear the world apart." He had no use for reasoned discourses; he did not want "to convince, or to explain." He wanted "to overwhelm and destroy." Bailyn, *Faces of Revolution: Personalities and Themes in the Struggle for American Independence* (New York: Knopf, 1990), 82–83. As we have seen, Paine's tools of destruction were often biblical.

6. Nathaniel Whitaker, *A Funeral Sermon, on the Death of the Reverend George Whitefield* (Salem, MA: Printed and sold by Samuel Hall, 1770), 33–34; Kidd, *God of Liberty*, 33. Mark Noll observed that "Whitefield was the colonies' most visible symbol of changing conceptions of hierarchy; he represented a new confidence in the religious powers of the people and a sharp, if implicit, rebuke to the authority of tradition." Even so, in substance, his preaching was not primarily political. And when he did address political themes, his "politics ... were much more determined by anti-Catholicism than by republicanism." Overall, he preached "spiritual liberty" rather than civil liberty; his was mostly "an apolitical gospel." Such was not the case with his followers, and Whitaker is but one example. Noll, *America's God*, 76–77. Various historians have well analyzed the social and political influence of Whitefield and of itinerant preaching in colonial America. See Timothy D. Hall, *Contested Boundaries: Itinerancy and the Reshaping of the Colonial American Religious World* (Durham, NC: Duke University Press, 2004), especially 41–100; Harry S. Stout, *The Divine Dramatist: George Whitefield and the Rise of Modern Evangelicalism*, Library of Religious Biography (Grand Rapids, MI: William B. Eerdmans, 1991); Frank Lambert, *"Pedlar in Divinity": George Whitefield and the Transatlantic Revivals, 1737–1770* (Princeton, NJ: Princeton University Press, 1994); Thomas S. Kidd, *The Great Awakening: The Roots of Evangelical Christianity in Colonial America* (New Haven, CT: Yale University Press, 2007), chapters 4, 7, 18.

7. Charles Royster, *A Revolutionary People at War: The Continental Army and American Character* (Chapel Hill: University of North Carolina Press, 1979), 24; J. T. Headley, *Chaplains and Clergy of the American Revolution* (New York: Charles Scribner, 1864), 92–93, 105; Kidd, *Great Awakening*, 288.

8. Harry S. Stout has critiqued historians' reliance almost exclusively on printed pamphlets. "The problem is pamphlets," Stout argued, "although central to the

rebellion and the articulation of classical republican theory in the colonies, they were not sufficient to explain the process of an egalitarian cultural transformation." Stout, "Religion, Communications, and the Ideological Origins of the American Revolution," *William and Mary Quarterly*, 3rd ser., 34, no. 4 (October 1977): 536–537. Here Stout poses a nuanced defense of Alan Heimert, *Religion and the American Mind, from the Great Awakening to the Revolution* (Cambridge, MA: Harvard University Press, 1966). Heimert's book was the classic statement for a direct link between the Great Awakening and the Revolution. For an insightful assessment of this intriguing historiographical debate, see Philip Goff, "Revivals and Revolution: Historiographic Turns since Alan Heimert's *Religion and the American Mind*," *Church History* 67, no. 4 (1998): 695–721. Making a similar point, Mark Noll argued that "Jonathan Mayhew, who had himself renounced the particular theology of the Awakening, displayed a rhetorical style that was as 'evangelistic' in the service of liberty as Whitefield's was in the service of the gospel." *Christians in the American Revolution* (Grand Rapids, MI: Christian University Press, 1977), 63. Elsewhere Noll stated the point well: "The political importance of the Awakening was not direct, as Heimert thought, but everywhere indirect....The revival opened up possibilities for the migration of political language into religious speech." Noll, "The American Revolution and Protestant Evangelicalism," *Journal of Interdisciplinary History* 23, no. 3, *Religion and History* (1993): 626. The latest and most authoritative religious history of the Revolution confirms this influence between revival and Revolution: "The evangelical view of limited government and its style of rhetoric colored America's Wars from the siege of Louisbourg in 1745 to the American Revolution. The evangelicals' challenge to authority from the Great Awakening to the Revolution helped forge an American style of resistance that propelled many into independence in 1776." Kidd, *God of Liberty*, 77. See also Kidd, *Great Awakening*, 288–289. Rhys Isaac has also well demonstrated the social and political effect of evangelicalism in colonial America in the following works: Isaac, "The Evangelical Revolt: The Nature of the Baptists' Challenge to the Traditional Order in Virginia, 1765 to 1775," *William and Mary Quarterly*, 3rd. ser., 31, no. 3 (1974): 345–368; "Preachers and Patriots: Popular Culture and the Revolution in Virginia," in Alfred F. Young, ed. *The American Revolution: Explorations in the History of American Radicalism* (Dekalb, IL: Northern Illinois University Press, 1976); and *The Transformation of Virginia : 1740–1790* (Chapel Hill: Published for the Institute of Early American History and Culture Williamsburg, VA, by University of North Carolina Press, 1982). The main critic of any influence of the Great Awakening on the American Revolution is Jon Butler. See Jon Butler, "Enthusiasm Described and Decried: The Great Awakening as Interpretive Fiction," *Journal of American History* 69 (September 1982): 305–325. Other excellent critiques include John Murrin, "No Awakening, No Revolution? More Counterfactual Speculations," *Reviews in*

American History 11, no. 2 (June 1983): 161–171; several of Nathan Hatch's works, including *The Sacred Cause of Liberty: Republican Thought and the Millennium in Revolutionary New England* (New Haven, CT: Yale University Press, 1977) and "New Lights and the Revolution in Rural New England," *Reviews in American History* 8, no. 3 (1980): 323–328. Gordon Wood argued that critiques such as Butler's tend to "misunderstand the nature of the historical process." Revivals did not cause the Revolution, but revivals "contributed to new social and cultural circumstances out of which the Revolution arose." Wood, "Religion and the American Revolution," in *New Directions in American Religious History,* ed. Harry S. Stout and D. G. Hart (New York: Oxford University Press, 1997), 180–181.

9. Thomas Kidd, *Great Awakening,* 289. Kidd argues that "the majority of evangelicals from Maine to Georgia (but not in Canada) were Patriots," although these patriotic evangelicals "did not necessarily become Patriots because they were evangelicals." Ibid., 289. In addition, Kidd organized evangelical responses to the Revolution into four categories, with "Patriot evangelicals" as the leading category. Ibid., 291–307.

10. Abigail Adams to John Adams, November 5, 1775. in *Familiar Letters of John Adams and his Wife Abigail Adams, During the Revolution,* ed. Charles F. Adams (New York: Hurd and Haughton, 1876), 122.

11. Judah Champion, *A Brief View of the Distresses, Hardships and Dangers Our Ancestors Encounter'd, in Settling New-England* (Hartford, CT: Green & Watson, 1770), unnumbered second page.

12. William MacDonald, ed., *Documentary Source Book of American History, 1606–1913* (New York: The Macmillan Company, 1920), 177–178.

13. Champion, *A Brief View,* 30. Similar to Champion, Presbyterian minister and chaplain Joseph Montgomery justified the conquering of Native American lands through war. "The Indian tribes, the natives of this land, cruel in their natures, barbarous in their customs, numerous in their nations, potent and artful in their wars, either are prevailed on to sell their right to the soil, or where they are refractory, are conquered." Montgomery justified such seizure of Indian lands, writing that "the Indians, in their savage state, occupy much more land than is necessary, by the laws of Nature for their support." Joseph Montgomery, *A Sermon Preached at Christiana Bridge* (Philadelphia, PA: James Humhreys, 1775), 24–25.

14. Jill Lepore, *The Name of War: King Philip's War and the Origins of American Identity* (New York: Knopf, 1998), x.

15. Stout, *New England Soul,* 77–83.

16. Ibid., 84; See also Ann M. Little, *Abraham in Arms: War and Gender in Colonial New England* (Philadelphia: University of Pennsylvania Press, 2007); Marie Ahearn, *The Rhetoric of War: Training Day, the Militia, and the Military Sermon,* Contributions in American History (Santa Barbara, CA: Praeger, 1989), 11–36.

17. Nathaniel Saltonstall quoted in Lepore, *Name of War*, 105. This was an unusual case, but ministers often warned that the people could not expect to win their wars if they neglected their Bibles. In an unprinted sermon from 1756, Matthew Bridge from Framingham preached: "If we should be carried into captivity among our persecuting foes, what sad reflections will such of you have upon your selves that ye have thus neglected the word of God." Matthew Bridge "Sermon on Lamentations 1:7, Sept. 12, 1756," in Sermons Collection, box 3, folder 35, American Antiquarian Society, Worchester, MA, 16–17. See also Marie L. Ahearn, *The Rhetoric of War* (New York: Greenwood Press, 1989).

18. Lepore, *Name of War*, 173. See also R. Don Higginbotham, "The Martial Spirit in the Antebellum South: Some Further Speculations in a National Context," *Journal of Southern History* 58, no. 1 (February 1, 1992): 7; John E. Ferling, *A Wilderness of Miseries: War and Warriors in Early America* (Westport, CT: Greenwood Press, 1980), 45.

19. John E. Ferling, *Almost a Miracle: The American Victory in the War of Independence* (Oxford: Oxford University Press, 2007), Kindle edition, loc. 482. See also R. Don Higginbotham, "The Early American Way of War: Reconnaissance and Appraisal," *William and Mary Quarterly* 3rd ser., 44, no. 2 (1987): 230–273; R. Don Higginbotham, *War and Society in Revolutionary America: The Wider Dimensions of Conflict* (Columbia: University of South Carolina Press, 1988).

20. Lepore, *Name of War*, xv–xxi.

21. On martial preaching in the context of the King Philip's War, see Stout, *New England Soul*, 77–85; Richard Slotkin and James K. Folsom, *So Dreadfull a Judgment: Puritan Responses to King Philip's War, 1676–1677* (Middletown, CT: Wesleyan University Press, 1978); Alden T. Vaughan, *New England Encounters: Indians and Euroamericans Ca. 1600–1850: Essays Drawn from The New England Quarterly* (Boston: Northeastern University Press, 1999); Samuel Willard, *The Heart Garrisoned or, The Wisdome, and Care of the Spiritual Souldier Above All Things to Safeguard His Heart. Delivered in a Sermon Which Was Preached to the Honoured Gentlemen of the Artillery Company, on the Day of Their Election, at Boston in New-England June, 5. 1676* (Cambridge: Samuel Green, 1676); Joshua Moodey, *Souldiery Spiritualized, or The Christian Souldier Orderly, and Strenuously Engaged in the Spirirual Warre, and so Fighting the Good Fight: Represented in a Sermon Preached at Boston in New England on the Day of the Artillery Election There, June 1. 1674* (Cambridge: Samuel Green, 1674); Urian Oakes, *The Unconquerable, All-conquering, & More-then-conquering Souldier: Or, The Successful Warre Which a Believer Wageth with the Enemies of His Soul: As Also the Absolute and Unparalleld Victory That He Obtains Finally over Them Through the Love of God in Jesus Christ, as It Was Discoursed in a Sermon Preached at Boston in New-England, on the Day of the Artillery-election There, June 3d. 1672* (Cambridge: Samuel Green, 1674); Wait Winthrop, *Some Mediations Concerning Our Honourable Gentlemen and Fellow-Souldiers, in*

Pursuit of Those Barbarous Natives (New London, CT, 1675); Thomas Wheeler, *A Thankefull Remembrance of Gods Mercy* (Cambridge: Samuel Green, 1676); Samuel Nowell, *Abraham in Arms; or The First Religious General with His Army* (Boston: John Foster, 1678).

22. Stout, *New England Soul*, 233–235; Charles Chauncy, *Marvellous Things Done by the Right Hand and Holy Arm of God in Getting Him the Victory.* (Boston: T. Fleet, at the Heart and Crown in Cornhill, 1745), 9. In addition to Chauncy's, the many sermons preached in celebration of the victory at Cape Breton included: George Whitefield, "Britain's Mercies, and Britain's Duty," in Sandoz, *Political Sermons*, 1:119–136; Jared Eliot, *God's Marvellous Kindness, Illustrated in a Sermon Preach'd at the South Society in Killingworth, on the General Thanksgiving in the Colony of Connecticut, July 25. 1745. Occasion'd by Taking the City of Louisbourg on the Isle of Cape-Breton, by New-England Soldiers, Assisted by a British Squadron, June 17, 1745* (New London, CT: T. Green, 1745); Samuel Niles, *A Brief and Plain Essay on God's Wonder-working Providence for New-England, in the Reduction of Louisburg, and Fortresses Thereto Belonging on Cape-Breton.* (New London, CT: T. Green, 1747); Gilbert Tennent, *The Necessity of Praising God for Mercies Receiv'd a Sermon Occasion'd, by the Success of the Late Expedition, (under the Direction and Command of Gen. Pepperel and Com. Warren,) in Reducing the City and Fortresses of Louisburgh on Cape-Breton, to the Obedience of His Majesty King George the Second.* (Philadelphia: William Bradford at the Bible in Second Street, 1745). Thomas Prince, *Extraordinary Events the Doings of God, and Marvellous in Pious Eyes* (Boston: D. Henchman, 1745).

23. Noll, *America's God*, 78–80; Hatch, *Sacred Cause of Liberty.*

24. Bailyn, *Ideological Origins*, 70–73; Noll, *America's God*, 55–57, 567. Gordon Wood argued that the English people "everywhere simply made poor subjects for monarchy, and they were proud of it." *Radicalism*, 12–13. For a recent work that argues convincingly for Puritan influences on the development of republican ideas, see Michael P. Winship, *Godly Republicanism: Puritans, Pilgrims, and a City on a Hill* (Cambridge, MA: Harvard University Press, 2012).

25. Fred Anderson, *Crucible of War: The Seven Years' War and the Fate of Empire in British North America, 1754–1766* (New York: A. A. Knopf, 2000), 11–32; Fred Anderson, *The War That Made America: A Short History of the French and Indian War* (New York: Viking, 2005), Kindle edition, locations 60, 187, 241.

26. See Joseph J. Ellis, *His Excellency: George Washington* (New York: Vintage Books, 2005), 1–7; 12–14; Anderson, *Crucible*, 50–65.

27. Benjamin Franklin, *Memoirs of Benjamin Franklin; Written by Himself,* ed. Henry Stueber (New York: Harper & Brothers, 1839), 161; Ellis, *His Excellency,* 22; Anderson, *Crucible*, 52–66, 94–107; Richard Furman, *Humble Submission to Divine Sovereignty the Duty of a Bereaved Nation. a Sermon, Occasioned by the Death of His Excellency General George Washington* (Charleston, SC: W. P. Young, 1800), 6.

28. Letter to Colonel Adam Stephen, July 20, 1776, in *The Papers of George Washington Digital Edition*, ed. Theodore J. Crackel (Charlottesville: University of Virginia Press, Rotunda, 2008), 408–409,http://rotunda.upress.virginia.edu.proxy.library.vanderbilt.edu/founders/GEWN-03-05-02-0298. See also, Ellis, *His Excellency*, 12–18; Anderson, *War that Made America*, locations 711–737.

29. Anderson, *Crucible*, 199–200.

30. Samuel Davies, *Religion and Patriotism the Constituents of a Good Soldier.* (Philadelphia: James Chattin, 1755), 3–7. Davies was a renowned preacher in the Great Awakening. For much of his career he was an itinerant minister who drew the ire of Anglicans and others who feared revivalist excesses. Davies was an unabashed revivalist, but he was also a moderate like New England's Jonathan Edwards. Both attempted to defend revivalism from overzealous radicals who gave it a bad name. For background on Davies, see Kidd, *Great Awakening*, 236–242 and Kidd, *God of Liberty*, 76.

31. Samuel Davies, *The Curse of Cowardice* (Boston: Fowle and Draper, 1759), 4–5. See also Noll, *America's God*, 80–81.

32. On sermons in celebration of the victory, see Stout, *New England Soul*, 251. The many sermons include Samuel Cooper, *A Sermon Preached Before His Excellency Thomas Pownall, Esq; Captain-General and Governor in Chief, The Honourable His Majesty's Council and House of Representatives, Of the Province of the Massachusetts-Bay in New-England, October 16th, 1759. Upon Occasion of the Success of His Majesty's Arms in the Reduction of Quebec* (Boston: Green & Russell and Edes & Gill, 1759); Nathanael Appleton, *A Sermon Preached October 9. Being a Day of Public Thanksgiving, Occasioned by the Surrender of Montreal, and All Canada, September 8th. 1760. to His Britannic Majesty* (Boston: John Draper, 1760); Thomas Foxcroft, *Grateful Reflexions on the Signal Appearances of Divine Providence for Great Britain and Its Colonies in America, Which Diffuse a General Joy* (Boston: S. Kneeland, 1760); Byles Mather, *A Sermon, Delivered March 6th 1760. Being a Day Appointed, by Order of His Majesty, as a Public Thanksgiving, for the Late Signal Successes, Granted to the British Arms* (New London, CT: Timothy Green, 1760); Jonathan Townsend, *Sorrow Turned into Joy. A Sermon Deliver'd at Medfield, October 25, 1759. Being a Day of Public Acknowledgement of the Smiles of Heaven Upon the British Arms in America: More Especially in the Reduction of Quebec* (Boston: S. Kneeland, 1760); Solomon Williams, *The Relations of God's People to Him, and the Engagements and Obligations They Are Under to Praise Him, and Prepare Him an Habitation. With a Special View to New-England, and the Rest of the British Subjects in America. A Thanksgiving Sermon, on Occasion of the Smiles of Heaven on the British Arms in America, Particularly in the Reduction of Quebec* (New London, CT: Timothy Green, 1760). John Burt, *The Mercy of God to His People, in the Vengeance He Renders to Their Adversaries, the Occasion of Their Abundant Joy* (Newport: J. Franklin, 1759); Andrew Eliot, *A Sermon Preached October 25th, 1759. Being a Day of Public Thanksgiving Appointed by Authority, for*

the Success of the British Arms This Year; Especially in the Reduction of Quebec, the Captial of Canada (Boston: Daniel and John Kneeland, 1759); William Adams, *A Discourse Delivered at New-London, October 23d. A.D. 1760. On the Thanksgiving, (ordered by Authority) for the Success of the British Arms, in the Reduction of Montreal, and the Conquest of All Canada* (New London, CT: Timothy Green, 1761); Eli Forbes, *God the Strength and Salvation of His People; Illustrated in a Sermon Preached October 9, 1760. Being a Day of Public Thanksgiving Appointed by Authority for the Success of the British Arms in North-America, Especially in the Total Reduction of Canada to the Crown of Great-Britain* (Boston: Edes & Gill, 1761); David Hall, *Israel's Triumph. It Concerns the People of God to Celebrate the Divine Praises, According to All His Wonderful Works. A Sermon Preached at Sutton on a Publick Thanksgiving, October 9th, 1760. For the Entire Reduction of Canada* (Boston: J. Draper, 1761); Samuel Langdon, *Joy and Gratitude to God for the Long Life of a Good King, and the Conquest of Quebec* (Portsmouth: Daniel Fowle, 1760); Jonathan Mayhew, *Two Discourses Delivered October 9th, 1760. Being the Day Appointed to Be Observed as a Day of Public Thanksgiving for the Success of His Majesty's Arms, More Especially in the Intire [sic] Reduction of Canada* (Boston: R. Draper, Edes and Gill, and T. and J. Fleet, 1760); John Mellen, *A Sermon Preached at the West Parish in Lancaster, October 9, 1760. On the General Thanksgiving for the Reduction of Montreal and Total Conquest of Canada* (Boston: B. Mecom, 1760); Samuel Woodward, *A Sermon Preached October 9, 1760. Being a Day of Public Thanksgiving on Occasion of the Reduction of Montreal and the Entire Conquest of Canada, by the Troops of His Britannic Majesty, Under the Command of General Amherst* (Boston: Benjamin Mecom, 1760).

33. Joseph Yesurun Pinto, *The Form of Prayer, Which Was Performed at the Jews Synagogue, in the City of New-York, on Thursday October 23, 1760; Being the Day Appointed by Proclamation for a General Thanksgiving to Almighty God, for the Reducing of Canada to His Majesty's Dominions* (New York: W. Weyman, 1760).

34. Gordon S. Wood, *The American Revolution: A History* (New York: Modern Library, 2002), 17–18.

35. Ibid., 28.

36. Thomas S. Kidd, *Patrick Henry: First Among Patriots* (New York: Basic Books, 2011), 58–61; William Wirt Henry, *Patrick Henry; Life, Correspondence and Speeches* (New York: Charles Scribner's Sons, 1891), 92–93; Stout, *New England Soul*, 262.

37. Bailyn, *Faces*, 69–70; Wood, *Radicalism*, 97–98, 100–103.

38. Gordon S. Wood, *The Creation of the American Republic, 1776–1787* (Chapel Hill, NC: University of North Carolina Press, 1998), 14–16; Bailyn, *Ideological Origins*, 36–40.

39. [Trenchard and Gordon], *Cato's Letters, or Essays on Liberty, Civil and Religious, and Other Important Subjects*, ed. Ronald Hamowy (Indianapolis, IN: Liberty Fund, 1995), vol. 2, chapter "NO. 62. SATURDAY, JANUARY 20, 1722. An Enquiry

into the Nature and Extent of Liberty; with its Loveliness and Advantages, and the vile Effects of Slavery," http://oll.libertyfund.org/title/1238/64485/1598122; Wood, *Creation*, 17.

40. Stout, *New England Soul*, 262–263; Bernard Bailyn, *The Ordeal of Thomas Hutchinson* (Cambridge, MA: Belknap Press of Harvard University Press, 1974), 35–69. On Mayhew, see Bailyn, *Faces*, 125–136.

41. Stout, *New England Soul*, 264; Alice M. Baldwin, *The New England Clergy and the American Revolution* (New York: F. Ungar, 1958), 99–102; Bailyn, *Faces*, chapter 6.

42. [Stephen Johnson], *Some Important Observations, Occasioned by, and Adapted to, The Public Fast, Ordered by Authority, December 18th, A. D. 1765* (Newport: Samuel Hall, 1766), 28.

43. Bailyn, *Faces*, ibook location 235. Thomas Kidd correctly noted "the folly of trying to separate the sources of revolutionary ideology into 'secular' or 'religious' categories: patriots drew on religious sources as well as Enlightenment philosophers like Locke and saw no contradiction between them." Kidd, *God of Liberty*, 81.

44. With their eyes on the Revolution, some historians have tended to underemphasize the extent to which pre-Revolutionary colonists put implicit trust in Hanoverian monarchs. See Brendan McConville, *The King's Three Faces: The Rise & Fall of Royal America, 1688–1776* (Chapel Hill: University of North Carolina Press, 2006).

45. Johnson, *Some Important Observations*, 4, 16–18.

46. Ibid., 20.

47. Nathaniel Appleton, *A Thanksgiving Sermon on the Total Repeal of the Stamp-act* (Boston, 1766); Charles Chauncy, *A Discourse on "the Good News from a Far Country." Deliver'd July 24th. A Day of Thanks-giving to Almighty God, Throughout the Province of the Massachusetts Bay in New-England, on Occasion of the Repeal of the Stamp-Act* (Boston: Kneeland and Adams for Thomas Leverett, 1766); Joseph Emerson, *A Thanksgiving Sermon Preach'd at Pepperrell, July 24th, 1766. A Day Set Apart by Public Authority as a Day of Thanksgiving On the Account of the Repeal of the Stamp Act* (Boston: Edes & Gill, 1766); Elisha Fish, *Joy and Gladness: A Thanksgiving Discourse, Preached in Upton, Wednesday, May 28, 1766; Occasioned by the Repeal of the Stamp-Act* (Providence: Sarah Goddard and Company, 1767); Jonathan Mayhew, *The Snare Broken. A Thanksgiving-Discourse, Preached At the Desire of the West Church in Boston, N.E. Friday May 23, 1766. Occasioned by the Repeal of the Stamp-Act* (Boston: R. & S. Draper, Edes & Gill, and T. &. J. Fleet, 1766); William Patten, *A Discourse Delivered at Hallifax In the County of Plymouth, July 24th, 1766. On the Day of Thanks-giving to Almighty God, Throughout the Province of the Massachusetts-Bay in New England, for the Repeal of the Stamp Act* (Boston: D. Kneeland for Thomas Leverett, 1766); Samuel Stillman, *Good News from a Far Country. A Sermon Preached at Boston, May 17, 1766. Upon the Arrival*

of the Important News Of the Repeal of the Stamp-Act (Boston: Kneeland and Adams, 1766); Benjamin Throop, *A Thanksgiving Sermon, Upon the Occasion, of the Glorious News of the Repeal of the Stamp Act* (New London, CT: Timothy Green, 1766); John Joachim Zubly, *The Stamp-Act Repealed. A Sermon, Preached in the Meeting at Savannah in Georgia, June 25th, 1766* (Charleston: Peter Timothy, 1766). See also Edmund Sears Morgan, *Prologue to Revolution; Sources and Documents on the Stamp Act Crisis, 1764–1766*, Documentary Problems in Early American History (Chapel Hill: University of North Carolina Press, 1959).

48. Peter Oliver, *Peter Oliver's "Origin and Progress of the American Rebellion": A Tory View* (Palo Alto, CA: Stanford University Press, 1961), 53. Stout, *New England Soul*, 266.

49. Robert Middlekauff, *The Glorious Cause: The American Revolution, 1763–1789*, rev. ed., The Oxford History of the United States (New York: Oxford University Press, 2005), 74–98; Wood, *American Revolution*, 31–32.

50. John Dickinson, *Letters from a Farmer in Pennsylvania, to the Inhabitants of the British Colonies.* (Boston: Mein and Fleeming, 1768), 18–20.

51. John Joachim Zubly, "An Humble Enquiry into The Nature of the Dependency of the American Colonies Upon the Parliament of Great-Britain," in Sandoz, *Political Sermons*, 1:298.

52. Middlekauff, *Glorious Cause*, chapter 9; Wood, *American Revolution*, 32–34. See also Richard Archer, *As If an Enemy's Country: The British Occupation of Boston and the Origins of Revolution* (New York: Oxford University Press, 2010).

53. Stout, *New England Soul*, 272; see the larger discussion in 271–275.

54. Harry Stout determined that sermons on the Boston Massacre "exceeded anything in the annals of New England oratory" for "sheer fury and blood revenge." *New England Soul*, 272.

55. John Lathrop, *Innocent Blood Crying to God from the Streets of Boston* (Boston: Edes and Gill, 1771), 5–6. For a similar interpretation of the Boston Massacre in terms of blood vengeance, see Charles Chauncy, *Trust in God, the Duty of a People in a Day of Trouble* (Boston: Daniel Kneeland, 1770), 19, 35–37.

56. John Lathrop, *Innocent Blood*, 4, 9; Stout, *New England Soul*, 275–277. The speeches commemorating the Boston Massacre were published in Peter Edes, ed., *Orations Delivered at the Request of the Inhabitants of the Town of Boston, to Commemorate the Evening of the Fifth of March, 1770; When a Number of Citizens Were Killed by a Party of British Troops, Quartered Among Them, in a Time of Peace* (Boston: Peter Edes, 1785); see, for example, James Lovell, *An Oration Delivered April 2d, 1771* (Boston: Edes and Gill, 1771).

57. Stout, New England Soul, 282.

58. J. M. Bumsted and C. E Clark, "New England's Tom Paine: John Allen and the Spirit of Liberty," *William and Mary Quarterly* 3rd ser., 21, no. 4 (October 1964): 561–570; John Allen, "An Oration Upon the Beauties of Liberty," in Sandoz, Political Sermons, 1:302.

59. Allen, "Beauties," 305.

60. Ibid., 316, 321.

61. Ibid., 322–323.

62. Ibid.

63. Middlekauff, *Glorious Cause*, chapter 11.

64. Benson Bobrick, *Angel in the Whirlwind: The Triumph of the American Revolution* (New York: Simon & Schuster, 1997), 72; Wood, *American Revolution*, 36–38.

65. As quoted in Bobrick, *Angel*, 73–74.

66. Israel Holly, *God Brings About His Holy and Wise Purpose or Decree.* (Hartford, CT: Ebenezer Watson, 1774), 17–18.

67. Holly, *God Brings About*, 17–18. See also Kidd, *God of Liberty*, 77–78.

68. Holly, *God Brings About*, 21–22. See also Elisha Rich, *A Sermon On Ecclesiastical Liberty. Preached Soon After the Civil War, Between Great-Britain and the American Colonies. In the Year 1775. In Which the Free Bought Man's Liberty Is Vindicated* (Concord, MA: Nathaniel Coverly, 1776).

69. As quoted in Bobrick, *Angel*, 75.

70. Middlekauff, *Glorious Cause*, chapter 11.

71. Alexander Hamilton, *The Works of Alexander Hamilton* (New York: Haskell House, 1904), 181, 193–196; Kidd, *God of Liberty*, 69. Numerous ministers agreed with Hamilton's assessment. In effect, the Quebec Act established George III as "the head of the romish church in Canada," preached Moses Mather in 1775. Mather, "America's Appeal to The Impartial World," in Sandoz, *Political Sermons*, 1:480.

72. Samuel Sherwood, "A Sermon, Containing Scriptural Instructions to Civil Rulers, and All Free-born Subjects," in Sandoz, *Political Sermons*, 1:373–408, especially 378–379. The "Coercive Acts" were coercive to all the colonies, as many Americans understood. These were horrendous policies, most likely diabolical in their aims but at best shortsighted, because they would hurt Britain as much as America. As Timothy Hilliard, pastor in Barnstable, Massachusetts, preached, "the interests" of Britain and America were united: "The same weapon that stabs America, pierces the vitals of Britain." Hilliard, *The Duty of a People Under the Oppression of Man, to Seek Deliverance from God* (Boston: Greenleaf's Printing Office, 1774), 23.

73. David Tappan, "A Song of Praise to God from United America" in *A Discourse delivered At the Third Parish in Newbury* (Salem, MA: Samuel Hall, 1783), 19; Joseph Perry, *A Sermon, Preached Before the General Assembly of the Colony of Connecticut, at Hartford, on the Day of Their Anniversary Election, May 11, 1775* (Hartford, CT: Eben. Watson, 1775), 7, 16.

74. John Carmichael, *A self-defensive war lawful, proved in a sermon, preached at Lancaster, before Captain Ross's company of militia, in the Presbyterian Church, on Sabbath morning, June 4th, 1775* (Lancaster, PA: Francis Bailey, 1775), 6–8.

75. Headley, *Chaplains and Clergy*, 158. See also John Wingate Thornton, *The Pulpit of the American Revolution* (Boston: D. Lothrop & Company, 1876), 328; Frank

Moore, *Diary of the American Revolution* (New York: Charles Scribner, 1860), 66; Phillips Payson, *A Memorial of Lexington Battle, and of some signal Interpositions of Providence in the American Revolution. A Sermon Preached at Lexington, on the Nineteenth of April, 1782* (Boston: Edes & Sons, 1782), especially 20–22. It was not unusual for clergy to fight in the war. In the South, several preachers took up arms, including the Presbyterian John Simpson, whom the British considered to be particularly dangerous. See Walter B. Edgar, *Partisans and Redcoats: The Southern Conflict That Turned the Tide of the American Revolution* (New York: HarperCollins, 2003), 63, 65, 69, 70, 73, 75, 127, 142, 159.

76. Peter Thacher, "Sermon on 2 Samuel 10:12, Preached after Independence, 1777," in Sermons Collection, box 2, folder 37, American Antiquarian Society, Worchester, MA; *Papers of George Washington Digital Edition*, 54, 624, http://rotunda.upress.virginia.edu.proxy.library.vanderbilt.edu/founders/GEWN-03-01-02-0027and http://rotunda.upress.virginia.edu.proxy.library.vanderbilt.edu/founders/GEWN-03-02-02-0579.

77. George Washington to Governor Trumbull, December 15, 1775, in *The Writings of George Washington*, ed. Jared Sparks (Boston: Russell, Odiorne, and Metcalf, 1834), 3:198–199. In his history of the Continental Army, Charles Royster noted the importance of chaplains in maintaining revolutionary zeal among soldiers. "Soldiers eager to feel love of America, pride in military service, and strength in combat responded to chaplains who could foster such ardor and gave short shrift to those who could not." Royster, *Revolutionary People*, 163. As Royster demonstrated, not just ministers, but "most revolutionary spokesmen believed that service in the Continental Army had a clear religious meaning for the soldier." In ibid., 16. Royster observed that "a religious vocabulary voiced many of the calls to serve in the Continental Army and to promote its cause. A belief in God's design for the future of America and in His governance over the life of the individual influenced most Americans' understanding of their activities." Ibid., 13.

78. *Papers of George Washington Digital Edition*, 531, http://rotunda.upress.virginia.edu.proxy.library.vanderbilt.edu/founders/GEWN-03-03-02-0395.

79. Royster, *Revolutionary People*, 172.

80. John David Broome, ed., *The Life, Ministry, and Journals of Hezekiah Smith: Pastor of the First Baptist Church of Haverhill, Massachusetts, 1765 to 1805 and Chaplain in the American Revolution, 1775 to 1780*, 1st ed., Warren Association Series (Springfield, MO: Particular Baptist Press, 2004), 450–451.

81. Frederick Cook, ed., *Journals of the Military Expedition of Major General John Sullivan Against the Six Nations of Indians in 1779* (Auburn, NY: Knapp, Peck & Thomson, Printers, 1887), 251.

82. Kidd, *God of Liberty*, 116.

83. Quoted in Royster, *Revolutionary People*, 19. Royster correctly stated that "both those who admired the American Protestant ministry and those who ridiculed

it could agree that preachers carried the revolution to large numbers of Americans." Ibid.

CHAPTER 2

1. Thomas Paine, *Common Sense* (New York: Peter Eckler Publishing Company, 1918), 29. For other interpretations of Exodus in the American Revolution, see Catherine L. Albanese, *Sons of the Fathers: The Civil Religion of the American Revolution* (Philadelphia: Temple University Press, 1977), 88–90; Sacvan Bercovitch, *The American Jeremiad* (Madison: University of Wisconsin Press, 1978), 121. According to Stephen Prothero, "the Exodus story may be *the* American story—the narrative Americans tell themselves to make sense of their history, identity, and destiny." *The American Bible: How Our Words Unite, Divide, and Define a Nation* (New York: HarperOne, 2012), Kindle edition, location 405.

2. Long before the American Revolution, the book of Exodus had inspired political readings, often radical ones. In the Reformation, works by John Calvin and John Knox were examples of such readings. In the next century's English Civil War, Oliver Cromwell referred to the Exodus in a speech to Parliament after he had assumed power. Exodus, Cromwell said, was "the only parallel of God's dealing with us that I know in the world." In fact, the parallel could be all too perfect, Cromwell warned, because liberation enacted in the English Exodus could be as tenuous as the liberation spirit of the biblical Exodus. The fear persisted that liberation would give way again to bondage; the people could return to Egypt, or, in Cromwell's world, to another corrupt monarchy. Michael Walzer is correct: "Wherever people know the Bible, and experience oppression, the Exodus has sustained their spirits and (sometimes) inspired their resistance." Walzer argued that Exodus was "a paradigm of revolutionary politics." That is, "Exodus is a story, a big story, one that became part of the cultural consciousness of the West—so that a range of political events...have been located and understood within the narrative frame that it provides. This story made it possible to tell other stories." See Walzer, *Exodus and Revolution* (New York: Basic Books, 1985), 4–7.

3. Abigail Adams and John Adams, *The Book of Abigail and John: Selected Letters of the Adams Family, 1762–1784,* ed. Lyman Henry Butterfield, Marc Friedlaender, and Mary-Jo Kline (Boston: Northeastern University Press, 2002), 129.

4. Ibid., 155–156.

5. Gordon S. Wood, "Conspiracy and the Paranoid Style: Causality and Deceit in the Eighteenth Century," *William and Mary Quarterly*, 3rd ser., 39, no. 3 (July 1, 1982): 401.

6. Ibid., 421, 429.

7. The renowned chaplain Israel Evans made a typical application of this verse to the revolutionary experience in 1782. "In the spirit and style of Egyptian tyranny,

they call upon one another to unite in measures of cruelty and injustice. 'Come on,' say they, 'let us deal wisely with them, lest they multiply. Therefore they did set over them taskmasters, to afflict them with their burdens.' Such was the conduct of Britain towards the inhabitants of this continent. But the Lord helped us, and their secret councils and schemes, the most wisely planned, at least in the eye of human wisdom, were turned into foolishness." Evans, *A Discourse Delivered Near York in Virginia, on the Memorable Occasion of the Surrender of the British Army to the Allied Forces of America and France* (Philadelphia: Francis Bailey, 1782), 19; see also Israel Evans, *A Discourse, Delivered, on the 18th Day of December, 1777, the Day of Public Thanksgiving, Appointed by the Honourable Continental Congress* (Lancaster: Francis Bailey, 1778), 7; Silvanus Conant, *An Anniversary Sermon Preached at Plymouth, December 23, 1776. In Grateful Memory of the First Landing of Our Worthy Ancestors in That Place, An.Dom. 1620* (Boston: Thomas & John Fleet, 1777), 12; Samuel Webster, *The Misery and Duty of an Oppress'd and Enslav'd People* (Boston: Edes and Gill, 1774), 24.

8. Nicholas Street, *The American States Acting over the Part of the Children of Israel in the Wilderness, and Thereby Impeding Their Entrance into Canaan's Rest* (New Haven: Thomas and Samuel Green, 1777), 10–11. Similarly, Presbyterian minister George Duffield of Philadelphia preached that "the court of Britain appear carefully to have copied the Egyptian model; and their measures have produced a similar event." Duffield, *A Sermon, Preached in the Third Presbyterian Church, in the City of Philadelphia, On Thursday, December 11, 1783* (Philadelphia: F. Bailey, 1784), 4.

9. Street, *American States*, 12.

10. Elijah Fitch, *A Discourse, The Substance of Which Was Delivered at Hopkinton, on the Lord's Day, March 24th, 1776, Being the Next Sabbath Following the Precipitate Flight of the British Troops from Boston* (Boston: John Boyle in Marlborough Street, 1776), 3, 10, 19–21.

11. Ibid., 21–22.

12. Ibid., 3.

13. This parallel between the Egyptian Pharaoh and George III was crucially important for American patriots. Pharaoh was the perfect image of the tyrannical oppressor, and there had never been a better modern match for biblical Pharaoh than George III. Fitch listed "that proud and haughty Monarch Pharaoh" as one of the evil rulers of scripture who "court deception, when pursuing their malicious designs." Moreover, he preached that "proud Pharaoh...was lifted up on high, with sure expectations of destroying the Israelites and dividing the spoil, flushed with the hopes of certain success, he rushes forward, till his glory, his pomp and his multitude are altogether buried in the sea." Fitch, *Discourse*, 8, 14.

14. Revolutionaries often referred to the hardening of Pharaoh's heart when referring to George III's attitude toward the colonies. On April 15, 1776, Samuel Adams wrote to Joseph Hawley, "I scruple not to affirm it as my Opinion that

[George III's] Disposition toward the People of America is more unrelenting and malignant than was that of Pharaoh toward the Israelites in Egypt." Samuel Adams, *The Writings of Samuel Adams: 1773–1777*, vol. 3, ed. Harry Cushing (New York: G.P. Putnam's Sons, 1907), 280–281; Scott M. Langston, *Exodus through the Centuries*, Blackwell Bible Commentaries (Malden, MA, and Oxford, UK: Blackwell, 2006), 87–88. See also Nathan Strong, *The Agency and Providence of God* (Hartford, CT: Hudson and Goodwin, 1780), 13–14.

15. Fitch, *Discourse*, 17–18. Fitch was one among many ministers who applied the Exodus to the Revolution in this way. Near the end of the war in 1782, Phillips Payson preached that "the finger of God has indeed been so conspicuous in every stage of our glorious struggle, that it seems as if the wonders and miracles performed for Israel of old, were repeated anew for the American Israel, in our day." The main example was, of course, George III as pharaoh: "The hardness that possessed the heart of Pharaoh of old, seems to have calloused the heart of the British King; and the madness that drove that ancient tyrant and his hosts into the sea, appears to have possessed the British court and councils," driving them mad with tyrannical oppression. Phillips Payson, *A Memorial of Lexington Battle, and of Some Signal Interpositions of Providence in the American Revolution* (Boston: Benjamin Edes & Sons, 1782), 8, 17. See also Robert Smith, *Obligations of the Confederate States* (Philadelphia, PA: Bailey, 1782), 30–31. Likewise, Nathan Williams of Connecticut preached that God allowed the British to turn evil so that he could work out "one of the greatest revolutions that have taken place…the Independence of America." Nathan Williams, *A Sermon, Preached in the Audience of the General Assembly of the State of Connecticut* (Hartford, CT: Hudson and Goodwin, 1780), 26.

16. This verse had a history of defending militancy, and a militant God, in colonial America. As Puritan minister Samuel Nowell preached in an artillery sermon a couple of years after the devastation of King Philip's War, the proclamation that "the Lord is a Man of War" identified one of the main aspects of the divine character—his warlike nature. As Nowell reasoned, this Song of Moses was "the first song that ever was penned to celebrate God's praises," and the divine virtue that this first hymn to God celebrated was God's warlike character—not his power as creator, but his might as a warrior. Nowell, *Abraham in arms; or The first religious general with his army engaging in a vvar for which he had wisely prepared* (Boston: John Foster, 1678), 1–2. For a recent study on gender and colonial warfare that takes this sermon as its point of departure, see Ann Little, *Abraham in Arms: War and Gender in Colonial New England* (Philadelphia: University of Pennsylvania Press, 2007).

17. Exodus 15 was the third most cited biblical chapter in colonial American sermons on war, 1675–1800. There were 152 citations of this chapter. But even that high number does not fully communicate the popularity of this overall narrative of the deliverance at the Red Sea, because colonists often cited Exodus 14 and 15

interchangeably to refer to this story. Therefore, if we combine the citaitons of Exodus 14 and 15 the total number is 227 citations (seventy-five of those were in the Revolutionary Era). See appendix.

18. William Foster, *True Fortitude Delineated* (Philadelphia: John Dunlap, 1776), 20.

19. Frank Moore, *Diary of the American Revolution: From Newspapers and Original Documents* (New York: C. Scribner, 1860), 223.

20. For an insightful argument that most revolutionary ministers followed just war theory, see Melvin B. Endy, "Just War, Holy War, and Millennialism in Revolutionary America," *William and Mary Quarterly*, 3rd. ser., 42, no. 1 (January 1985): 3–25.

21. Jonas Clark, *The Fate of Blood-thirsty Oppressors, and God's Tender Care of His Distressed People. A Sermon, Preached at Lexington, April 19, 1776. To Commemorate the Murder, Blood-shed, and Commencement of Hostilities, Between Great-Britain and America* (Boston: Powars and Willis, 1776), 6–7, 17.

22. Clark, *Blood-thirsty Oppressors*, 18–19.

23. Ibid., 24.

24. Ibid., 27.

25. Jacob Cushing, "Divine Judgments Upon Tyrants: And Compassion to the Oppressed (1778)," in *Political Sermons of the American Founding Era, 1730–1805*, ed. Ellis Sandoz, 2nd ed. (Indianapolis: Liberty Fund, 1998), 618, 622. Several ministers drew on Deuteronomy 32 in wartime sermons. Sermons that made similar points about wartime vengeance from this particular verse (Dt. 32:43) included John Burt, *The Mercy of God to his People, in the Vengeance he renders to their Adversaries, the Occasion of their abundant Joy* (Newport: J. Franklin, 1759), 1, 7, 9; and Samuel Cooke, *The violent destroyed: And opressed delivered. A Sermon, Preached at Lexington, April 19, 1777. For a Memorial of the Bloody Tragedy, barbarously acted, by a party of British Troops, in that Town and the Adjacent, April 19, 1775* (Boston: Draper and Phillips, 1777), 19.

26. Cushing, "Divine Judgments Upon Tyrants," 621.

27. Ibid., 623–624.

28. John Wesley, "A Calm Address to our American Colonies," in *The Works of the Reverend John Wesley*, vol. 6, ed. John Emory (New York: J. Emory and B. Waugh for the Methodist Episcopal Church, 1831), 294. Jacob Green, *A Sermon Delivered at Hanover, (in New-Jersey) April 22d, 1778* (Chatham, NJ: Shepard Kollock, 1779), 12, 16. See also Levi Hart, *Liberty Described and Recommended* (Hartford, CT: Ebenezer Watson, 1775), 16–17.

29. As Gordon Wood observed, "the Revolution suddenly and effectively ended the cultural climate that had allowed black slavery, as well as other forms of bondage and unfreedom, to exist…without serious challenge." *The Radicalism of the American Revolution*, vol. 1 (New York: Knopf, 1992), 186. For histories of slavery in Revolutionary America, see Sylvia R. Frey, *Water from the Rock: Black Resistance in a Revolutionary Age* (Princeton, NJ: Princeton University Press, 1991); Simon

Schama, *Rough Crossings: Britain, the Slaves, and the American Revolution* (New York: Ecco, 2006). For an unconventional argument that "two revolutions were actually underway in the 1770s and 1780s," the American Revolution and a revolution against slavery, see Alan Gilbert, *Black Patriots and Loyalists: Fighting for Emancipation in the War for Independence* (Chicago: University of Chicago Press, 2012), 6. See also Douglas R. Egerton, *Death or Liberty: African Americans and Revolutionary America* (New York: Oxford University Press, 2009). For an examination of the slavery metaphor, its persistence in Revolutionary America, and its influence on the institution of slavery, see Peter A. Dorsey, *Common Bondage: Slavery as Metaphor in Revolutionary America* (Knoxville: University of Tennessee Press, 2009).

30. Albert J. Raboteau, "African-Americans, Exodus, and the American Israel," in *Religion and American Culture*, ed. David G. Hackett (New York: Routledge, 2003), 81; Eddie S. Glaude, *Exodus! Religion, Race, and Nation in Early Nineteenth-century Black America* (Chicago: University of Chicago Press, 2000).

31. James Habersham, "The Letters of Hon. James Habersham, 1756–1775," *Collections of the Georgia Historical Society*, (Savannah, GA: Savannah Morning News Print, 1904), 6:243–244; Frey, *Water from the Rock*, 62–63.

32. *A Sermon on the Evacuation of Charlestown. By an Aethiopian* (Philadelphia: Will Woodhouse, 1783), 6.

33. Ibid., 6–9.

34. Ibid., 7.

35. Sarah J. Purcell, *Sealed with Blood: War, Sacrifice, and Memory in Revolutionary America* (Philadelphia: University of Pennsylvania Press, 2002), 70.

36. William C. Nell, *The Colored Patriots of the American Revolution* (Boston: Robert F. Wallcut, 1855), 5–6.

37. *Evacuation of Charlestown*, 10.

38. Ruth Bogin, "'Liberty Further Extended': A 1776 Antislavery Manuscript by Lemuel Haynes," *William and Mary Quarterly*, 3rd ser., 40, no. 1 (January 1, 1983): 94.

39. Ibid., 94–96, 104.

40. Ibid., 102–103. This argument was not original with Haynes. For instance, see Samuel Hopkins, *Dialogue Concerning the Slavery of the Africans*, in *The Works of Samuel Hopkins: With a Memoir of His Life and Character*, ed. Edwards Amasa Park, vol. 2 (Boston: Doctrinal Tract and Book Society, 1854), 586–588.

41. Hopkins, *Dialogue*, 549–550.

42. Hopkins, *Dialogue*, 562–563, 570, 573, 580; Joseph A. Conforti, *Samuel Hopkins and the New Divinity Movement: Calvinism, the Congregational Ministry, and Reform in New England Between the Great Awakenings* (Grand Rapids, MI: Christian University Press, 1981), 127–128. David Brion Davis, *The Problem of Slavery in the Age of Revolution, 1770–1823* (New York: Oxford University Press, 1999), 280–281. Jonathan Edwards, Jr., another leading New Divinity minister,

neglected the Exodus in his influential sermon, *The Injustice and Impolicy of the Slave Trade, and of the Slavery of the Africans*, published in 1791, as did Levi Hart in his *Liberty Described and Recommended*, published in 1775. See Jonathan Edwards, Jr., *The Injustice and Impolicy of the Slave Trade, and of the Slavery of the Africans* (Boston: Wells and Lilly, 1822).

43. Hopkins, *Dialogue*, 549, 563, 573.

44. Ibid., 550–552, 584–585.

45. Nathaniel Niles, *Two Discourses on Liberty* (Newbury-Port, MA: I. Thomas and H. W. Tinges, 1774), 39; Elisha Rich, *On the Bloody engagement that was Fought on Bunker's Hill* (Chelmsford, MA: Coverly, 1775), stanzas XV–XVI. Among others who agreed with Hopkins, Niles, and Rich on this point was minister John Murray of Massachusetts. In 1779, he warned against supporting slavery in the state constitutions. To do so, he preached, would be to provoke "the curse of heaven on all our struggles for the defense of our own" liberty. John Murray, *Nehemiah, Or the Struggle for Liberty Never in Vain* (Newbury, MA: John Mycall, 1779), 9

46. Hopkins, *Dialogue*, 570–571. See also Davis, *Slavery*, 275–276; Raboteau, "African-Americans, Exodus, and the American Israel"; Glaude, *Exodus!*. Scott Langston noted that Exodus was used to motivate the slave rebellion of Denmark Vesey in Charleston, South Carolina, in 1822, but it was not used in the earlier revolt of Gabriel in Virginia in 1800. He also noted that some proponents of slavery used the Exodus to argue against colonization movements that would free the slaves and transport them to Africa. *Exodus!* 143–145.

47. Edmund S. Morgan, *The Meaning of Independence: John Adams, George Washington, and Thomas Jefferson* (Charlottesville: University of Virginia Press, 2004), 38. See, for instance, Abraham Keteltas, *The Religious Soldier: Or, the Military Character of King David* (Elizabeth-Town: H. Gaine, 1759). Moses' military leadership did not go completely unnoticed, however. Moses figured prominently, for instance, in Nathanael Walter, *The Character of a True Patriot* (Boston: D. Henchman, 1745).

48. Michael Walzer made a similar observation about the Exodus narrative itself, arguing that "though Moses plays a critical role" in the Exodus history, "the people are central. And Moses' importance is not personal but political—as leader of the people or mediator between the people and God—for this is a *political* history: it is about slavery and freedom, law and rebellion." *Exodus and Revolution*, 12.

49. Adams and Adams, *Book of Abigail and John*, 129.

50. Gordon S. Wood, *Revolutionary Characters: What Made the Founders Different* (New York: Penguin, 2006), 31–33.

51. Ezra Stiles, *The United States Elevated to Glory and Honor*, in *God's New Israel: Religious Interpretations of American Destiny*, 2nd ed., ed. Conrad Cherry (Chapel Hill: University of North Carolina Press, 1998), 88–89. Numerous sermons

featured exuberant praise for Washington as the war ended. See, for example, Benjamin Trumbull, *God is to be praised for the Glory of his Majesty* (New Haven, CT: Thomas and Samuel Green, 1784), 24. Among the sermons that celebrated the Treaty of Paris and God's work in bringing about "the birthday of [a] New Empire" was Joseph Buckminster, *A Discourse Delivered in the First Church of Christ at Portsmouth, on Thursday December 11, 1783* (Portsmouth, NH: Robert Gerrish, 1784), 3, 27.

52. Thomas Brockway, *America Saved, or Divine glory displayed, in the late war with Great Britain* (Hartford, CT: Hudson & Goodwin, 1784), 18–19.

53. As Charles Royster noted, "Americans depended on [Washington's] virtue, and some of them warned against such dependence. They exalted his character but not his authority." Royster, *A Revolutionary People at War: The Continental Army and American Character* (Chapel Hill: University of North Carolina Press, 1979), 255.

54. Wood, *Revolutionary Characters*, 48–54.

55. John Adams to Benjamin Rush, April 4, 1790, in *Old Family Letters*, ed. Alexander Biddle (Philadelphia: J. B. Lippincott, 1892), 55.

56. Adams and Adams, *Book of Abigail and John*, 129.

57. For example, see Stiles, *United States Elevated*, 42.

58. Robert P. Hay, "George Washington: American Moses," *American Quarterly* 21, no. 4 (winter 1969): 780–791. In addition to depictions of Washington as America's Moses, ministers eulogized Washington with 2 Samuel 3:38, "Know ye not that there is a prince and a great man fallen this day in Israel?" See Mark A. Noll, "The Image of the United States as a Biblical Nation, 1776–1865," in *The Bible in America: Essays in Cultural History*, ed. Nathan O. Hatch and Mark A. Noll (New York: Oxford University Press, 1982), 41.

59. Cyprian Strong, *A Discourse Delivered at Hebron, At the Celebration of the Anniversary of American Independence, July 4th, 1799* (Hartford, CT: Hudson and Goodwin, 1799), 18, 6. For more on Strong and his political views, see Jonathan D. Sassi, *A Republic of Righteousness: The Public Christianity of the Post-Revolutionary New England Clergy* (New York: Oxford University Press, 2001), 46, 61, 82.

60. Thomas Paine, *The Writings of Thomas Paine*, vol. 3, ed. Moncure Daniel Conway (New York: G. P. Putnam's Sons, 1895), 214–217.

61. Richard N. Rosenfeld and Edmund S. Morgan, *American Aurora: A Democratic-Republican Returns: The Suppressed History of Our Nation's Beginnings and the Heroic Newspaper That Tried to Report It* (New York: Macmillan, 1998), 33.

62. Strong, *Discourse Delivered at Hebron*, 6. These kinds of references to Washington were typical even before his death. In 1797, Samuel Austen preached in a thanksgiving sermon at Worcester that Washington was "the rich gift of a merciful God to the Republic of North America." Moreover, he preached that God "raised up a deliverer, to us, the children of his American Israel, even George

Washington." Samuel Austin, *A Sermon, Delivered at Worcester, on the Day of Public Thanksgiving, Observed Throughout the Commonwealth of Massachusetts, December 15th, 1796* (Worcester, MA: Leonard Worcester, 1797), 8, 10.

63. David Barnes, *Discourse Delivered at South Parish in Scituate, February 22, 1800* (Boston: Manning & Loring, 1800), 7.

64. Ibid., 10, 8.

65. Wood, *Radicalism*, 206.

66. Gary Wills, *Cincinnatus: George Washington and the Enlightenment* (Garden City, NY: Doubleday, 1984), 23.

67. Quoted in Wood, *Radicalism*, 206.

68. Hay, "George Washington," 14.

69. Peter Folsom, *An Eulogy on Geo. Washington* (Gilmanton, NH: E. Russell, 1800), 11.

70. Thadeus Fiske, *A Sermon, Delivered Dec. 29, 1799* (Boston: James Cutler, 1800), 14.

71. John Carroll, *A Discourse on General Washington; Delivered in the Catholic Church of St. Peter, in Baltimore* (Baltimore: Warner & Hanna, 1800), 19, 23.

72. Eli Forbes, *An Eulogy Moralized on the Illustrious Character of the Late General George Washington* (Newburyport, MA.: Edmund M. Blunt, 1800).

73. Fiske, *A Sermon, Delivered*, 17.

74. Barnes, *Discourse*, 13.

75. Richard Furman, *Humble Submission to Divine Sovereignty the Duty of a Bereaved Nation* (Charleston, SC: 1800), 13–15. Furman's fellow Baptist Samuel Stillman agreed, and he also preached up Washington's heroism and his religious character working to "prove him to be the warm friend of religion." Samuel Stillman, *A Sermon, Occasioned by the Death of George Washington, Late Commander in Chief of the Armies of the United States of America, Who Died December 14, 1799, Aged 68* (Boston: Manning & Loring, 1800), 14.

76. Barnes, *Discourse*, 13.

77. See the reprint of the "Farewell Address" in Forbes, *Eulogy*, 32.

78. Folsom, *Eulogy*, 6

79. Barnes, *Discourse*, 13–14.

80. Forbes, *Eulogy*, 14.

81. Nathan R. Perl-Rosenthal, "The 'divine right of republics': Hebraic Republicanism and the Debate over Kingless Government in Revolutionary America," *William and Mary Quarterly*, 3rd ser., 66, no. 3 (July 2009): 535–564. For an example of Hebraic republicanism similar to Paine's usage, see Samuel Langdon's sermon from the previous year, *Government corrupted by Vice, and recovered by Righteousness* (Watertown, CT: Benjamin Edes, 1775), 11–12. Perl-Rosenthal stated that Langdon's paragraph "is the only known public discussion of the constitution of the Hebrew Republic in the revolutionary period before the publication of *Common Sense*." "The 'divine right of republics,'" 551, footnote 22. Yet there were a few other examples of such appeals to the Hebrew Republic in the 1770s

prior to Paine. See Dan Foster, *A Short Essay on Civil Government* (Hartford, CT: Ebenezer Watson, 1775), 3–5; John Joachim Zubly, *The Law of Liberty. A Sermon on American Affairs, Preached At the Opening of the Provincial Congress of Georgia* (Philadelphia: Henry Miller, 1775), 30–31; and Gad Hitchcock, *A Sermon Preached at Plymouth, December 22d, 1774* (Boston: Edes and Gill, 1775), 22–23.

82. Paine, *Common Sense*, 12.

83. John Adams, *A Defence of the Constitutions of Government of the United States of America* (London and New York: H. Caine, 1787), 147. Americans' Hebraic republicanism owed much to seventeenth-century English thinkers, including John Locke, Thomas Hobbes, and Algernon Sidney, particularly his *Discourses Concerning Government* (1680), which was reprinted in several forms for American readers. The quote from Adams here referred to Sidney's thought. In Sidney's view, the Mosaic republic of the Old Testament consisted of a judge, a council ("Sanhedrin"), and an assembly of the people. In this way, the government of Moses conformed to the three tenants of government in the classical tradition because it featured elements of "monarchy, aristocracy, and democracy." See Eran Shalev, " 'A Perfect Republic': The Mosaic Constitution in Revolutionary New England, 1775–1788," *New England Quarterly* 82, no. 2 (2009): 240–245; Algernon Sidney, *Discourses Concerning Government*, ed. Thomas G. West (Indianapolis, IN: Liberty Fund, 1996), section 16.

84. Samuel Langdon, *The Republic of the Israelites an Example to the American States* (Exeter, MA: Lamson and Ranlet, 1788), 8–9; Shalev, " 'A Perfect Republic,' " 256–260.

85. Bruce S. Feiler, *America's Prophet: Moses and the American Story* (New York: William Morrow, 2009).

CHAPTER 3

1. The most famous sermon on the Curse of Meroz in the English Civil War is Stephen Marshall, *Meroz Cursed* (London: 1642). Scholars who have studied the Curse of Meroz have most often focused on the curse itself without assessing either the context of the curse in scripture or the interpretation of other elements of Judges 5 in American warfare. A helpful discussion of the curse occupies the final chapter in Alan Heimert, *Religion and the American Mind: From the Great Awakening to the Revolution* (Cambridge, MA: Harvard University Press, 1966). The statistics are impressive. I counted 227 references to the Song of Deborah (Judges 5) in war sermons published between King Philip's War and the American Revolution. This was by far the most-cited biblical chapter in the period. The statistics are even more impressive if we add the forty-four citations to Judges 4, which colonists often cited interchangeably with Judges 5 because both chapters told the story of Deborah and Jael. The total citations of Judges 4–5 equals 271. The statistics on the popularity of violent prophecies are even

more striking if we add the thirty-six citations of Jeremiah 48:10, which was a related curse often cited alongside the curse of Meroz (Judges 5:23).

2. Melvin B. Endy, Jr., "Just War, Holy War, and Millennialism in Revolutionary America," *William and Mary College Quarterly* 42, no. 1 (1985): 3–25.

3. Drew Gilpin Faust, *This Republic of Suffering: Death and the American Civil War* (New York: A. A. Knopf, 2008), 32.

4. Historians have long extolled the importance of the jeremiad in America—a rhetorical form, modeled after the prophet Jeremiah, who warned Israel of coming judgments if it did not repent of its sins and return to God. Perry Miller influenced many historians and literary scholars in his view of the jeremiad. Miller, *The New England Mind: From Colony to Province* (Cambridge, MA: Harvard University Press, 1953), chapter 2. The classic study, which revised Miller's views, is Sacvan Bercovitch, *The American Jeremiad* (Madison: University of Wisconsin Press, 1978). See also a newer work that traces the theme to contemporary views: Andrew R. Murphy, *Prodigal Nation: Moral Decline and Divine Punishment from New England to 9/11* (New York: Oxford University Press, 2009).

5. Moses Mather, "America's Appeal to The Impartial World," in *Political Sermons of the American Founding Era, 1730–1805*, 2nd ed., ed. Ellis Sandoz (Indianapolis: Liberty Fund, 1775), 438–492.

6. William Foster, *True Fortitude Delineated* (Philadelphia, PA: John Dunlap, 1776), 20–21.

7. Samuel Davies, *The Curse of Cowardice* (Boston: Fowle and Draper, 1759), 4.

8. Ibid., 15–16.

9. Ibid., 8–11.

10. Ibid., 4, 15–16, 20–22.

11. Samuel Finley, *The Curse of Meroz; or, the Danger of Neutrality, in the Cause of God, and Our Country* (Philadelphia: James Chattin, 1757), 6–8, 13, 16, 22. Cf. Gilbert Tennent, *The Happiness of Rewarding the Enemies of our Religion and Liberty* (Philadelphia: James Chattin, 1756), 21–22.

12. Ibid., 28–30.

13. Ibid., 22.

14. Ebenezer Prime, *The Importance of the Divine Presence with the Armies of God's People* (New York: Samuel Parker, 1759), 8.

15. Ibid., 9.

16. See Faust, *Republic of Suffering*, 32.

17. George Whitefield, *A Short Address to Persons of All Denominations, Occasioned by the Alarm of an Intended Invasion* (Boston: Green & Russell, 1756), 9, 13–14. For discussions of verse 23, see Jeremy Belknap, *A Sermon on Military Duty* (Salem: S. and E. Hall, 1773), 13; Daniel Brewer, *God's Help to Be Sought, in Time of War* (Boston: B. Green, 1724), 12; John Carmichael, *A self-defensive war lawful* (Lancaster: Francis Bailey, 1775), 11; Judah Champion, *Christian and Civil Liberty*

and Freedom Considered (Hartford: E. Watson, 1776), 20; Silvanus Conant, *The Art of War, the Gift of God* (Boston: Edes and Gill, 1759), 11; Jacob Cushing, *Divine judgments upon tyrants* (Boston: Powars and Willis, 1778), 22; Samuel Davies, *Religion and patriotism the constituents of a good soldier.* (Philadelphia: James Chattin, 1755), 14; Davies, *Curse of Cowardice*, 11; Jonathan Edwards, "The Curse of Meroz" in *Sermons and Discourses, 1739–1742, The Works of Jonathan Edwards Online, Yale University*, ed., Harry S. Stout, 489–500, http://edwards.yale.edu; Hobart Estabrook, *The praying warrior.* (New Haven: James Parker and Company, 1758), 14; Finley, *Curse of Meroz*, 5, 7, 14, 19, 22, 29; Jonathan Judd, *Soldiers directed and urged, to inlist under Jesus Christ.* (Boston: S. Kneeland, 1759), 7; Cotton Mather, *The Present State of New-England...Upon the news of an invasion by bloody Indians and French-men, begun upon us.* (Boston: Samuel Green, 1690), 24; Cotton Mather, *Things to be look'd for* (Boston: Samuel Green & Barth, 1691), 75; Ebenezer Pemberton, *A Sermon Preached to the Ancient and Honourable Artillery-Company in Boston, New-England; June 7, 1756* (Boston: Edes and Gill, 1756), 21; Samuel Phillips, *Soldiers counselled and encouraged. A sermon preached at the request, and in the audience of the Ancient and Honourable Artillery-Company in Boston, June 1st, 1741* (Boston: Tho. Fleet, for John Phillips, 1741), 29; Thomas Prentice, *When the people, and the rulers among them, willingly offer themselves to a military expedition against their unrighteous enemies, and are successful therein, the Lord is to be praised, and they to be loved and honoured therefor* (Boston: Rogers and Fowle, 1745), 6, 27, 33; Josiah Stearns, *Two Sermons, Preached at Epping* (Newbury-Port, MA: John Mycall, 1777), 26; William Stearns, *A View of the Controversy subsisting between Great-Britain and the American Colonies* (Watertown, MA: Benjamin Edes, 1775), 31; Thomas Symmes, *Good Soldiers Described, and Animated* (Boston: S. Kneeland, 1720), 20; Gilbert Tennent, *The late association for defence, encourag'd, or The lawfulness of a defensive war. Represented in a sermon preach'd at Philadelphia December 24, 1747* (Philadelphia: William Bradford, 1748), 15, 52; Benjamin Throop, *Religion and Loyalty, the Duty and Glory of a People* (New London: Timothy Green, 1758), 30; Benjamin Wadsworth, *Good Souldiers a Great Blessing; Being So Represented in a Sermon Preached on the Day for Election of Officers, in the Honourable Artillery Company in Boston, June 3d, 1700* (Boston: B. Green, and J. Allen, 1700), 24; Benjamin Wadsworth, *A letter of wholesome counsels, directed to Christian souldiers [sic], going forth to war* (Boston: Bartholomew Green, 1709), 20; Benjamin Wadsworth, *True piety the best policy for times of war.* (Boston: B. Green, 1722), 3; Samuel West, *A Sermon preached before the Honorable Council, and the Honorable House of Representatives, of the Colony of the Massachusetts-Bay, in New-England* (Boston: John Gill, 1776), 55; Nathaniel Whitaker, *An Antidote Against Toryism. Or The Curse of Meroz, In a Discourse on Judges 5th 23. Dedicated to his Excellency, General Washington* (Newbury-Port, MA: John Mycall, 1777), 3, 7, 8, 14, 16, 19, 21, 23, 26–28, 32–34.

18. Phillips, *Soldiers Counselled*, 30. Here Tennent compared the victorious troops of New England with the brave tribes of Zebulun and Naphtali from the Song of Deborah (Judges 5:18–23). Others made a similar association. For other discussions of Judges 5:18–23 in military applications, see Zabdiel Adams, *The Grounds of Confidence and Success in War, Represented.* (Boston: Mills and Hicks, 1775), 13; John Allen, "An Oration Upon the Beauties of Liberty," in Sandoz, *Political Sermons*, 318; Brewer, *God's Help to Be Sought*, 12; Thomas Brockway, *America Saved, or Divine Glory Displayed, in the Late War with Great Britain* (Hartford, CT: Hudson & Goodwin, 1784), 15; Samuel Checkley, *Prayer a Duty, When God's People Go Forth to War* (Boston: B. Green, 1745), 6, 9; Edwards, "Curse of Meroz," in Stout, *Works*, 40; Thomas Foxcroft, *Grateful Reflexions on the Signal Appearances of Divine Providence for Great Britain and Its Colonies in America, Which Diffuse a General Joy* (Boston: S. Kneeland, 1760), i; Cotton Mather, *Things to Be Look'd For*, 82; Joshua Moodey, *Souldiery spiritualized, or The Christian souldier orderly, and strenuously engaged in the spirirual warre, and so fighting the good fight: represented in a sermon preached at Boston in New England on the day of the artillery election there, June 1, 1674* (Cambridge, MA: Samuel Green, 1674), 34; Ebenezer Pemberton, *The Souldier Defended & Directed* (Boston: B. Green and F. Allen, 1701), 20; Thomas Prentice, *When the People*, 8, 14, 37; Gilbert Tennent, *The Happiness of Rewarding*, 29; Jonathan Todd, *The Soldier Waxing Strong and Valiant in Fight through Faith* (New London, CT: T. Green, 1747), 26; Benjamin Wadsworth, *Good Souldiers a Great Blessing*, 24; Benjamin Wadsworth, *A Letter of Wholesome Counsels*, 19; George Whitefield, "Britain's Mercies, and Britain's Duty," in Sandoz, *Political Sermons*, 132; John Williams, *God in the Camp: Or, the Only Way for a People to Engage the Presence of God with Their Armies.* (Boston: B. Green, 1707), 11; John Joachim Zubly, *The Stamp-Act Repealed. A Sermon, Preached in the Meeting at Savannah in Georgia, June 25th, 1766* (Charleston, SC: Peter Timothy, 1766), 6; Samuel Bird, *The Importance of the divine Presence with our Host* (New Haven, CT: James Parker, and Company, 1759), 5; Samuel Chandler, *A Sermon Preached at Glocester* (Boston: Green & Russell, 1759), 23; Samuel Checkley, *The duty of God's people when engaged in war.* (Boston: D. Fowle and Z. Fowle, 1755), 15; Peter Clark, *Religion to be minded, under the greatest Perils of Life* (Boston: S. Kneeland, 1755), 17, 19; Henry Cumings, *A sermon preached in Billerica, December 11, 1783* (Boston: T. and J. Fleet, 1784), 24; John Cushing, *A Discourse, Delivered at Ashburnham, July 4th, 1796* (Leominster, MA: Charles Prentiss, 1796), 23; Timothy Dwight, *The Duty of Americans, at the Present Crisis, Illustrated in a Discourse, preached on the Fourth of July, 1798* (New Haven, CT: Thomas and Samuel Green, 1798), 26; Joseph Emerson, *The fear of God, an antidote against the fear of man* (Boston: Kneeland, 1758), 18; Finley, *Curse of Meroz*, 9; David Hall, *Israel's triumph* (Boston: J. Draper, 1761), 13.

19. Finley, *Curse of Meroz*, 10–12; my emphasis. Cf. James Cogswell, *God, the Pious Soldier's Strength & Instructor* (Boston: John Draper, 1757), 18–19.

20. Prime, *Importance of the Divine Presence*, 6. Jonathan Edwards used the "curse of Meroz" to condemn disloyalty in the spiritual warfare over the Great Awakening. In his *Distinguishing Marks*, Edwards warned ministers who did not advocate the revivals that they may bring the curse of Meroz on themselves for being "silent and unactive" in response to God's great work in manifesting "himself in so wonderful a manner in this land . . ." *The Distinguishing Marks* in *Works of Jonathan Edwards*, vol. 4, *The Great Awakening*, ed. C. C. Goen (New Haven, CT: Yale University Press, 1972), 276. Numerous sermons focused on this point of balancing human means and divine assistance in war. An example of an unprinted sermon on this topic is Thomas Fessenden, "Sermon on Exodus 17:11, June 22, 1777," Sermons Collection, American Antiquarian Society.

21. Hezekiah Smith recorded in his journal that he preached from Jeremiah's curse in 49:10 in March of 1776. John David Broome, ed., *The Life, Ministry, and Journals of Hezekiah Smith: Pastor of the First Baptist Church of Haverhill, Massachusetts, 1765 to 1805 and Chaplain in the American Revolution, 1775 to 1780*, 1st ed., Warren Association Series (Springfield, MO: Particular Baptist Press, 2004), 432.

22. West, *Sermon Preached before the Honorable Council*, 54.

23. Ibid., 54–55.

24. Ibid., 55–57.

25. George Washington, *The Writings of George Washington*, vol. 5, ed. Worthington Chauncey Ford (New York and London: G. P. Putnam's Sons, 1890), the chapter "General Washington's Proclamation," http://oll.libertyfund.org/title/2403/227163.

26. Whitaker, *Antidote*, unnumbered introductory pages. On the basis of his two sermons on the curse of Meroz, Alan Heimert called Whitaker "the first orator of American Democracy." *American Mind*, 509. For additional background on Whitaker, see ibid., 500–509.

27. Whitaker, *Antidote*, 9–10, 13–14.

28. Robert Ross, *A Sermon, in Which the Union of the Colonies is Considered and Recommended; And the Sad Consequences of Divisions are Represented* (New York: John Holt, 1776), 4, 8–9, 16–19.

29. Whitaker, *Antidote*, 7.

30. Ibid., 7.

31. Ibid., 21–22, 26.

32. Ibid.

33. Ibid., 15–16, 19.

34. Ibid., 4.

35. Ibid., 4, 30, 32.

36. Ibid., 7–8.

37. Ibid., 8.

38. Ibid., 19. For an interpretation similar to Whitaker's, see John Carmichael, *A Self-defensive War Lawful, Proved in a Sermon, Preached at Lancaster, Before Captain Ross's Company of Militia, in the Presbyterian Church, on Sabbath Morning, June 4th, 1775* (Lancaster: Francis Bailey, 1775), 12, 18.

39. Nathaniel Whitaker, preface to *The Reward of Toryism. A Discourse on Judges V.23, Delivered at the Tabernacle in Salem, May, 1783* (Boston: Yankee Office, 1813), 3.

40. Article 5th and Article 6th in "Transcript of the Treaty of Paris," Our Documents website, www.ourdocuments.gov.

41. Henry quoted in Moses Coit Tyler, *Patrick Henry* (Boston: Houghton, Mifflin and Company, 1898), 298. See also Thomas S. Kidd, *Patrick Henry: First among Patriots* (New York: Basic Books, 2011), 163–164.

42. Whitaker, *Reward of Toryism*, 10–11.

43. Ibid., 18–19, 21.

44. Ibid., 19–20.

45. Brockway, *America Saved*, 7, 8, 12–16.

46. Ibid., 19–20.

47. See Heimert, *American Mind*, chapter 9.

48. William Tennent, *An Address, Occasioned by the Late Invasion of the Liberties of the American Colonies* (Philadelphia: William and Thomas Bradford, 1774), 5.

49. Zabdiel Adams, *Grounds of Confidence*, 5.

CHAPTER 4

1. Silvanus Conant, *The Art of War, the Gift of God* (Boston: Edes and Gill, 1759), 4 (emphasis added).

2. Timothy Dwight, *A Sermon, Preached at Stamford, in Connecticut, Upon the General Thanksgiving, December 18th, 1777* (Hartford, CT: Watson and Goodwin, 1778), 13. Dwight preached the sermon on December 18, 1777.

3. Abraham Keteltas, *The Religious Soldier: or, the Military Character of King David* (Elizabeth-Town: H. Gaine, 1759), ii–iii. The biblical citation is 1 Samuel 13:14, which includes Samuel's words to Saul about David: "But now thy kingdom shall not continue: the LORD hath sought him a man after his own heart, and the LORD hath commanded him to be captain over his people, because thou hast not kept that which the LORD commanded thee" (KJV).

4. Nathan Perkins, *A Sermon, Preached to the Soldiers, who went from West-Hartford, in Defence of their Country.* (Hartford, CT: Ebenezer Watson, 1775), 9.

5. These texts were 2 Samuel 10, 1 Samuel 17, and Psalms 126, 118, 144, and 124. In addition, the sixth most popular biblical chapter in the Revolutionary era (1763–1800) was 1 Kings 12, which included the people's rejection of the Davidic line due to Rehoboam's tyranny. This chapter includes verse 16, "when all Israel saw that the king hearkened not unto them, the people answered the king, saying,

What portion have we in David? neither have we inheritance in the son of Jesse: to your tents, O Israel: now see to thine own house, David."

6. When addressing war, colonial preachers referred to the story of David and Goliath at least 114 times in sermons, making it the seventh most cited biblical chapter from 1674 to 1800. Sermons that cite David and Goliath in the Revolutionary era include Samuel Baldwin, *A Sermon, Preached at Plymouth, December 22, 1775* (Boston: Powars and Willis, 1776), 34; Thomas Brockway, *America saved, or Divine glory displayed, in the late war with Great Britain* (Hartford, 1784), 15; Robert Cooper, *Courage in a good cause, or The lawful and courageous use of the sword* (Lancaster, PA: Francis Bailey, 1775), 15–16; John Fletcher, "The Bible and the Sword," in *Political Sermons of the American Founding Era, 1730–1805*, ed. Ellis Sandoz (Indianapolis, IN: Liberty Fund, 1998), 564; David Jones, *Defensive War in a just Cause Sinless* (Philadelphia: Henry Miller, 1775), 22; Samuel McClintock, *A Sermon preached before the Honorable the Council, and the Honorable the Senate, and House of Representatives, of the State of New-Hampshire, June 3, 1784. On Occasion of the Commencement of the New Constitution and Form of Government* (Portsmouth, NH: Robert Cerrish, 1784), 19; John Murray, *Nehemiah, Or the Struggle for Liberty never in vain, when managed with Virtue and Perseverance* (Newbury, MA: John Mycall, 1779), 41; John Joachim Zubly, *The Law of Liberty. A Sermon on American Affairs, Preached At the Opening of the Provincial Congress of Georgia* (Philadelphia: Henry Miller, 1775), 10. Page numbers listed are for first citations only. Sermons that cited the story of David and Goliath prior to the American Revolution include: John Ballantine, *The Importance of God's Presence with an Army, going against the Enemy; and the Grounds on which it may be expected* (Boston: Edes and Gill, 1756), 18; Samuel Chandler, *A Sermon Preached at Glocester* (Boston: Green & Russell, 1759), 19; John Chaplin, *War, Temporal and Spiritual, Considered* (Boston: 1762), 2; Jonathan Ellis, *The Justice of the Present War* (Newport, RI: J. Franklin, 1755), 3; Samuel Mather, *War is lawful, and arms are to be proved. A sermon preached to the Ancient and Honourable Artillery Company, on June 4, 1739* (Boston: T. Fleet, for Daniel Henchman, 1739); Isaac Morrill, *The soldier exhorted to courage in the service of his king and country, from a sense of God and religion* (Boston: J. Draper, in Cornhill, 1755), 18; Urian Oakes, *The Soveraign Efficacy of Divine Providence* (Boston: Samuel Sewell, 1682), 10; Ebenezer Pemberton, *The Souldier Defended & Directed* (Boston: B. Green and F. Allen, 1701), 21; Ebenezer Prime, *The Importance of the Divine Presence with the Armies of God's People* (New York: Samuel Parker, 1759), 37; John Richardson, *The necessity of a well experienced souldiery. Or, A Christian common wealth ought to be well instructed & experienced in the military art. Delivered in a sermon, upon an artillery election June the 10th: 1675* (Cambridge, MA: Samuel Green, 1679), 10; Thomas Symmes, *Lovewell lamented. Or, A sermon occasion'd by the fall of the brave Capt. John Lovewell and several of his valiant company, in the late heroic action at Piggwacket* (Boston: B. Green for S. Gerrish, 1725), 18; Benjamin Wadsworth,

A letter of wholesome counsels, directed to Christian souldiers [sic], going forth to war (Boston: Bartholomew Green, 1709), 24; Samuel Wigglesworth, *The blessedness of such as trust in Christ, the King whom God hath exalted.* (Boston: S. Kneeland, 1755), 20; Joseph Fish, *Angels ministring to the People of God, for their Safety and Comfort in Times of Danger and Distress* (Newport, RI: J. Franklin, 1755), 26; Samuel Frink, *The marvelous works of creation and providence, illustrated* (Boston: S. Kneeland, 1763), 36; Gilbert Tennent, *The late association for defence, farther encourag'd, or The consistency of defensive war, with true Christianity. Represented in two sermons preach'd at Philadelphia, January 24, 1747–8* (Philadelphia: William Bradford, 1748), 55; John Williams, *God in the camp: or, The only way for a people to engage the presence of God with their armies* (Boston: B. Green, 1707), 19; Cotton Mather, *Souldiers counselled and comforted. A discourse delivered unto some part of the forces engaged in the just war of New-England against the northern & eastern Indians* (Boston: Samuel Green, 1689), unnumbered fourth page; Jonathan Todd, *The soldier waxing strong and valiant in fight through faith. Or, Religion recommended to soldiers in a sermon preached at East-Guilford, July 6th, 1746* (New London, CT: T. Green, 1747), 25; George Whitefield, *A Short Address to Persons of all Denominations, Occasioned by the Alarm of an intended Invasion* (Boston: Green & Russell, 1756), 3; Benjamin Wadsworth, *Good souldiers a great blessing; being so represented in a sermon preached on the day for election of officers, in the Honourable Artillery Company in Boston, June 3d, 1700* (Boston: B. Green, and J. Allen, 1700), 10–11. A selection of Revolutionary-era sermons that cite David and Goliath is noted later. Page numbers listed are for first citations only.

7. Jonathan Edwards, "In The Name Of The Lord Of Hosts" [1755] in *Sermons and Discourses, 1743–1758, Works of Jonathan Edwards* (hereafter abbreviated as *WJE*), vol. 25, ed. Wilson H. Kimnach (New Haven, CT: Yale University Press, 2006), 680–685. In this way, Edwards posed a martial reading of David and Goliath that paralleled his spiritual interpretation of the text in his great treatise on revival, *Religious Affections*. Jonathan Edwards, *Religious Affections* in *WJE* vol. 2, ed. John Smith (New Haven, CT: Yale University Press, 1959), 140. For a similar interpretation of God's deliverance in war as compared to the inadequacy of human means, see Daniel Brewer, *God's Help to Be Sought, in Time of War with a Due Sense of the Vanity of What Help Man Can Afford* (Boston: B. Green, 1724).

8. Edwards's sermon was just one of many that took this approach in the French and Indian War. See a prominent example in Keteltas, *The Religious Soldier*. David's military exploits filled numerous wartime sermons. In an unpublished sermon that celebrated the British defeat of the Spanish at Havana 1762, Ezra Stiles cited David's defeat of the Syrans from 2 Samuel 10. Here "David killed seven hundred charioteers and forty thousand horsemen of the Syrians, and struck Shobach the commander of their army, who died there." Stiles, 2 Sam 10:18–19, Sept. 15, 1762, Stiles Sermons, folder 41, Beinecke Rare Book and Manuscript Library, Yale University, New Haven, CT.

9. During the American Revolution, preachers understandably cast the story of David and Goliath in revolutionary terms, pitting the undermatched but divinely inspired David against the haughty (and tyrannical) Goliath. For instance, in relating the battles of Lexington and Concord in a 1775 sermon delivered in Plymouth, Massachusetts, Samuel Baldwin praised the "brave and determined" Americans who succeeded despite stronger British forces that looked upon the Americans "with as much contempt and disdain, as Goliath of Gath did upon David the stripling." *Sermon...at Plymouth*, 33–34. Even with this change, however, Revolutionary-era preachers continued to stress the theme established earlier that the biblical pronouncement of David as a "man after God's own heart" was tied both to his military capacities and to his piety. For instance, in a 1775 sermon preached in Chester county, Pennsylvania and later published in Philadelphia, David Jones connected the description of David as both godlike and warlike: "David, a man eminent for pure religion, the sweet psalmist of Israel, David, a man after God's own heart, yet all his life is a scene of war." *Defensive War in a just Cause Sinless* (Philadelphia: Henry Miller, 1775), 10–11. Also, Belknap asserted that David was the "man after God's own heart" because he defeated Israel's "enemies,...leaving the kingdom in peace..." Jeremy Belknap, *A Sermon on Military Duty* (Salem: S. and E. Hall, 1773), 12.

10. McClintock, *Sermon Preached Before the Honorable the Council*, 19. John E. Ferling, *Almost a Miracle: The American Victory in the War of Independence* (Oxford: Oxford University Press, 2007), Kindle edition, location 503. Gordon S. Wood noted that, in contrast to the professional British soldiers, on the American side "there were innkeepers who were captains and shoemakers who were colonels." *The American Revolution: A History* (New York: Modern Library, 2002), 77. For statistics on the social and economic makeup of the Continental Army, see Charles Royster, *A Revolutionary People at War: The Continental Army and American Character* (Chapel Hill: University of North Carolina Press, 1979), 373–378.

11. United States, Continental Congress, *Journals of Congress: Containing the Proceedings from Sept. 5, 1774 to [3d Day of November 1788]...*(Philadelphia: Printed by David C. Claypoole, 1782), 224.

12. Baldwin, *Sermon...at Plymouth*, 34.

13. Hugh Henry Brackenridge, *Six Political Discourses Founded on the Scripture* (Lancaster, PA: Francis Bailey, 1778), 64–65.

14. For background on Jones, see William Cathcart, ed., *The Baptist Encyclopedia* (Philadelphia: Louis H. Everts, 1881), 610–612; Benson J. Lossing, *Our Countrymen* (New York: Ensign, 1855), 140–141; George Truett Rogers, ed., *The Life, Journal and Works of David Jones, 1736–1820: Pastor of Baptist Churches in New Jersey and Pennsylvania and Chaplain in the American Army*, The Philadelphia Association Series (Springfield, MO: Particular Baptist Press, 2007).

15. David Jones, *Defensive War in a Just Cause Sinless* (Philadelphia: Henry Miller, 1775), 6–11, 20–22.

16. Jared Sparks, ed., *The Works of Benjamin Franklin*, vol. 1 (Boston: Charles Tappan, 1844), 408.

17. Quoted in Joseph J. Ellis, *Founding Brothers: The Revolutionary Generation* (New York: Random House, 2000), 4–5; Richard N. Rosenfeld and Edmund S. Morgan, *American Aurora: A Democratic-Republican Returns: The Suppressed History of Our Nation's Beginnings and the Heroic Newspaper That Tried to Report It* (New York: Macmillan, 1998), 282.

18. John Fletcher, "The Bible and the Sword," 563–564. Here Fletcher quoted Richard Price, *Observations on the Nature of Civil Liberty, the Principles of Government, and the Justice and Policy of the War with America* (London: Printed for T. Cadell, 1776), 98.

19. John Fletcher, *American Patriotism Farther Confronted with Reason, Scripture, and the Constitution* (Shrewsbury, England: J. Edrowes, 1776), 98.

20. Fletcher, *American Patriotism*, 98; and "Bible and the Sword," 563–564.

21. Mark A. Noll, *Princeton and the Republic, 1768–1822: The Search for a Christian Enlightenment in the Era of Samuel Stanhope Smith* (Princeton, NJ: Princeton University Press, 1989), 34; Varnum L. Collins, *President Witherspoon: A Biography* (Princeton, NJ: Princeton University Press, 1925), 1:159.

22. John Witherspoon, *The Dominion of Providence over the Passions of Man* (Philadelphia: R. Aitken, 1776), 36–37. On Witherspoon and his revolutionary importance, see Jeffry H. Morrison, *John Witherspoon and the Founding of the American Republic*, 1st ed. (Notre Dame, IN: University of Notre Dame Press, 2007).

23. By my count, wartime sermons included at least 2815 citations of the Psalms, compared with only 559 citations from the Book of Revelation.

24. The original title was *The Whole Booke of Pslames Faithfully Translated into English Metre* (Cambridge: Stephen Daye, 1640).

25. When addressing the topic of war, colonial preachers referred to Psalm 144 at least ninety times in sermons during the years 1674–1800. By comparison, Psalm 126 received two more citations (ninety-two total), and Psalm 118 received one more citation (ninety-one total). Unlike Psalm 144, however, these other psalms were psalms of thanksgiving, not war psalms. Psalm 126 was cited primarily for verse 3: "the Lord hath done great things for us; whereof we are glad." Likewise, Psalm 188 was cited for verse 23 "This is the Lord's doing; it is marvellous in our eyes." Ministers usually cited these two psalms without much commentary rather than making them central to their arguments for war, as they did with Psalm 144. Sermons that cite Psalm 144 include Jeremy Belknap, *An Election Sermon, Preached Before The General Court, of New-Hampshire at Portsmouth, June 2, 1785* (Portsmouth: Melcher and Osborne, 1785), 4; Samuel Checkley, *Prayer a duty, when God's people go forth to war.* (Boston: B. Green,

1745), 7–8; Amos Adams, *The Expediency and Utility of War, in the present State of Things, considered* (Boston: Fowle and Draper, 1759), 14; Zabdiel Adams, *The Grounds of Confidence and Success in War, represented* (Boston: Mills and Hicks, 1775), 21; Thomas Barnard, *A Sermon Preached to the Ancient and Honourable Artillery Company in Boston, New-England, June 5, 1758* (Boston: Edes and Gill, 1758), 25; Samuel Bird, *The Importance of the divine Presence with our Host* (New Haven, CT: James Parker, and Company, 1759), 19; Brewer, *God's Help*, 12; Charles Chauncy, *Marvellous Things done by the right Hand and holy Arm of God in getting him the Victory* (Boston: T. Fleet, 1745), 10; Samuel Checkley, *The duty of God's people when engaged in war* (Boston: D. Fowle and Z. Fowle, 1755), 25; James Cogswell, *God, the Pious Soldier's Strength & Instructor* (Boston: John Draper, 1757), 6; Samuel Davies, *Religion and Patriotism the Constituents of a Good Soldier* (Philadelphia: James Chattin, 1755), 24; Cotton Mather, *Things to be Look'd for. Discourses on the Glorious Characters, with Conjectures on the Speedy Approaches of that State, which is Reserved for the Church of God in the Latter Dayes* (Boston: Samuel Green & Barth, 1691), 71–72; Jonathan Mayhew, *Two Discourses Delivered October 9th, 1760. Being the Day appointed to be observed As a Day of public Thanksgiving for the Success of His Majesty's Arms, More Especially in the intire [sic] Reduction of Canada* (Boston: R. Draper, Edes and Gill, T and J. Fleet, 1760), 29; Richardson, *The Necessity of a Well Experienced Souldiery*, unnumbered first page, 8, 13; Zephaniah Ross, *An Oration Upon the Gloomy Aspects of the Times, Delivered in the precint Meeting-House in Attleborough on Nov. 2, 1774* (Springfield, MA: 1795) 10; Robert Smith, *The Obligations of the Confederate States of North America to Praise God* (Philadelphia: Francis Bailey, 1782), 14; Thomas Symmes, *Good Soldiers Described, and Animated* (Boston: S. Kneeland, 1720), 32; Gilbert Tennent, *A Sermon Preach'd at Philadelphia, January 7, 1747–8. Being the Day appointed by The Honourable the President and Council, to be observed throughout this Province, as a Day of Fasting and Prayer. With some Enlargement* (Philadelphia: W. Bradford, 1748), 13; Jonathan Todd, *The soldier waxing strong and valiant in fight through faith. Or, Religion recommended to soldiers in a sermon preached at East-Guilford, July 6th, 1746* (New London: T. Green, 1747), 12–13; Benjamin Wadsworth, *Good souldiers a great blessing; being so represented in a sermon preached on the day for election of officers, in the Honourable Artillery Company in Boston, June 3d, 1700* (Boston: B. Green, and J. Allen, 1700), 27; Benjamin Wadsworth, *A Letter of Wholesome Counsels, Directed to Christian Souldiers [sic], going Forth to War* (Boston: Bartholomew Green, 1709), 13; Benjamin Wadsworth, *True piety the best policy for times of war. A sermon preacht at Boston-lecture on August 16, 1722. Soon after a declaration of war, against the Eastern Indians & rebels* (Boston: B. Green, 1722), 10; Charles Chauncy, *The accursed Thing must be taken away from among a People, if they would reasonably hope to stand before their Enemies* (Boston: Thomas & John Fleet, 1778), 27. Page number listed for first citation only.

26. Joseph Yesurun Pinto, *The Form of Prayer, Which was performed at the Jews Synagogue, in the City of New-York, on Thursday October 23, 1760; being the Day appointed by Proclamation for a General Thanksgiving to Almighty God, for the Reducing of Canada to His Majesty's Dominions* (New York: W. Weyman, 1760), 1–7; Jacob Rader Marcus, *United States Jewry, 1776–1985* (Detroit, MI: Wayne State University Press, 1989), 346–347; Pinto, *Form of Prayer*, 1–5.

27. Conant, *The Art of War*. For background information on Conant, see Thomas Weston, *History of the Town of Middleboro, Massachusetts* (Boston: Haughton-Miffin, 1906), 3.

28. Conant, *Art of War*, 4.

29. Ibid., 3–4.

30. Ibid., 5–6, 9–10.

31. Ibid., 6, 8.

32. Ibid., 8.

33. Ibid., 10–11.

34. Ibid., 13–14.

35. Ibid., 9.

36. Adams, *Grounds of Confidence*, 12–13. See also Charles Chauncy, *The accursed Thing*, 27.

37. William Stearns, *A View of the Controversy Subsisting Between Great-Britain and the American Colonies* (Watertown, MA: Benjamin Edes, 1775), 25–26. David was, as chaplain Israel Evans preached in October, 1779, "a conqueror" and "a saint, equally brave, pious and successful." David was no less than a "divine hero" because his victories on the battlefield issued from the guidance of God. No biblical hero could do more than David to support Evans's main argument that "God is the author of military skill and strength," and, therefore, the successful solider will depend on God and praise God for all successes. *A Discourse, Delivered at Easton, On the 17th of October, 1779, To the Officers and Soldiers of the Western Army, After Their Return from an Expedition Against the Five Nations of Hostile Indians* (Philadelphia: Thomas Bradford, 1779), 7–11.

38. Robert Cooper, *Courage in a Good Cause*, 15, 24–25. Other ministers made precisely this point. As Baldwin asserted, "Providence usually works by means," and so even though the Americans were on God's side of liberty, they must be aware not "to neglect any exertions of which we are capable," for to do so would be "to render ourselves unworthy" and "to provoke heaven" against the American cause. Baldwin, *Sermon...at Plymouth*, 23, 35.

39. Keteltas, *Religious Soldier*, ii–iii.

40. Ibid., 7–8. See 1 Samuel 24.

41. Abraham Keteltas, *God Arising and Pleading his People's Cause; Or the American War in Favor of Liberty, Against the Measures and Arms of Great Britain, Shewn to be the Cause of God* (Newbury-Port: John Mycall for Edmund Sawyer, 1777), 8–10; 1 Samuel 24:15. On David as the ultimate loyalist even to corrupt Saul, see Paul

A. Rahe, *Republics Ancient and Modern: Classical Republicanism and the American Revolution* (Chapel Hill: University of North Carolina Press, 1992), 482.

42. Thomas Paine, *Common Sense* (New York: Peter Eckler Publishing Company, 1918), 8–9. See Nathan R. Perl-Rosenthal, "The 'divine right of republics': Hebraic Republicanism and the Debate over Kingless Government in Revolutionary America," *William and Mary Quarterly*, 3rd ser., 66, no. 3 (July 2009): 535–564.

43. Elaine Forman Crane, "Religion and Rebellion: Women of Faith in the American War for Independence," in *Religion in a Revolutionary Age*, ed. Ronald Hoffman and Peter J. Albert (Charlottesville: University Press of Virginia, 1994), 54–74. For a reflection on the Absalom story in relation to the post-Revolutionary era and the Constitution, see Nathanael Emmons, A Discourse, Delivered May 9, 1798 (Wrentham, MA: Benjamin Heatons, 1798), 3–5, passim.

44. For a loyalist interpretation of "The Character of Absalom," see Jonathan Boucher, *A View of the Causes and Consequences of the American Revolution* (London: G. C. and J. Robinson, 1797), 376–401.

45. 1 Kings 12, which narrated the downfall of Rehoboam and the Davidic line, was the seventh most popular biblical text in the Revolutionary Era. John Allen, "An Oration Upon the Beauties of Liberty," in Sandoz, *Political Sermons*, 321.

46. Israel Holly, *God Brings About His Holy and Wise Purpose or Decree*,.... (Hartford, CT: Eben. Watson, 1774). The British were guilty of mimicking Rehoboam in denying the rights of the people, Holly argued, and God would punish the British nation for it. And yet Holly also found much to complain about with the colonies, particularly their hypocritical cries for civil liberty while denying religious liberty to Separatists and others. In all likelihood, Holly warned, God would punish both Britain and America as the crisis escalated. As Holly warned, "the colonies now, are in a sad and woeful plunge let them turn which way they will, either submit to or reset these parliament acts; and what adds to the calamity is, the divided testaments among us concerning what is right." Ibid., 23. Holly worried that British tyranny hid within it a conspiracy with Catholicism that, if it overtook the colonies, would bind America with "Popish chains" of oppression. Ibid., 21–22. For background on Holly see Mark A. Noll, *America's God: From Jonathan Edwards to Abraham Lincoln* (New York: Oxford University Press, 2002), 145–146; Thomas S. Kidd, *God of Liberty: A Religious History of the American Revolution* (New York: Basic Books, 2010), 77–78.

47. *A Sermon, on the Present Situation of the Affairs of America and Great-Britain. Written by a Black* (Philadelphia: T. Bradford and P. Hall, 1782), 9.

48. Peter Whitney, *American Independence Vindicated* (Boston: E. Draper, 1777). Whitney quoted directly the Hebraic republican argument from Paine's *Common Sense* on pages 43–44 of his sermon, and then credited Paine on page 47. See Harry S. Stout, *New England Soul: Preaching and Religious Culture in Colonial New England* (New York: Oxford University Press, 1986), 303–305.

49. Following the logic of Hebraic republicanism, Whitney did not have a posi-
    tive view of kings in general. Israel's first king, Saul, "was a silly prince,"
    while "David was in the main a good king, though he had his faults," Whitney
    remarked, alluding to David's sins with Bathsheba and Uriah. And Solomon,
    the son of David and Bathsheba, "was a wise and good king, and in general
    ruled well," though "he was led away, by his wives, from God" and "there were
    some things in his reign grievous and oppressive to the people," which is
    why the people first came to Rehoboam to ask for better treatment. Whitney,
    American Independence, 11–12. For all their praise of David, ministers in revo-
    lutionary America also saw his famous sins as biblical examples of how vices
    could spell doom for entire nations. See Nathan Williams, *A Sermon, Preached
    in the Audience of the General Assembly of the State of Connecticut* (Hartford,
    CT: Hudson and Goodwin, 1780), 10.

50. Williams, *A Sermon, Preached in the Audience of the General Assembly*, 5–6;
    13–16.

51. Ibid., 7, 10, 37–38, 50–51. See also Daniel Batwell, *A Sermon, Preached at
    York-Town, Before Captain Morgan's and Captain Price's Companies of Rifle-Men,
    On Thursday, July 20, 1775* (Philadelphia: John Dunlap, 1775), 12.

CHAPTER 5

1. Examples of such republican readings of Romans 13 came from both tradi-
   tional Protestant clergy and liberals such as Jonathan Mayhew. See Mayhew,
   *A Discourse Concerning Unlimited Submission and Non-Resistance to the Higher
   Powers: With some Reflections on the Resistance made to King Charles I* (Boston:
   D. Fowle and D. Gookin, 1750). See a discussion of Mayhew's interpretation of
   Romans 13 in Mark A. Noll, *America's God: From Jonathan Edwards to Abraham
   Lincoln* (New York: Oxford University Press, 2002), 79–80.

2. The many websites devoted to Romans 13 and the American Revolution
   include "Romans 13 and the American Revolution The Founding Fathers
   Believed Government was of God and UnGodly Tyranny Must be Resisted,"
   http://vftonline.org/EndTheWall/romans13rev.htm; "Was the American
   Revolution a Biblically Justified Act? A New Testament examination of the
   Founding Fathers' motives," http://www.beliefnet.com/News/2003/07/Wa
   s-The-American-Revolution-A-Biblically-Justified-Act.aspx#ixzz10N84XEbk;
   "Romans 13 and the American Revolution," http://lutheranguest.blogspot.
   com/2007/09/romans-13-and-american-revolution.html; "Was the American
   Revolution a violation of Romans 13:1–7?" http://www.gotquestions.org/
   American-Revolution-Romans-13.html; "The American Revolution And
   Romans 13," http://homebrewedtheology.com/the-american-revolution-an
   d-romans-13.php; "The American Revolution vs. the Bible and Romans 13,"
   http://americancreation.blogspot.com/2009/10/american-revolution-vs-

bible-and-romans.html; "Romans 13 and the American Revolution" http://amer-icanrevolutionblog.blogspot.com/2007/11/romans-13-and-american-revolution.html; "Was the American Revolution Sinful?" http://adampowers.wordpress.com/2009/03/13/was-the-american-revolution-sinful/; "Romans 13 and the American Revolutionary War," http://mattstone.blogs.com/christian/2010/01/romans-13-and-the-american-revolutionary-war-.html.

3. See the appendix for details on ranking and citations.

4. In the Reformation period, for example, John Calvin and Philipp Melanchthon, who were strong advocates of the magistrate's power in religious affairs, were both uncomfortable with Paul's seemingly unqualified loyalty to civil author-ity. David C. Steinmetz, *Calvin in Context* (New York: Oxford University Press, 1995), 207. This interest carried over to colonial America, where Romans 13 was involved in just about any discussion of the relationship between civil and reli-gious authority. In the seventeenth century, when Puritan minister John Cotton engaged in a famous debate with Roger Williams over church, state, and reli-gious persecution, they spent numerous pages arguing over the ramifications of Romans 13. See James P. Byrd, *The Challenges of Roger Williams* (Macon, GA: Mercer University Press, 2002), chapter 4.

5. Samuel Lockwood, *Civil Rulers an Ordinance of God, For Good to Mankind.* New London: Timothy Green, 1774), 11.

6. John Wesley, "A Calm Address to Our American Colonies," in *Political Sermons of the American Founding Era, 1730–1805*, ed. Ellis Sandoz, 2nd ed. (Indianapolis: Liberty Fund, 1775), 410, 417–418. Wesley's *Calm Address* was based largely on Samuel Johnson's book, *Taxation No Tyranny*, published in 1775. See also Paul A. Rahe, *Republics Ancient and Modern: Classical Republicanism and the American Revolution* (Chapel Hill: University of North Carolina Press, 1992), 483.

7. John Fletcher, "Bible and the Sword," in Sandoz, *Political Sermons*, 560.

8. Ibid., 574.

9. Ibid., 571.

10. Ibid., 567.

11. Ibid., 575–575.

12. Charles Inglis, *The Duty of Honouring the King, explained and recommended: in a Sermon, Preached at St. George's and St. Paul's Chapels, New York, On Sunday, January 30, 1780; Being the Anniversary of the Martyrdom of King Charles I* (New York: Hugh Gaine, 1780), 24–25. On Inglis, see Maya Jasanoff, *Liberty's Exiles: American Loyalists in the Revolutionary World* (New York: A. A. Knopf, 2011), 29–30, 31, 33, 36; 147–148.

13. Inglis, *Duty*, 6.

14. Ibid., 5. See Noll, *America's God*, 68–69.

15. Inglis, *Duty*, 9–10.

16. Ibid., 11.

17. Ibid., 22.

18. Ibid., 23–24.

19. Ibid., 24.

20. Ibid., 25.

21. Ibid., 27.

22. John Adams, *The Works of John Adams, Second President of the United States*, vol. 1, ed. Charles F. Adams (Boston: Little, Brown and company, 1856), 287–288.

23. Jonathan Mayhew, *A Discourse Concerning Unlimited Submission and Non-Resistance to the Higher Powers: With Some Reflections on the Resistance Made to King Charles I* (Boston: D. Fowle and D. Gookin, 1750); Noll, *America's God*, 80. Pauline Maier, *From Resistance to Revolution: Colonial Radicals and the Development of American Opposition to Britain, 1765–1776* (New York: W. W. Norton, 1992), 31–35.

24. Mayhew, *Discourse*, 3–10.

25. Ibid., 10; emphasis mine.

26. Ibid.; emphasis original.

27. Ibid., 16.

28. Ibid., 30.

29. Ibid., 21.

30. Ibid., 20.

31. Ibid., 24.

32. Noll, *America's God*, 80.

33. Gad Hitchcock, *A Sermon Preached at Plymouth, December 22d, 1774* (Boston: Edes and Gill, 1775), 29.

34. Zabdiel Adams, *A Sermon Preached Before His Excellency John Hancock, Esq; Governor* (Boston: T. & J. Fleet and J. Gill, 1782), 11–13.

35. Again David Jones declared that Peter did not endorse an unqualified submission to rulers, "for this would condemn the conduct of the midwives" during the Exodus, as well as "Daniel, Shadrach, Meshach and Abednego." *Defensive War in a Just Cause Sinless* (Philadelphia: Henry Miller, 1775), 12–15.

36. Ibid., 12–15. Jones was one among several who made this argument. See also Josiah Stearns, *Two Sermons, Preached at Epping, in the State of New-Hampshire, January 29th, 1777, on a Public Fast, Appointed by Authority, on Account of the Un-natural and Distressing War with Great-Britain, in Defence of Liberty* (Newbury-Port, MA: John Mycall, 1777), 10–11.

37. On David Griffith, see John A Ragosta, *Wellspring of Liberty: How Virginia's Religious Dissenters Helped Win the American Revolution and Secured Religious Liberty* (Oxford: Oxford University Press, 2010), 97; Patricia U. Bonomi, *Under the Cope of Heaven: Religion, Society, and Politics in Colonial America*, updated ed. (New York: Oxford University Press, 2003), 213–214.

38. David Griffith, *Passive Obedience Considered: In a Sermon Preached at Williamsburg, December 31st, 1775* (Williamsburg: Alexander Purdie, 1776), 11.

39. As Griffith wrote, the issue was not the words of Peter and Paul, but their interactions with political officials, which were hardly submissive in all cases.

This behavior countered any claim that Romans 13, for instance, required unlimited submission. "I doubt not to prove, from the example of St. Paul's conduct, that he never meant, by the declaration in [Romans 13] to give sanction to the crimes of wicked and despotic men." Griffith, *Passive*, 11. Other ministers also employed this strategy of narrating the patriotic lives of Peter and Paul as a means of countering their supposedly loyalist rhetoric about absolute obedience to civil authorities. For an illuminating example, see Hitchcock, *Sermon Preached at Plymouth*, 26–30.

40. See Acts 22; Griffith, *Passive*, 15–16.

41. Griffith, *Passive*, 16–17.

42. Ibid., 17–18.

43. Ibid., 18.

44. Ibid., 22.

45. Ibid., 22–23.

46. John Joachim Zubly, *The Law of Liberty. A Sermon on American Affairs, Preached At the Opening of the Provincial Congress of Georgia* (Philadelphia: Henry Miller, 1775), 17.

47. Harry S. Stout, *The New England Soul: Preaching and Religious Culture in Colonial New England* (New York: Oxford University Press, 1986), 299. This verse gained usage as the revolutionary crisis escalated. In July of 1774, Nathan Fisk of Brookfield preached, "We have no design to oppose any authority that is constitutionally founded and exercised; but only to stand fast in the liberty wherewith God, and our charter, hath made us free." Nathan Fiske, *The Importance of Righteousness to the Happiness, and the Tendency of Oppression to the Misery of a People; Illustrated in Two Discourses Delivered at Brookfield, July 4, 1774* (Boston: John Kneeland, 1774), 37. Galatians 5 was the third most cited biblical chapter of the Revolutionary era (1763–1800). See appendix for details.

48. John Dickinson, *Letters from a Farmer in Pennsylvania, to the Inhabitants of the British Colonies* (Boston: Mein and Fleeming, 1768), 27–28. On Dickinson and his influence, see Gordon S. Wood, *The Radicalism of the American Revolution* (New York: A. A. Knopf, 1992), 210.

49. Jacob Duché, *The Duty of Standing Fast in Our Spiritual and Temporal Liberties* (Philadelphia: James Humphreys, Jr., 1775), 2–3.

50. Jacob Duché and John Butler, *Washington at Valley Forge: Together with the Duché Correspondence...* (Philadelphia: J. M. Butler, 1858), 68–69. See also *Letters from General Washington, to Several of his Friends in the Year 1776* ([New York], 1778).

51. Quoted in Joel T. Headley, *The Chaplains and Clergy of the Revolution* (New York: C. Scribner, 1864), 320. See also Benson Bobrick, *Angel in the Whirlwind: The Triumph of the American Revolution* (New York: Simon & Schuster, 1997), 299.

52. Judah Champion, *Christian and Civil Liberty and Freedom Considered and Recommended* (Hartford: E. Watson, 1776), 9. See also Stout, *New England Soul*, 298–299.

53. Champion, *Christian and Civil Liberty*, 5–6.

54. Ibid., 18.

55. Ibid., 13.

56. Ibid., 13–14.

57. Ibid., 17.

58. Nathaniel Whitaker, *An Antidote Against Toryism. Or The Curse of Meroz, In a Discourse on Judges 5th 23. Dedicated to His Excellency, General Washington* (Newbury-Port: John Mycall, 1777), dedication page.

59. Zabdiel Adams, *The Grounds of Confidence and Success in War, represented* (Boston: Mills and Hicks, 1775), 25.

60. Ibid., 27–28.

61. Jonathan Parsons, *Freedom From Civil and Ecclesiastical Slavery, the Purchase of Christ* (Newbury-Port: I. Thomas and H. W. Tinges, 1774), 5.

62. Ibid., 13, 16.

63. Thomas S. Kidd, *God of Liberty: A Religious History of the American Revolution* (New York: Basic Books, 2010), 90.

64. Parsons, *Freedom*, 10.

65. John Leland, *The Writings of the Late Elder John Leland*, ed. L. F. Greene (New York: G. W. Wood, 1845), 184.

66. Isaac Backus, *An Appeal to the Public for Religious Liberty Against the Oppressions of the Present Day* (Boston: John Boyle, 1773). On Backus's use of republican arguments for religious reform, see Noll, *America's God*, 82–83; Bernard Bailyn, *The Ideological Origins of the American Revolution* (Cambridge, MA: Belknap Press of Harvard University Press, 1992), 263, 266, 269, 305.

67. Backus, *Appeal*, 12–16.

68. Ibid., 54–56.

69. Ibid., 52–53.

70. Isaac Backus, *A History of New England with Particular Reference to the Denomination of Christians Called Baptists* (Newton, MA: Backus Historical Society, 1871), 202. See also Kidd, *God of Liberty*, 171.

71. Isaac Backus, "Chapter XXIV. Reasons Why the Baptists Joined in This War," in *A History of New England with Particular Reference to the Denomination of Christians Called Baptists*, vol. 2 (Newton, MA: Backus Historical Society, 1871), 197–217.

72. Henry Cumings, *A Sermon Preached Before His Honor Thomas Cushing, Esq; Lieutenant-Governor* (Boston: T. & J. Fleet, 1783), 52–53.

73. Thomas Paine, *Common Sense* (Philadelphia: R. Bell, 1776), iii.

74. Z. Adams, *Sermon before Hancock*, 36–37.

75. For an excellent treatment of the French Revolution's reception in America, see Gordon S. Wood, *Empire of Liberty: A History of the Early Republic, 1789–1815* (New York: Oxford University Press, 2009), chapter 5.

76. John Prince, *A Discourse, Delivered at Salem, on the Day of the National Fast, May 9, 1798; Appointed by President Adams, on Account of the Difficulties Subsisting*

Between the United States and France (Salem, MA: Thomas C. Cushing at Essex-Street, 1798), title page.

77. Ibid., 21, 24–25.
78. Ibid., 27–28.
79. Ibid., 26–27.
80. Ibid., 5–7.
81. Ibid., 17–18.
82. Jonathan Mayhew, *The Snare Broken. A Thanksgiving-Discourse, Preached At the Desire of the West Church in Boston, N.E. Friday May 23, 1766. Occasioned by the Repeal of the Stamp-Act* (Boston: R. & S. Draper, Edes & Gill, and T. &. J. Fleet, 1766), 24, 44.

CHAPTER 6

1. Thomas Jefferson to Alexander Smyth, January 17, 1825, in James H. Hutson, ed., *The Founders on Religion* (Princeton, NJ: Princeton University Press, 2005), 175. On America's longtime interest in Antichrist, see Robert C. Fuller, *Naming the Antichrist: The History of an American Obsession* (New York: Oxford University Press, 1996).
2. Gordon S. Wood, "Religion and the American Revolution," in *New Directions in American Religious History*, ed. Harry S. Stout and D. G. Hart (New York: Oxford University Press, 1997), 197.
3. Samuel Sherwood, "The Church's Flight into the Wilderness: An Address on the Times," in *Political Sermons of the American Founding Era, 1730–1805*, ed. Ellis Sandoz, 2nd ed. (Indianapolis, IN: Liberty Fund, 1998), 523. Sherwood's sermon was atypical in its millennial claims. It was, as Harry Stout categorized it, "the most explicitly millennial sermon to appear in 1776." Stout, *The New England Soul: Preaching and Religious Culture in Colonial New England* (New York: Oxford University Press, 1986), 308. Millennialism was an important component of Alan Heimert's massive argument for the influence of the Great Awakening on the American Revolution. Heimert traced revolutionary enthusiasm for the millennium to Jonathan Edwards's postmillennial zeal for revival. *Religion and the American Mind: From the Great Awakening to the Revolution* (Cambridge, MA: Harvard University Press, 1966), especially 59–94, 413–509. Heimert's book provoked significant dialog and substantial criticism. Many historians since Heimert have examined the influence of millennial thought during the Revolutionary era, with the excellent work of Nathan Hatch and Ruth Bloch heading the field on this topic. Leading off with Sherwood's famous sermon, Hatch argued that many of the New England clergy believed that "America's victory would initiate Christ's millennial kingdom," and that "America would become the principal seat of Christ's earthly rule." Hatch, "The Origins of Civil Millennialism in America: New England Clergymen, War with France, and the

Revolution," *William and Mary Quarterly,* 3rd ser., 31, no. 3 (July 1974): 407, 409. See also, Hatch, *The Sacred Cause of Liberty: Republican Thought and the Millennium in Revolutionary New England* (New Haven, CT: Yale University Press, 1977), in which Hatch argued that the New England clergy "rallied to the American Revolutionary cause as a veritable crusade." Ibid., 13. In this millennial, crusading spirit, "the American republic actually became the *primary agent of redemptive history.*" Ibid., 17, my emphasis. Moreover, Hatch argued that many in the clergy interpreted "existing American society *as the model upon which the millennial kingdom would be based.*" Ibid., 24–25, my emphasis. In another influential book, Ruth Bloch argued that millennialism "can illuminate how many Americans understood the ultimate meaning of the revolutionary crisis and the birth of the American nation." *Visionary Republic: Millennial Themes in American Thought 1756–1800* (Cambridge, MA: Cambridge University Press, 1985), xiii. For an excellent analysis of Sherwood's sermon, see Stephen J. Stein, "An Apocalyptic Rationale for the American Revolution," *Early American Literature* 9, no. 3 (winter 1975): 211–225. For an excellent historiographical critique of civil religion and millennialism in the Revolutionary period, see Gerald R. McDermott, "Civil Religion in the American Revolutionary Period: An Historiographical Analysis," *Christian Scholar's Review* 18, no. 4 (June 1989): 346–362. See also James West Davidson, *The Logic of Millennial Thought: Eighteenth-Century New England* (New Haven, CT: Yale University Press, 1977). For classic arguments for millennialism and religious nationalism beyond the Revolution, see Sacvan Bercovitch, *The American Jeremiad* (Madison: University of Wisconsin Press, 1978) and Ernest Lee Tuveson, *Redeemer Nation: The Idea of America's Millennial Role* (Chicago: University of Chicago Press, 1968). The main historiographical themes in revolutionary millennialism and beyond are assessed admirably in Reiner Smolinski, "Apocalypticism in Colonial North America" in *The Encyclopedia of Apocalypticism,* vol. 3, ed. Stephen J. Stein (New York: Continuum, 1998), 36–71. See also Reiner Smolinski, "Israel Redivinus: The Eschatological Limits of Puritan Typology in New England," *New England Quarterly* 63 (1990): 357–395.

4. This information confirms the conclusions of some historians who have doubted the dominance of millennialism in the colonies, at least to some extent. Melvin Endy argued that only about "one-sixth of the documents dealing with public events published in Revolutionary America by ministers placed the nation in the context of millennial history, and this estimate includes sermons with only very brief millennial suggestions in the rhetorical flourish at the end" of the sermons. Melvin B. Endy, "Just War, Holy War, and Millennialism in Revolutionary America," *William and Mary Quarterly,* 3rd. ser., 42, no. 1 (January 1985): 17. Similarly, focusing on New England preaching, Harry S. Stout discovered that "Prior to Lexington and Concord millennial speculations played no significant part in justifying resistance or in explaining the historical and constitutional

grounds of protest; it was not a major topic in regular or occasional preaching, nor was it conspicuous in print." All that changed with the Revolution, Stout argued. *New England Soul,* 306–307. Even though Nathan Hatch asserted the importance of millennial discourse for revolutionary politics, he noted that it was not until 1776 that a Massachusetts election sermon focused primarily on "an explicitly apocalyptic text." The preacher was Samuel West, and the text was from Revelation 17. Hatch, *Sacred Cause,* 55. See Samuel West, *A Sermon preached before the Honorable Council, and the Honorable House of Representatives, of the Colony of the Massachusetts-Bay, in New-England* (Boston: John Gill, 1776). Ruth Bloch stated that millennialism did not "pervade revolutionary ideology" until "the mid-1770s," when it enabled "Americans to perceive the outbreak of the war and the assertion of national independence as steps toward the realization of God's kingdom on earth." Bloch, "Religion and Ideological Change in the American Revolution" in *Religion and American Politics: From the Colonial Period to the Present,* ed. Mark A. Noll and Luke E. Harlow (New York: Oxford University Press, 2007), 55. Moreover, optimistic, revolutionary millennialism was short lived. After the war, millennial aspirations for America subsided as controversies and conflicts plagued the new nation. See Marini, "Uncertain Dawn: Millennialism and Political Theology in Revolutionary America," in *Anglo-American Millennialism, From Milton to the Millerites,* ed. Richard Connors and Andrew Collin Gow (Boston: Brill, 2004), 167–169. Early on, Perry Miller argued that revolutionary millennialism shifted into revivalism. "From the Covenant to the Revival," in *Nature's Nation* (Cambridge, MA: Harvard University Press, 1967). Nicholas Guyatt surmised that historians' assertions that "American national providentialism was millennial owes more to a weak definition of 'millennialism' or a limited survey of providential rhetoric than to the evidence from the Revolutionary period. Historians have tended to offer minimal or vague definitions of eschatological thinking, or to collapse all categories of religious appeal into a single 'millennialism.'" Guyatt is correct in his conclusion that "the most grandiose visions of America's future tended to be either non-millennial, in the sense that they made no specific reference to the realization of the Book of Revelation, or extremely tentative in their predictions. A small minority of patriots made explicit reference to biblical prophecy." Nicholas Guyatt, "'The Peculiar Smiles of Heaven': Providence and the Invention of the United States, 1607–1865" (PhD dissertation, Princeton University, 2003), 155–156. See also Guyatt, *Providence and the Invention of the United States, 1607–1876* (New York: Cambridge University Press, 2007), 106–107. Furthermore, in his study of Edwardseans in the Revolutionary era, Mark Valeri noted that they "eschewed civil millennialism. Unlike preachers who viewed the Revolution as the fulfillment of prophecy and the establishment of a divinely preordained nation, they predicted no eschatological intervention in behalf of American interests." Mark Valeri, "The New Divinity and the American Revolution,"

William and Mary Quarterly, 3rd. ser., 46, no. 4 (October 1989): 745. At least some contemporary clergy, including Baptist (and loyalist) Morgan Edwards, actually expressed concern with the large-scale neglect of millennial interest in the Revolutionary period. Edwards cited in Bloch, *Visionary Republic*, 121.

5. Ruth Bloch observed that many Revolutionary-era ministers, even those who preached on the millennium, were reluctant to make precise claims about when the millennium would begin. Bloch, *Visionary Republic*, 30. In an insightful essay on revolutionary millennialism, Stephen Marini pointed out the inherent instability and variety of millennial images and arguments. As Marini argued, "millennialism... is an element of religious culture whose meaning cannot be restricted to any one political movement in a given period." Moreover, "millennialism is... an indeterminate and culturally unstable religious belief because the imagery of [apocalyptic] biblical texts is ahistorical....The opacity of millennial and eschatological symbols makes them the most contested of Christian images and the most applicable to political use." Marini, "Uncertain Dawn," 162–163.

6. Ebenezer Baldwin, *The Duty of Rejoicing under Calamities and Afflictions* (New York: Hugh Gaine, 1776), 38. Baldwin was pastor of the First Church in Danbury, Connecticut, which was where he preached this thanksgiving sermon. In addition to Sherwood's *Church's Flight* and Baldwin's *The Duty of Rejoicing*, another millennial sermon that received the most attention from historians was West, *Sermon preached before the Honorable Council*. Likewise Timothy Dwight, in a sermon preached to celebrate the defeat of Cornwallis in 1781, preached that the Revolution was important in God's plan of history but the Revolution did not launch the millennium. The millennium, Dwight speculated, would begin approximately "near the year 2000." Moreover, the victory in the Revolutionary War was not so "that we might enjoy the exultation of victory, or a deliverance from the rapacity of Britain," nor was it so that Americans may glory "in the pride of independence and empire." Rather, the victory was so "that the work of Divine providence might be carried on, and a way opened for the arrival of scenes, which shall respect happier ages, and influence in their consequences the events of eternity." Dwight, *A Sermon, Preached at Northampton, on the Twenty-eighth of November, 1781: Occasioned by the Capture of the British Army, Under the Command of Earl Cornwallis* (Hartford, CT: Nathaniel Patten, 1781), 26–27.

7. The most cited apocalyptic text in sermons that addressed war was Revelation chapter 2, with fifty-seven total citations from 1675 to1800. A close second place in the rankings, with only one citation fewer, was Revelation chapter 19, with fifty-six citations. In the Revolutionary era, Revelation 12 led with thirty-two citations, which placed it at twenty-ninth overall.

8. Timothy P. Weber, "Millennialism," *The Oxford Handbook of Eschatology*, ed. Jerry L. Walls (New York: Oxford University Press, 2008), 365. Millennialism is a subcategory of apocalyptic thought, which originated in the Jewish apocalyptic

literature of 250 BCE to 200 CE. Among the various biblical writings that contain apocalyptic ideas and forms, two biblical books are explicitly apocalyptic: Daniel, from the Hebrew Bible, and Revelation, from the New Testament.

9. We should also note that not all revolutionary millennialism was patriotic. For some colonists, the graphic visions of Revelation warned American patriots that the war would bring not liberating victory but divine judgment for America's sins. In one of the few Revolutionary-era sermons that focused primarily on an apocalyptic text, Eliphalet Wright, a Separatist Congregationalist from Killingly, Connecticut, predicted destruction for American patriots in the war. In his thanksgiving sermon of December 1776, he preached: "How foolish is it for us to contend with the rod, and overlook the hand that useth it. We are full of our complaints against Great Britain, and say, they are seeking to deprive us of all our liberties civil and religious. Well, suppose this should be the case, hath not God a right to deprive us of every favour, and to use what instruments he pleaseth to effect his own purposes?" *A People Ripe for Harvest* (Norwich, CT: J. Trumbull, 1776), 16

10. Although most biblical arguments in support of American patriotism were not millennial, most writers of millennial literature in the period were patriots. For an impressive study of the social contexts of writers and readers of millennial literature in the period, see Ruth H. Bloch, "The Social and Political Base of Millennial Literature in Late Eighteenth-Century America," *American Quarterly* 40, no. 3 (September 1988), 378–396.

11. Drew Gilpin Faust, *This Republic of Suffering: Death and the American Civil War* (New York: A. A. Knopf, 2008), 32.

12. Fred Anderson, *The War That Made America: A Short History of the French and Indian War* (New York: Viking, 2005) Kindle edition, loc. 1584–1591.

13. Ebenezer Prime, *The Importance of the Divine Presence with the Armies of God's People* (New York: Samuel Parker, 1759), 38–39. See also Fred Anderson, *Crucible of War: The Seven Years' War and the Fate of Empire in British North America, 1754–1766* (New York: A. A. Knopf, 2000), 297–329; Fred Anderson, *The War That Made America: A Short History of the French and Indian War* (New York: Viking, 2005), Kindle edition, locations 1578–1659.

14. Zabdiel Adams, *The Grounds of Confidence and Success in War, Represented* (Boston: Mills and Hicks, 1775), 34; See also Z. Adams, *A Sermon Preached Before His Excellency John Hancock, Esq; Governor* (Boston: T. & J. Fleet and J. Gill, 1782), 59.

15. Catherine A. Brekus, *Strangers & Pilgrims: Femal Preaching in America, 1740–1845* (Chapel Hill: University of North Carolina Press, 1998), 70. This vision gained popularity in the Revolutionary era to become the top apocalyptic text and the twenty-eighth ranked text overall during the years 1763–1800.

16. Sherwood, *Church's Flight*, 514, 522. Note here Sherwood's focus on the church. The Revolution was a glorious cause for him because the war was God's means

of preserving the church in America. As Stephen Marini correctly observed, "Sherwood consistently named the church, and not the American patriots, as the object of God's providential protection." Marini, "Uncertain Dawn," 165. Sherwood's reading of the wilderness as the American refuge for the church was similar to other readings that also located the church's refuge in the West, though not in the American colonies. Nearly thirty years before Sherwood's sermon, Jesuit Francisco Javier Carranza interpreted Revelation 12 to identify Mexico as the church's refuge from Antichrist. See Francisco Javier Carranza, *The Transmigration of the Church to Guadalupe* (1749); Alain Milhou, "Apocalypticism in Central and South American Colonialism" in *Encyclopedia of Apocalypticism*, ed. Stephen Stein, 24. For brief application of this text to the Revolution that is similar to Sherwood's but predates Sherwood's sermon by two months, see Henry Cumings, *A Sermon, Preached in Billerica, on the 23d of November, 1775. Being the Day Appointed by Civil Authority, for a Public Thanksgiving Throughout the Province of Massachusetts-Bay* (Worcester, MA: I. Thomas, 1776), 11–12. See also the later interpretation just as the war ended, Robert Smith, *Obligations of the Confederate States* (Philadelphia: Bailey, 1782), 27. The quote from Elisha Fish is from *The Art of War Lawful, and Necessary for a Christian People* (Boston: Thomas and John Fleet at the Heart and Crown, 1774), 10–11.

17. Sherwood, *Church's Flight*. Note that the dedication page, included in this original version of the sermon, was not included in the reprinted version in Sandoz, *Political Sermons*.

18. Ibid., 521–522.

19. Ibid., 504, 506. Sherwood was not isolated in couching his millennial predictions with cautious qualifiers. Though his sermon was the most extreme statement of revolutionary millennialism, the few other ministers who made similar claims, like Sherwood, were careful to qualify their predictions. As Nicholas Guyatt argued, even those who held "the most grandiose visions of America's future" were often "extremely tentative in their predictions." Guyatt cited the example of Ebenezer Baldwin, noted earlier, who was careful to qualify his predictions, stating their speculative nature, especially in making specific claims for the America's fulfillment of the millennium. Guyatt, "Peculiar Smiles of Heaven," 155–156.

20. Sherwood, *Church's Flight*, 501–503. Thomas Kidd notes the exceptional nature of Sherwood's sermon, calling it "the most elaborate case for the American Revolution as a fight against Catholicism, which he equated with Antichrist." Thomas S. Kidd, *God of Liberty: A Religious History of the American Revolution* (New York: Basic Books, 2010), 71.

21. Sherwood, "Church's Flight," 497.

22. *Concerning the Number of the Beast* (unknown publisher: 1777), unnumbered second page. See also Kidd, *God of Liberty*, 92. Revelation 13 was the second most cited apocalyptic text in the Revolutionary era, ranking fifty-ninth overall.

23. West, *A Sermon Preached Before the Honorable Council*, 64–65. Two years earlier Samuel Langdon published an extensive interpretation of Revelation 13, intended clearly to prove that the second beast in the chapter referred to the Pope's religious and civil tyranny. See Samuel Langdon, *A Rational Explication of St. John's Vision of the Two Beasts, in the XIIIth Chapter of the Revelation. Shewing That the Beginning, Power, and Duration of Popery Are Plainly Predicted in That Vision, and That These Predictions Have Hitherto Been Punctually Verified.* (Portsmouth: Daniel Fowle, 1774). Chaplain Hugh Henry Brackenridge also preached on Revelation 13, specifically verse 5: "And there was given unto him a mouth, speaking great things and blasphemies." With understanding that the Pope most likely uttered these blasphemies, Brackenridge noted a resemblance between them and the boastings of British General John Burgoyne. Brackenridge, *Six Political Discourses* (Lancaster, PA: Francis Bailey, 1777), 62–63, 68.

24. Ibid., 65–67. West strongly rejected the standard reading of the beasts in this text to refer exclusively to "the pope and the clergy" (63–65). According to West, the first beast represented "the tyranny of arbitrary princes" as in "the emperors and kings of the eastern and western roman empire, and not the tyranny of the pope and the clergy" (63). The second beast represented religious tyranny of pope and clergy (64).

25. Ibid., 54, 67–68. Several revolutionary ministers referred to tyranny as a "monster," both inside and outside of apocalyptic texts. See Jonathan Bascom, *A Sermon Preached at Eastham, on Thanksgiving-Day, December 15, 1774* (Boston: Edes and Gill, 1775), 19.

26. West, *Sermon preached before the Honorable Council*, 57–59.

27. Ibid., 58–59.

28. Simeon Howard, *A Sermon Preached to the Ancient and Honorable Artillery-Company, in Boston, New-England, June 7th, 1773* (Boston: John Boyles, 1773), 17.

29. Ibid., 17–19. This image of a pacifist Christ was everywhere in Revolutionary America, and it was an obstacle that ministers encountered often in military sermons. See, for instance, Jeremy Belknap, *A Sermon on Military Duty* (Salem: S. and E. Hall, 1773), 13–14.

30. Anthony Benezet, *Serious Considerations on Several Important Subjects; Viz. On War and Its Inconsistency with the Gospel. Observations on Slavery. And Remarks on the Nature and Bad Effects of Spirituous Liquors* (Philadelphia: Joseph Crushank, 1778), 6, 11–12; Anthony Benezet, *Thoughts on the Nature of War, &c.* (Philadelphia, 1776), 4; Anthony Benezet, *Serious Reflections Affectionately Recommended to the Well-disposed of Every Religious Denomination, Particularly Those Who Mourn and Lament on Account of the Calamities Which Attend Us; and the Insensibility That so Generally Prevails* (Philadelphia, 1778), 1. On Benezet, see Maurice Jackson, *Let This Voice Be Heard: Anthony Benezet, Father of Atlantic Abolitionism* (Philadelphia: University of Pennsylvania Press, 2010).

31. Eighteenth-century wartime and military sermons with citations of Revelation 19 include James Allen, *Magistracy an Institution of Christ Upon the Throne* (Boston: John Draper, 1744); Peter Clark, *The Captain of the Lord's Host Appearing with His Sword Drawn* (Boston: S. Kneeland and T. Green, 1741); Henry Cumings, *A Sermon Preached at Lexington, on the 19th of April, 1781. Being the Anniversary of the Commencement of Hostilities Between Great-Britain and America, Which Took Place in That Town, on the 19th of April, 1775* (Boston: Benjamin Eades & Sons, 1781); Abraham Cummings, *The Present Times Perilous* (Castine, MN: David J. Waters, 1799); Samuel Davies, "The Mediatorial Kingdom and Glories of Jesus Christ," in *Political Sermons*, ed. Ellis Sandoz; Timothy Dwight, *The Duty of Americans, at the Present Crisis, Illustrated in a Discourse, Preached on the Fourth of July, 1798* (New Haven, CT: Thomas and Samuel Green, 1798); Jonathan Ellis, *The Justice of the Present War* (Newport: J. Franklin, 1755); Elisha Fish, *Joy and Gladness: A Thanksgiving Discourse, Preached in Upton, Wednesday, May 28, 1766; Occasioned by the Repeal of the Stamp-Act* (Providence, RI: Sarah Goddard and Company, 1767); Joseph Fish, *Angels Ministring to the People of God, for Their Safety and Comfort in Times of Danger and Distress* (Newport, RI: J. Franklin, 1755); Nathan Fiske, *An Oration Delivered at Brookfield, Nov. 14, 1781. In Celebration of the Capture of Lord Cornwallis and His Whole Army at York-Town and Gloucester, in Virginia, by the Combined Army Under the Command of His Excellency General Washington, on the 19th of October, 1791* (Boston: Thomas and John Fleet, 1781); Eli Forbes, *The Dignity and Importance of the Military Character Illustrated* (Boston: Richard Draper, 1771); Samuel Frink, *The Marvelous Works of Creation and Providence, Illustrated* (Boston: S. Kneeland, 1763); Timothy Harrington, *Prevailing Wickedness, and Distressing Judgments, Ill-boding Symptoms on a Stupid People* (Boston: Edes and Gill, 1756); Timothy Hilliard, *The Duty of a People Under the Oppression of Man, to Seek Deliverance from God* (Boston: Greenleaf's Printing Office, 1774); William Hobby, *The Happiness of a People, Having God for Their Ally* (Boston: S. Kneeland, 1758); Simeon Howard, *A Sermon preached to the Ancient and Honorable Artillery-Company, in Boston, New-England, June 7th, 1773* (Boston: John Boyles, 1773); Jonathan Judd, *Soldiers Directed and Urged, to Inlist Under Jesus Christ, the Captain of the Lord's Host* (Boston: S. Kneeland, 1759); Samuel Langdon, *Joy and Gratitude to God for the Long Life of a Good King, and the Conquest of Quebec* (Portsmouth, NH: Daniel Fowle, 1760); Samuel E. McCorkle, *A Sermon, on the Comparative Happiness and Duty of the United States of America, Contrasted with Other Nations, Particularly the Israelites* (Halifax: Abraham Hodge, 1795); Jonathan Mayhew, *Two Discourses Delivered October 25th, 1759* (Boston: Richard Draper, Edes & Gill, and Thomas & John Fleet, 1759); Jonathan Mayhew, *Two Discourses Delivered October 9th, 1760. Being the Day Appointed to Be Observed as a Day of Public Thanksgiving for the Success of His Majesty's Arms, More Especially in the Intire [sic] Reduction of Canada* (Boston: R. Draper, Edes & Gill, T and J. Fleet, 1760); Jonathan Mayhew, "A Sermon Preach'd

in the Audience of His Excellency William Shirley (1754)," in *The Wall and the Garden: Selected Massachusetts Election Sermons, 1670–1775*, ed. A. W. Plumstead (Minneapolis: University of Minnesota Press, 1968), 289–319; Joshua Moodey, *Souldiery Spiritualized, or The Christian Souldier Orderly, and Strenuously Engaged in the Spirirual Warre, and so Fighting the Good Fight: Represented in a Sermon Preached at Boston in New England on the Day of the Artillery Election There, June 1, 1674* (Cambridge, MA: Samuel Green, 1674); Urian Oakes, *The Unconquerable, All-conquering, & More-then-conquering Souldier: Or, The Successful Warre Which a Believer Wageth with the Enemies of His Soul: As Also the Absolute and Unparalleld Victory That He Obtains Finally over Them Through the Love of God in Jesus Christ: as It Was Discoursed in a Sermon Preached at Boston in New-England, on the Day of the Artillery-election There, June 3d, 1672* (Cambridge, MA: Samuel Green, 1674); David Osgood, *Reflections on the Goodness of God in Supporting the People of the United States Through the Late War, and Giving Them so Advantageous and Honourable a Peace* (Boston: T. and J. Fleet, 1784); Moses Parsons, *A Sermon Preached at Cambridge, Before His Excellency Thomas Hutchinson, EESQ; Governor* (Boston: Edes & Gill, 1772); Ebenezer Prime, *The Importance of the Divine Presence with the Armies of God's People* (New York: Samuel Parker, 1759); Joseph Sewall, *A Sermon Preached at the Thursday-lecture in Boston, September 16, 1762. Before the Great and General Court of the Province of the Massachusetts-Bay, in New-England. On the Joyful News of the Reduction of the Havannah* (Boston: John Draper, 1762); Gilbert Tennent, *The Late Association for Defence, Encourag'd, or The Lawfulness of a Defensive War. Represented in a Sermon Preach'd at Philadelphia December 24, 1747.* (Philadelphia: William Bradford, 1748); Gilbert Tennent, *The Late Association for Defence, Farther Encourag'd, or The Consistency of Defensive War, with True Christianity. Represented in Two Sermons Preach'd at Philadelphia, January 24, 1747–8* (Philadelphia: William Bradford, 1748); Charles Turner, *A Sermon, Preached at Plymouth, December 22d, 1773* (Boston: Greenleaf, 1773); Samuel Webster, *Soldiers, and Others, Directed and Encouraged, When Going on a Just and Important, Tho' Difficult, Enterprize, Against Their Enemies* (Boston: Edes and Gill, 1756); Samuel West, *A Sermon Preached Before the Honorable Council, and the Honorable House of Representatives, of the Colony of the Massachusetts-Bay, in New-England* (Boston: John Gill, 1776); Samuel West, *An Anniversary Sermon, Preached at Plymouth, December 22d, 1777* (Boston: Draper and Folsom, 1778); John Williams, *God in the Camp: Or, The Only Way for a People to Engage the Presence of God with Their Armies* (Boston: B. Green, 1707).

32. Joseph A. Leo Lemay, *The Life of Benjamin Franklin*, vol. 3, *Soldier, Scientist, and Politician, 1748–1757* (Philadelphia: University of Pennsylvania Press, 2009), 28–29; Milton J. Coalter, *Gilbert Tennent, Son of Thunder: A Case Study of Continental Pietism's Impact on the First Great Awakening in the Middle Colonies* (New York: Greenwood Press, 1986), 131.

33. Tennent, *Lawfulness of a Defensive War*, 36–37.

34. Ibid., 35; Benjamin Franklin, *Plain truth: or, Serious considerations on the present state of the city of Philadelphia, and province of Pennsylvania* (Philadelphia, 1747), 5–7, 22. In citing the biblical example of Laish to defend wartime defense, Franklin picked up on a prominent military theme in colonial sermons. See, for example, Charles Chauncy, *Character and Overthrow of Laish Considered and Applied. A Sermon Preached at the Desire of the Honourable Artillery-Company In Boston, June 3, 1734* (Boston: S. Kneeland and T. Green, 1734).

35. Benjamin Franklin also realized the need for New Testament defenses of war. His argument for wartime preparation included an examination of Matthew 26:51–54, which includes Jesus's warning that "they that take the sword shall perish with the sword." See Lemay, *The Life of Benjamin Franklin*, 29; Tennent, *Lawfulness of a Defensive War*, 11, 14. The Sermon on the Mount (Matthew 5:7), with its depiction of Jesus as inherently peaceful and arguably pacifist, received a lot of attention in Revolutionary America. By my count, it ranked as the twelfth most-cited text during the French and Indian War and the American Revolution, with fifty-nine citations. If we consider all of the eighteenth century, there were 116 citations of Matthew 5, making it the sixth most cited biblical text among colonial wartime and military sermons.

36. Tennent, *Lawfulness of a Defensive War*, 24, 39–40.

37. Tennent also asserted the martial influence of Christ the "victorious WARRIOR" in one of two sermons preached in Philadelphia on January 24, 1748. The sermons shared the agenda of the previous sermon in fortifying Pennsylvania's defenses for war. In defending Christ's military relevance, Tennent quoted Christ's victorious ride on the apocalyptic white horse with eyes blazing and wearing a blood-soaked garment, prepared to "smite the Nations." Given the ferociousness of the warrior Jesus in Revelation 19 and other texts, Tennent asked, "may we not gather, from all the particulars mentioned, Christ's Approbation of War?" One could demonstrate that "the Lord Jesus Christ, the second Person of the adorable Trinity, approves of WAR" by citing the many "martial Characters, Weapons, and Exploits, ascribed to him in the Holy Scriptures." And, to be sure, these texts were not about spiritual warfare only, but they clearly evidenced military war, "temporal Death and Destruction," as well as spiritual death. Gilbert Tennent, *The late association for defence, farther encourag'd, or The consistency of defensive war, with true Christianity. Represented in two sermons preach'd at Philadelphia, January 24, 1747–8* (Philadelphia: William Bradford, 1748), 33–36; Tennent, *Lawfulness of a Defensive War*, 24. Tennent was not alone. Virginia's Samuel Davies also found this heroic, patriotic Christ revealed dramatically in Revelation 19, which Davies called "one of the most majestic descriptions" of Jesus as the "all-conquering hero and his army," fully engaged in battle. In this apocalyptic scene, the warrior Christ had "eyes" like "a flame of fire" and wore "many crowns," and his clothing was "dipt in blood," which Davies read as "the blood of his enemies," further proof of his righteous

victory. In Davies's description of Christ's character, martial images dominated. Davies even referred to Christ's atonement as a patriotic act. Christ's chief attribute was a "generous patriotism," enacted in the bloody battle over evil. Those who shared Christ's "generous patriotism" would follow him into battle. There, Christ's followers would, "like brave soldiers," fight and die for an ultimately victorious mandate, a "cause" that was "immortal and invincible." Davies, "Mediatorial Kingdom," 195–197, 203.

38. Forbes, *Dignity*, 15–16; for background on Forbes, see William Buell Sprague, *Annals of the American pulpit: or, Commemorative notices of distinguished American clergymen of various denominations*, vol. 1 (New York: Robert Carter & Brothers, 1857), 493–495, and Heimert, *Religion and the American Mind*, 418–419.

39. Forbes, *Dignity*, i–ii, 23.

40. Ibid., 4–5.

41. Ibid., 11–12.

42. Ibid., 4–6, 20.

43. John Adams to Thomas Jefferson, February 10, 1812, in Hutson, ed., *Founders on Religion*, 173–174.

EPILOGUE

1. David Avery, *The Lord Is to Be Praised for the Triumphs of His Power* (Norwich, CT: Green & Spooner, 1778), 3–4. For background on Avery, see Thomas S. Kidd, *God of Liberty: A Religious History of the American Revolution* (New York: Basic Books, 2010), 1–4; Joel Tyler Headley, *The Chaplains and Clergy of the Revolution* (New York: C. Scribner, 1864), chapter 29.

2. John Mellen, *The Great and Happy Doctrine of Liberty* (Boston: Hall, 1795), 9, my emphasis. For the latest research on the republican influence of Puritanism, see Michael P. Winship, *Godly Republicanism: Puritans, Pilgrims, and a City on a Hill* (Cambridge, MA: Harvard University Press, 2012).

3. In an unprinted sermon from 1758, Ezra Stiles warned: "It will be said—Religion is unfashionable in the Camp—it is not modest in the present Age to fight under the Banner of the Lord of Hosts—that since the holy Wars in Palestine, true Britons fight no more under Standard of Jehovah." Sermon on Psalms 60:11, 1758, in Stiles Sermons, folder 41, Beinecke.

4. Peter Thacher, "Sermon on 2 Samuel 10:12, Preached after Independence, 1777," Sermons Collection, box 2, folder 37, American Antiquarian Society, 5, 8, 14, my emphasis.

5. George M. Marsden, "The American Revolution: Partisanship, 'Just Wars,' and Crusades," in *Wars of America*, ed. Ronald A. Wells (Grand Rapids, MI: Eerdmans, 1981), 11–12.

6. Josiah Whitney, *A Sermon Addressed to a military company belonging to the 13th Regiment of the Infantry* (Windham, CT: John Byrne, 1800), 10.

7. John Devotion, *The Duty and Interest of a People to Sanctify the Lord of Hosts* (Hartford, CT: Ebenezer Watson, 1777), 33.

8. *An Address to General St. Clair's Brigade, at Ticonderoga, When the Enemy Were Hourly Expected, October 20, 1776* (Philadelphia: Steiner & Cist, 1777), 3–4. The chaplain may have been David Jones, prominent chaplain and Baptist minister.

9. Richard Lee, ed., *The American Patriot's Bible: The Word of God and the Shaping of America* (Nashville: Thomas Nelson, 2009), 1–15. For an example of media coverage, see Steve Rabey, "New 'American Patriot's Bible' Sees USA's 'Godly Roots'," *USA Today*, July 2, 2009, http://www.usatoday.com/news/religion/2009-07-01-patriots-bible_N.htm.

10. Headley, *Chaplains and Clergy of the Revolution*, 158. See also John Wingate Thornton, *The Pulpit of the American Revolution: Or, The Political Sermons of the Period of 1776. With a Historical Introduction, Notes, and Illustrations* (Boston and New York: Gould and Lincoln; Sheldon and company, 1860); Frank Moore, *The Patriot Preachers of the American Revolution. With Biographical Sketches. 1776–1783* ([New York]: Printed for the subscribers, 1860). As Jon Butler wrote, all these men were "religious activists" who were looking "for models that could be used to guide clerical activity in the North-South conflict." Jon Butler, *Awash in a Sea of Faith: Christianizing the American People* (Cambridge, MA: Harvard University Press, 1990), 195.

11. Again, the pivotal essay that called for a reassessment of religion and war in America, including the militant tenor of much of American religion, is Harry S. Stout, "Review Essay: Religion, War, and the Meaning of America," *Religion and American Culture: A Journal of Interpretation* 19, no. 2 (Summer 2009): 275.

APPENDIX

1. When colonists referred to the Red Sea deliverance, they often used Exodus 14 and 15 interchangeably, because both chapters focus on that event.

2. When colonists referred to the story of Deborah and Jael, they often used Judges 4 and 5 interchangeably, because both chapters focus on that event. The popular Curse of Meroz is part of that story (Judges 5:23).

Index